D0804787

Multicultural Student Services on Campus

ACPA Books and Media Contact Information

ACPA Central Office

Vernon Wall
Director of Educational Programs
Suite 360-A
One Dupont Circle, NW
Washington, DC 20036-1110
(202) 835-2272 Ext. 068
FAX (202) 296-3286
Vernon.Wall@gmail.com

ACPA Books and Media

Dr. Denise Collins, Editor
Associate Professor
Educational Leadership
and Women's Studies
Bayh College of Education
Indiana State University
Terre Haute, IN 47809
(812) 237-2868
FAX (812) 237-8041
Denise.Collins@indstate.edu

ACPA Books and Media Editorial Board: 2010–2011

Denise Collins (2010–2014), Indiana State University, Editor and Chair
Holley Belch (2008–2011), Indiana University of Pennsylvania, Associate Editor
Vanessa Diaz de Rodriguez (2008–2011), Texas A & M
Patrick Dilley (2009–2012), Southern Illinois University
Karen Haley (2009–2012), Northern Illinois University
Steve Janosik (2008–2011), Virginia Polytechnic Institute and State University
Heidi Levine (2009–2012), Cornell College
John Mueller (2008–2011), Indiana University of Pennsylvania
Penny A. Pasque (2008–2011), University of Oklahoma
Cissy Petty (2008–2011), Loyola University New Orleans
Lisa Severy (2009–2012), University of Colorado, Boulder
Paul Shang (2008–2011), University of Oregon
Deborah J. Taub (2008–2011), University of North Carolina, Greensboro
Michele Welkener (2009–2012), University of Dayton
Maureen Wilson (2009–2012), Bowling Green State University
Timothy L. Wilson (2008–2011), Seattle University

Multicultural Student Services on Campus

Building Bridges, Re-Visioning Community

Edited by

DAFINA LAZARUS STEWART

STERLING, VIRGINIA

COPYRIGHT © 2011 BY ACPA, COLLEGE STUDENT
EDUCATORS INTERNATIONAL

Published by Stylus Publishing, LLC
22883 Quicksilver Drive
Sterling, Virginia 20166-2102

The vignettes that open each chapter were written by Dafina
Lazarus Stewart, except in the case of chapters 5, 6, and 7,
which were written by the chapter authors.

All rights reserved. No part of this book may be reprinted
or reproduced in any form or by any electronic, mechanical,
or other means, now known or hereafter invented, including
photocopying, recording, and information storage and
retrieval, without permission in writing from the publisher.

Library of Congress Cataloging-in-Publication-Data
   Multicultural student services on campus : building
bridges, re-visioning community / edited by Dafina Lazarus
Stewart.
      p.   cm.
   Includes bibliographical references and index.
   ISBN 978-1-57922-373-1 (cloth : alk. paper)
   ISBN 978-1-57922-374-8 (pbk. : alk. paper)
   ISBN 978-1-57922-617-6 (library networkable e-edition)
   ISBN 978-1-57922-618-3 (consumer e-edition)
   1. Minority college students—Services for—United
States.   2. Minorities—Education (Higher)—United
States.   I. Stewart, Dafina Lazarus, 1973–
LB2342.92.M85   2011
378.1'97089—dc22   2010045288

13-digit ISBN: 978-1-57922-373-1 (cloth)
13-digit ISBN: 978-1-57922-374-8 (paper)
13-digit ISBN: 978-1-57922-617-6 (library networkable
e-edition)
13-digit ISBN: 978-1-57922-618-3 (consumer e-edition)

Printed in the United States of America

All first editions printed on acid free paper
that meets the American National Standards Institute
Z39-48 Standard.

Bulk Purchases

Quantity discounts are available for use in workshops
and for staff development.
Call 1-800-232-0223

First Edition, 2011

10   9   8   7   6   5   4   3   2

This book is dedicated to
the multicultural office directors and advisors of the
Ohio Black Student Task Force, 2005–2006

Contents

Acknowledgments

THIS BOOK would not have been possible without the determined and persistent efforts of many people. I particularly would like to thank the authors who contributed to this book. Many of them are full-time practitioners and some of them were also working on doctoral degrees. Each of them added their work on this book to an already over-full plate of responsibilities. I am sincerely grateful to each of the contributing authors for seeing my vision for this work and bringing their wisdom and insights to bear toward making it a reality.

Many thanks are also due to the editorial board for ACPA's Books and Media Board and the three editors who oversaw the development of this book. Many thanks also go to Vernon Wall and his interns at ACPA's International Office. I also appreciate John von Knorring and the staff at Stylus for their dedication to getting this book in print.

I also acknowledge my daughter's encouragement and excitement as each step in this process was completed. Her patience, grace, and mercy overwhelm me.

Finally, a special debt of gratitude goes to those who have worked in multicultural student services, past, present, and future. Without their work, service, and support, many college students would not see their dreams of achieving a college degree manifested. I am such a student. Thank you.

Dafina Lazarus Stewart
October 5, 2010
Bowling Green State University
Bowling Green, OH

Introduction

Building Bridges, Re-Visioning Community

Dafina Lazarus Stewart

Pauline searches online for some information that would help her understand the history and development of multicultural affairs offices. She wonders if other campus multicultural affairs professionals deal with the same issues she does. Jaime, a senior student affairs officer, is well aware of the history of exclusion that demarcates higher education in the United States, but wonders how to negotiate the need to provide social and cultural support for the underrepresented students on his campus with positioning the multicultural student services office as a resource for the entire campus. He calls a colleague for help in finding a good resource. Both Pauline and Jaime make an exciting discovery and come across a recently published book . . .

COLLEGES IN THE UNITED STATES first served as intellectual and spiritual enclaves for economically privileged, White, young men. Inspired by classic notions regarding the freeing power of education (Giamatti, 1990), politically and economically disenfranchised communities began to demand education in greater numbers as the dominant pathway to social mobility (Anderson, 1988). Later, pragmatism and the progressive social movement provided the philosophical backdrop for the push to educate more of this nation's citizens during the twentieth century (Thelin, 2004).

Slowly, new populations of students gained entrance to the nation's colleges and universities. However, the admission of a more diverse student body that reflected the nation's citizenry did not typically result in transformational change to the institutional norms and policies governing life on campus. For instance, even Oberlin, often praised for its commitment to the education of women and African Americans from its inception, required women students to do the men's laundry and serve food in the dining hall and forbade African American students from living on campus (Thelin, 2004). Although college enrollments began to reflect the nation's population, college life and administration continued to reflect the nation's bigotry and oppression. This juxtaposition proved to be untenable, and faculty and students protested during the late 1960s and 1970s. The result of this activism was the formal, organized delivery of programs and services to marginalized students by college administrators, usually within student affairs.

Since the 1960s, however, there has been little scholarship elucidating the work of these professionals. The publication of *The Handbook of Minority Student Services,* edited by Charles Taylor in 1986, seems to be the first text to specifically and uniquely address multicultural student services. Taylor's edited volume depicted an emerging functional area primarily concerned with defining its role on campus and delimiting its responsibilities, largely focused on students of color and Black and Chicano students most especially. Taylor also included a variety of resources, including a self-evaluation instrument, advice on getting evaluations completed for minority student programs, and a needs assessment survey. The next year, Doris Wright's (1987) monograph on the needs of culturally diverse students, although arguing for the presence of institutionalized multicultural student services, does not review such units.

Nine years later, a chapter on multicultural affairs as a functional area within student affairs appeared, in the second edition of *Student Affairs Practice in Higher Education* (Rentz & Associates, 1996). In that volume, Palmer and Shuford (1996) provided an overview of the history of racial and ethnic minorities in higher education, the historical development of multicultural affairs and cultural centers, and how such units could attend to diversity issues within student affairs through student developmental theory, cultural environment transitions model, and the concept of cultural brokering. Shuford and Palmer updated their treatment in 2004 to include the expansion of services to lesbian, gay, bisexual, and transgender students and issues, international students, and religious diversity, as well as considering challenges faced in the future.

The time has come for a more thorough treatment of these units than can be accomplished by a single chapter (although the efforts made have been rich and laudable) and one that is reflective of the increased scope of this area over the last quarter century. Shifts in language and representation have mirrored or reflected the shifts in how issues of difference, power, and community have been conceived in colleges and universities in the United States and are important considerations for its future. Also important are issues of representation and accountability: Who can represent the issues of marginalized and underrepresented groups on campus, and who should be accountable for making sure these groups are supported? Approaches to these issues have evolved over time and are reflected in the ways that multicultural student services (MSS) units are structured and organized.

This text presents a substantive treatment of the history and philosophy of MSS units, their range of services and educational offerings, their character at different types of institutions, and what challenges and opportunities the future holds for the operation of multicultural student services in higher education. In effect, it is a handbook for both the new professional in multicultural student services and the senior practitioner offering new strategies, common issues, and inspiration to continue the work.

The book's subtitle reflects the dual role of MSS on campus. On the one hand, MSS seeks to "build bridges" between minoritized student populations and the broader institutional environment, between different groups of minoritized student populations, and across differences in cultural values and traditions, as well as communication styles. On the other hand, MSS also compels colleges and universities to "re-vision" or redefine what makes a community. In the past, higher education institutions have relied on the homogeneity of faculty and student cultures to construct a campus community (Tierney, 1993). Now, MSS has the opportunity to lead institutions to new definitions of community that use difference as an opportunity for community development, through educating for multicultural competence and social justice advocacy across the campus commons. It is from this vision that this book was conceived.

ORGANIZATION OF THE BOOK

This book is organized in four sections, moving the reader from the past to the present to the future and from a service mission to an educational one. Each chapter begins with a vignette that portrays a fictional student, undergraduate or graduate, or staff member who is attempting to deepen or clarify his or her understanding of the history, purpose, organization, and services of multicultural student services. I have attempted to reflect a broad range of diversity across the students and staff represented in these vignettes. In terms of race, ethnicity, and religion, this is accomplished at times through the explicit naming of racial, ethnic, or religious identifiers for the individuals involved. At other times, the depiction of racial and ethnic diversity across the characters is attempted more subtly by using names that are reflective of different languages and cultural groups. I have also paid attention to diversifying the gender identities of the characters which open each chapter by varying the use of men, women, and transgender individuals and signaling this diversity through the use of both conventional (e.g., he/she, her/him) and gender-neutral pronouns like *ze* and *hir* that are preferred by some transgender and gender-queer individuals. Readers are encouraged to review Judith Butler's (2004) essays in *Undoing Gender* for her discussion of gender and the need to disrupt the gender binaries which serve to render invisible transgender and gender-queer members of college and university communities, and society at large. In this way, I seek to use this text as a *practice of freedom* (hooks, 1994) and illustration of the re-visioned community that multicultural student services can help to promote.

Part One, "History and Evolution of Multicultural Student Services," begins with a snapshot of the present and then looks backward. Leilani Kupo begins with a discussion of the history of social oppression in the United States and how it has shaped the social, political, and institutional context within which MSS functions. Multicultural student services embraced the challenge to help support and spearhead a revolution in values in the United States and in colleges and universities. Over time, MSS expanded from a singular focus on race and ethnicity to a multifaceted focus that reflected the many ways in which people have experienced oppression based on their identities. Therefore, Bettina Shuford explores further the philosophical development and evolution of multicultural student services on campus. Following this, Dafina Lazarus Stewart and Brian Bridges provide a demographic profile of MSS, filling a gap in empirical knowledge about the nature and structure of these units and how professionals themselves perceive their needs and challenges.

Part Two, "Multicultural Student Services Affirming and Integrating Diversity," moves the discussion past history and philosophy to look at some of the issues that currently are included under the umbrella of multicultural student services: race/ethnicity, sexual orientation and gender identity, and religion/faith diversity. Other issues surely could have been covered in this area, such as disability, social class, and international student issues. However, education about issues and services for the students who identify in these ways are often located in administrative units or centers on the campus separate from MSS. Certainly, working as partners with these units is important for MSS, and this is also addressed. However, as part of the purview for MSS, these issues are not as commonly represented as have become issues of sexual orientation, gender identity, and religious diversity.

Moreover, great tension exists regarding the treatment of issues of race and ethnicity alongside issues of sexual orientation and gender identity. Discussions that depict the groups as mutually exclusive, as well as recent media portrayals of the gay rights movement as usurping issues of racial and ethnic equality (Gross, 2008), put MSS in a critical role to build alliances across these student groups and take a stand for multiculturally competent treatment and social justice advocacy on behalf of multiple student groups. Further, as Patel (2007) has noted, religion is quickly becoming a key source of difference, hostility, and marginalization in the United States and on college campuses. Moreover, the intersections of religion and faith with racial and ethnic culture, as well as sexual orientation and gender identity, call for greater attention to this facet of student diversity. If MSS can find common ground between and among issues of race, sexuality, gender identities, religion, and faith, then certainly this can serve as a model for how to incorporate other social issues and student groups under the MSS umbrella.

Lori D. Patton, Jessica Ranero, and Kimberly Everett challenge the reader to consider why race and critical race theory should remain the primary critical lens through which MSS makes meaning of its work, while reaching out to include other issues and advocacy groups. Following, Nicholas Negrete and Chris Purcell argue that one reason lesbian, gay, bisexual, and transgender (LGBT) students and issues should be included in MSS is that students of color and LGBT students are not discrete, mutually exclusive groups. The existence of students of color who identify as LGBT requires attention to issues of sexual orientation and gender identity. Moreover, given the common roots and practices of oppression, dismantling both is the only way to erase either as definers of students' experiences on campus. Jenny Small then gives a cogent treatment of the rationale for including religious diversity within the purview of MSS, pointing to the unique ways that culture manifests in religious expression, creating overlapping and intersecting social groups and issues.

Such a segmented approach hides the true value of MSS on campus. Mary Grace Almandrez and Felicia Lee address the ways in which administrators within MSS offices provide integration and coherence among these multiple foci. In this chapter, the authors discuss the intersections of multiple identities for students seeking services and support from MSS. The synergistic potential of MSS for realizing transformative, democratic campuses can come only by its recognition of the multiple facets of students' identities and the intersections of oppression and privilege on campus.

Part Three, "Diverse Contexts, Similar Goals," acknowledges the fact that institutional context plays a large role in the structure and organization of MSS units. Who is MSS serving? What kind of support services and educational programming can MSS provide? Is MSS responsible and accountable for providing these services? The answers to these questions differ based on the structural diversity of the campus, its legacy of inclusion and exclusion, and the climate both within and between underrepresented students and the larger campus. Institutional type diversity plays a significant role in how MSS shapes, understands, and addresses these issues, as well as the amount of human and fiscal resources that are available. For instance, as discussed by Kimberly Ferguson and Timeka Thomas-Rashid, liberal arts colleges have limited structural diversity and have smaller overall student populations. Therefore, MSS units are often one-person outfits with programmatic and support services focused on a much more narrowly defined group of students than is likely the case at a larger, public institution. Dorian McCoy deals with public institutions next, demonstrating how the more bureaucratic, complex structure of student affairs at such institutions can provide both opportunities and challenges to professionals working within MSS. Further, Eboni Zamani-Gallaher and Stanley Bazile review the treatment of diversity and multicultural student services in the community college context. This sector now serves as the primary entry point to higher education for the majority of college students, particularly for students of color and first-generation students. Moreover, at minority-serving institutions (MSIs), diversity takes on a different range of meaning and is handled differently both in philosophy and organizational structure. By looking at historically Black institutions and tribal colleges, Kevin Rome, and Les Riding In and

Robert Longwell-Grice, respectively, explore this at institutions that are some-times assumed to have no diversity within their student populations because of their racial homogeneity. Their chapters depict the relevance of diversity discussions on these campuses, as well as the challenge of meeting the needs of non-majority students (not defined by race/ethnicity) in the absence of a specific, organizational unit that is responsible and accountable for doing so.

Although single-gender institutions, Hispanic-serving institutions (HSIs), and other population-specific colleges and universities could have also been highlighted in this section, they were not included here, given that most of these institutions are still predominantly White in their student enrollments. Although the argument could be made that the significant Hispanic/Latino student population at HSIs (at least 25%; U.S. Department of Education, 2006) represents a critical mass altering the institutional context, it should be noted that HSIs are identified as such on the basis of their enrollment, not their mission (Excelencia in Education, 2009). Institutions that were founded specifically to educate populations excluded on the basis of their race from receiving higher education (e.g., historically Black colleges and universities [HBCUs] and tribal colleges and universities [TCUs]) provide compelling case studies for how MSS is conducted when racial difference is not the primary diversity issue on campus and where diversity and social justice define the rationale for the institution's existence. Further, it is at such institutions like HBCUs and TCUs where the need to expand the conversations about diversity and multiculturalism beyond race is the most pressing.

The goals of MSS to build transformative and democratic campus com-munities cannot be realized if it remains as marginalized on campus as the students it exists to serve. Skills in building bridges and developing alliances and coalitions are fundamental. This is the terrain tackled in Part Four, "Building Bridges." Becky Petitt and David McIntosh address the impor-tance of knowing and understanding the campus environment through assessment. They argue that understanding the campus climate for diversity, its history of inclusion and exclusion, and how the MSS unit is currently viewed on campus is important to defining the mission and goals of the unit.

Although MSS is usually housed in student affairs and not academic affairs, it cannot be assumed that collaborating with other student services offices happens naturally or easily. In fact, MSS units can be isolated and marginalized within student affairs. Walter Kimbrough and Caretta Cooke discuss specifically how practitioners working in MSS form coalitions and alliances with other student services colleagues and the benefits these new or strengthened relationships have for students and the office itself. Following this, Corinne Maekawa Kodama and Kisa Takesue assert that coalitions with academic affairs units are also needed. Kodama and Takesue demonstrate how MSS can work with faculty, academic advising units, and other academic units to advance its mission, enlist advocates, and enhance services and support to students.

MSS does not only provide social and academic support services to nonmajority or underrepresented students. The MSS office also often provides educational programming for the larger campus to build awareness and knowledge about issues of difference, power, and community. Jamie Washington discusses ways to approach educating majority students to understand the experiences and needs of underrepresented students, identifying allies for social justice and supporting the development of those students as well. Related to this are the ways in which multicultural educators and professionals in MSS are prepared. Carney Strange and Dafina Lazarus Stewart refer to them as "diversity change leaders" and propose two seemingly contradictory models for preparing professionals to work in and with MSS in the context of student affairs graduate preparation. Strange and Stewart advocate for a third model that integrates the other two as perhaps a better way both to prepare diversity change leaders and to socialize emerging professionals to be advocates for multicultural education on their campuses.

The origins of MSS were in environments demarcated by privilege and oppression. Multicultural student services continue to provide accurate and perceptive statements of this as a problem; however, a clear vision for how higher education can truly reflect freedom is also needed. The book concludes by looking at how MSS can re-vision community. By integrating multicultural competence training and social justice advocacy, multicultural student services units can ensure their continued relevance to the college or university community, as asserted by Robert Reason and Kenjus Watson. Finally, Kathleen Manning and Frank Muñoz consider future challenges and opportunities for MSS. Manning and Muñoz contend that it takes an intentional focus on social justice advocacy to transform the ways in which higher education does its business.

MOVING AHEAD, LOOKING BACK

There is a traditional African principle called "sankofa," represented by a bird with its feet pointing forward but with its head turned back. The symbol means that as we move toward the future, we must remain mindful of the lessons of the past. It is in this spirit that I offer this text. It is my hope that reading, exploring, and considering the questions raised and answers given herein, would challenge, inspire, and better prepare the reader to do the work of MSS and to support those who are.

REFERENCES

Anderson, J. D. (1988). *The education of Blacks in the south, 1860–1935*. Chapel Hill: University of North Carolina Press.

Butler, J. (2004). *Undoing gender*. New York, NY: Routledge.

Excelencia in Education. (2009). *Hispanic-serving institutions*. Retrieved from http://www.edexcelencia.org/research/hsi

Giamatti, A. B. (1990). A city of green thoughts. In *A free and ordered space: The real world of the university* (pp. 127–137). New York, NY: W. W. Norton.

Gross, M. J. (2008, December 16). Gay is the new black: The last great civil rights struggle. *The Advocate, 1021,* pp. 30–33.

Palmer, C. J., & Shuford, B. C. (1996). Multicultural affairs. In A. L. Rentz & Associates (Eds.), *Student affairs practice in higher education* (2nd ed., pp. 214–237). Springfield, IL: Charles C Thomas.

Patel, E. (2007). Religious diversity and cooperation on campus. *Journal of College and Character, 9*(2), 1–8.

Rentz, A. L., & Associates. (Eds.). (1996). *Student affairs practice in higher education* (2nd ed.). Springfield, IL: Charles C Thomas.

Shuford, B. C., & Palmer, C. J. (2004). Multicultural affairs. In F. J. D. MacKinnon & Associates (Eds.), *Rentz' student affairs practice in higher education* (3rd ed., pp. 218–238). Springfield, IL: Charles C Thomas.

Taylor, C. (1986). *The handbook of minority student services*. Madison, WI: National Minority Campus Chronicle.

Thelin, J. R. (2004). *A history of American higher education*. Baltimore, MD: Johns Hopkins University Press.

Tierney, W. G. (1993). *Building communities of difference: Higher education in the twenty-first century*. Westport, CT: Bergin & Garvey.

U.S. Department of Education. (2006). *Higher education act of 1965: Title V program statute* [as amended through September 2006]. Retrieved from http://www.ed.gov/programs/idueshsi/title5legislation.pdf

Wright, D. J. (Ed.). (1987). *Responding to the needs of today's minority students.* New Directions for Student Services, no. 38. San Francisco, CA: Jossey-Bass.

Part One

History and Evolution of Multicultural Student Services

THE CHAPTERS IN THIS SECTION explore the current picture of Multicultural Student Services (MSS) in colleges and universities in the United States and look back to its historical development.

1

Remembering Our Past to Shape Our Future

V. Leilani Kupo

Jennifer is concerned about the presence of student services "just for minority students" on her campus and doesn't understand what circumstances led to their existence. "Haven't colleges always been open to anyone who was qualified to enter?" she wonders. Her student organization advisor, Sayyid, attempts to explain that, in fact, that has not always been the case.

A 'ohe pau ka 'ike I ka halau ho 'ikahi
(All knowledge is not taught in the same school).

KĀNAKA MAOLI/NATIVE HAWAIIAN PROVERB

A DISCUSSION OF multicultural student services must begin with understanding the historical roots and framework that have shaped U.S. society. "Colleges and universities are historical institutions. They may suffer from amnesia or may have selective recall, but ultimately heritage is the lifeblood of our campuses" (Thelin, 2004, p. xiii). As Thelin (2004) pointed out, "History does matter" (p. xiv). It is how we begin to define ourselves as institutions and as professionals and how we define our work. Understanding how events have shaped our attitudes, values, and needs and how they have influenced not only access to education but the dialogue concerning the purpose and relevance of multicultural student services is critical as we begin to define, redefine, and defend our work on college campuses across the nation. It can be argued that societal attitudes and systems of power, privilege, and oppression have created a need for multicultural student services on college campuses as a remedy for communities that have historically been barred from receiving formal primary, secondary, and higher education.

USING THE PAST TO INFORM
THE PRESENT AND FUTURE

Understanding the historical influence of segregation on U.S. education is essential (Hurtado, Milem, Clayton-Pedersen, & Allen, 1998). The remnants of segregated schools and colleges continue to impact institutional climates for racial/ethnic diversity on college campuses. "The best example is resistance to desegregation in communities and specific campus settings, the maintenance of old campus policies at [predominantly] White institutions that best serve a homogeneous population, and attitudes and behaviors that prevent interaction across race and ethnicity" (Hurtado et al., 1998, p. 283). Historically, institutions of higher education have responded to issues of segregation through policy changes with limited attention to campus culture. More importantly, because cultural expectations are typically built on a history of segregation that can hinder interaction across race and ethnicity, many campus communities sustain long-term, and often invisible, benefits for specific student groups based on racial privilege (Duster, 1993; Hurtado et al., 1998).

Desegregation policies in schools and colleges were intended to alter the racial/ethnic composition of the student body, improve educational opportunity, and ultimately, change the environments of educational institutions (Hurtado et al., 1998). Research on the outcomes of desegregation suggests that individuals who attend desegregated schools and colleges accept desegregation as adults in other educational settings, occupations, and social situations. In addition, White adults who attended desegregated schools have fewer racial stereotypes and less fear of hostile interactions in interracial settings (Braddock, 1980, 1985; Braddock, Crain, & McPartland, 1984; Braddock & Dawkins, 1981; Braddock & McPartland, 1982).

Though some campuses have admitted and graduated students of color since their inception (Thelin, 2004), most predominantly White institutions (PWIs) have historically limited access to students of color and have a history of exclusion. According to Hurtado (1992), a college's legacy of exclusion can shape the dominant climate and impact existing practices and policies. Success in creating supportive campus environments often depends on an institution's initial response to the entrance of students of color. Among important factors were the institution's philosophy of education for students of color, commitment to affirmative action, intent for minority specific programs, and attention to the psychological climate and intergroup relations on campus (Peterson et al., 1978).

Examining history makes it clear that higher education has had a long history of resistance to desegregation (Hurtado et al., 1998; Thelin, 2004). Legal pressures were often needed to require institutions to accept their obligation to serve a more diverse student population equitably. This need for legal pressure has conveyed not only the message of institutional resistance but, in some cases, outright hostility toward people whose backgrounds were not accepted by the dominant culture.

EXCLUSION AND INCLUSION

Any discussion of diversity and multiculturalism in U.S. higher education must acknowledge the elitist and restrictive purposes this education served. Higher education in the new colonies was intended for White, economically privileged men, and their colleges reflected the religious traditions dominant in the colony. "The Puritans as college-founders were committed to a rigorous demanding education of young men who would become Christian gentlemen. They were in line to inherit family commercial enterprises in shipping and selling" (Thelin, 2004, p. 24). This was an elitist educational enterprise not intended for the masses.

Despite this elitist goal, diversity still found a place. Early school founders developed grammar schools and Indian schools to increase enrollments and resources for their institutions (Thelin, 2004). The education of American Indians had great appeal to English donors as a missionary tool for Christian conversion, which drew donor funding to the colonial colleges.

There were many problems with this method of education. These school experiments were usually disastrous, and most innovative and forward thinking college officials who got involved in these enterprises quickly looked for ways to remove themselves. Most of the American Indian students who attended these schools contracted measles, developed consumption, or became addicted to alcohol (Juneau, 2001). In addition, education was used as a colonization tool and forced students to adopt Western cultural norms and shed their indigenous culture and identity (Benham, 2003; Juneau, 2001). Colleges that enrolled American Indian students noticed high attrition of these students (Juneau, 2001). Because of this, the "colleges had to construct a strategy for holding on to the missionary endowments while shifting attention away from educating heathens" (Thelin, 2004, p. 30) and had to refocus on educating young, White men.

According to Thelin (2004), there is little evidence that the colonists' dedication to Christian education of the American Indian was comparable to any similar concern for African Americans. There is no record of colonial commitment to the collegiate education of African American students, whether in regular courses of study or at special affiliated schools. In addition, women were excluded from colleges by statute. There are occasional accounts of young women being considered for entrance examinations. However, there would have never been any intention to allow any woman to enroll even if she had excelled in the entrance examination (Thelin, 2004). It is clear that the American higher education system was founded on tenets of exclusion. It is this history of exclusion and privilege that has shaped and influenced contemporary campus climates across the nation.

THE LAW AND EDUCATION

U.S. law has played a significant role in shaping the practice of exclusion and inclusion in colleges and universities. Until *Brown v. Board of Education of Topeka* (1954), laws had been used to limit or deny access to education. Legal restrictions created a foundation for institutions to become elite and exclusionary in ways that impacted several different groups.

African Americans

Laws that prohibited the education of slaves in the eighteenth and nineteenth centuries provide some of the clearest examples of exclusion. Not only did these laws and codes prohibit the education of slaves, but they also defined slaves as nonhuman. According to Goodell (1853/1968), the U.S. Slave Codes included the following:

> EDUCATION PROHIBITED: The Slave not being regarded as a member of Society, nor as a human being, the Government, instead of providing for his education, takes care to forbid it, as being inconsistent with the condition of chattelhood. CHATTELS are not educated! And if human beings are to be held in chattelhood, education must be withheld from them. (p. 319)

In addition, many states had specific laws that prohibited the education of slaves.

> South Carolina.—Act of 1740:
> Whereas, the having of slaves taught to write, or suffering them to be employed in writing, may be attended with great inconveniences; Be it enacted, that all and every person and persons whatsoever, who shall hereafter teach or cause any slave or slaves to be taught to write, or shall use or employ any slave as a scribe, in any manner of writing whatsoever, hereafter taught to write, every such person or persons shall, for every such offense, forfeit the sum of one hundred pounds, current money. (2 Brevard's Digest, p. 243, as cited in Goodell, 1853/1968, p. 319)

Many other states such as Georgia, Louisiana, South Carolina, and Virginia had similar laws that banned not only the education of slaves, but the education of mulattos and free African Americans. Besides reading and writing, the laws also denied African Americans the right to attend school, forbade the distribution of any reading materials, including the Bible, and barred attendance at assemblies and gatherings (Goodell, 1853/1968).

American Indians

As discussed earlier, American Indians have also had a long history of educational inequity enforced by the U.S. government. The assimilationist policies of the federal government forced indigenous people to learn American customs and values. These policies were created so that American Indians would integrate with European American culture and merge with the greater society (Benham, 2003; Juneau, 2001). Indian boarding schools, primarily run by Christian missionaries, were established in the United States during the late

19th century to educate American Indian youths according to Euro-American standards. Children who attended these schools were forbidden to speak their native languages, were taught Christianity instead of their native religions, and were forced to abandon their indigenous identity and adopt European American culture (Benham, 2003). These schools were not designed to educate, but rather to assimilate and Christianize the students attending them.

Asian Americans

Long before the 1954 Brown decision, *Tape v. Hurley* (1885) served as legal precedent to support the goal of educational equality in the state of California. In 1884, 8-year-old Mamie Tape, a Chinese American born in San Francisco, was denied admission to the Spring Valley School because of her Chinese descent. The principal refused to admit Mamie, citing school board policy barring Chinese children from attending public schools. Her parents sued the San Francisco Board of Education in 1885, arguing that the school board's decision was a violation of the California Political Code (Thompson, 2004).

On January 9, 1885, the Superior Court handed down a decision in favor of the Tapes. School officials defended their position by arguing that the California constitution declared the Chinese population to be "dangerous to the well-being of the state" (Soo, 2006, "Chinese Americans Overlooked," para. 5), and thus the city had no obligation to educate Chinese children. On appeal, the California Supreme Court upheld the ruling based on California state law and the U.S. Constitution.

After the decision, the San Francisco school board lobbied for a separate school system for Chinese and other "Mongolian" children. A bill passed through the California state legislature giving the board the authority to establish the Oriental Public School in San Francisco. Though the Tape family won the case, a state-supported "separate but equal" educational system was created for children from a racially marginalized group. "Separate but equal" education would become a common educational philosophy. In 1896, the U.S. Supreme Court in *Plessy v. Ferguson* decided that mandating separate but equal accommodations for Blacks and Whites on intrastate railroads was constitutional. However, separate education was not usually equal education and led to the creation of a stratified, hierarchical, and segregated society.

Mexican Americans

During the 1920s and 1930s, as the number of Mexican immigrants increased following the Mexican Revolution, several school districts created "Americanized" schools for children of Mexican ancestry. Similar to Native Americans in the colonial period, both recent immigrants and Mexican American U.S. citizens were placed in these separate schools, primarily to learn the English language and American culture. Although school boards justified this practice by claiming Mexican American children would better integrate into American society if they learned to assimilate into the dominant culture, in most cases stereotypical assumptions and racism toward Mexican Americans motivated school board officials to treat Mexican American students differently and provide them with inferior education (Valencia, Garcia, Flores, & Juarez, 2004). Much like African American schoolchildren, Mexican American schoolchildren were segregated because of deepseated prejudices.

The *Tape* decision was not the only case to challenge segregation in education before 1954. Before the Supreme Court's landmark decision in *Brown v. Board of Education*, state and federal courts were struggling with the issues of Mexican American segregation in public education (Valencia et al., 2004). In the early 1930s, organizations such as the League of United Latin American Citizens (LULAC) led the drive in the courts for educational rights. Of these early cases, the most noted was *Mendez v. Westminster School District of Orange County* (1946). As a precursor to the *Brown* decision, this case was closely watched by members of the National Association for the Advancement of Colored People (NAACP) as a potential test case (Valencia et al., 2004). The case was brought by the parents of Mexican American children in southern California who had been segregated based on their Mexican ancestry. The federal trial court held that the Fourteenth Amendment's Equal Protection clause was not met by furnishing a separate school for Mexican American children. In addition, a Texas federal court in 1948 also ruled that segregation of Mexican Americans violated the Fourteenth Amendment (Valencia et al., 2004). It is important to note that both *Mendez* and *Brown* addressed educational segregation but they failed to address the discrimination that persisted in other systems such as housing, employment, and social attitudes and norms (Valencia et al., 2004).

Brown v. Board of Education: Separate Is Not Equal

The 1954 U.S. Supreme Court decision in *Brown v. Board of Education* is one of the most significant judicial decisions in the development of our country and educational system. The *Brown* case was not simply about a family whose little girl was denied access to an all-White school and then sued so that she could attend the all-White school in her neighborhood rather than be bussed to another school. The story of *Brown v. Board of Education* is far more complex. In December 1952, the U.S. Supreme Court had on its docket cases from Kansas, Delaware, the District of Columbia, South Carolina, and Virginia, all of which challenged the constitutionality of racial segregation in public schools. The Court consolidated these five cases under one name, *Oliver Brown et al. v. the Board of Education of Topeka*. One of the justices later explained that the Supreme Court felt it was better to have representative cases from different parts of the country.

The suit, originally led by NAACP lawyer Charles H. Houston and later Thurgood Marshall, led to dismantling the legal basis for racial segregation in schools and other public facilities. By declaring that the discriminatory nature of racial segregation violated the Fourteenth Amendment to the United States Constitution, which guarantees all citizens equal protection under the law, *Brown v. Board of Education* laid the foundation for shaping future national and international policies regarding views on segregation and human rights. According to Justice Ruth Bader Ginsberg (2004), the *Brown* decision inspired and galvanized human rights struggles across the country and around the world, has been used to advance the movement for social change in countries such as Canada, Israel, South Africa, and Trinidad and Tobago, and demonstrated a direct tie between education and democracy.

Brown v. Board of Education was not simply about children and education. The laws and policies struck down by this decision were products of the human tendency to prejudge, discriminate against, and stereotype other people by their ethnic, religious, physical, or cultural characteristics. Ending this behavior as a legal practice caused far-reaching social and ideological implications, which continue to be felt throughout our country.

Education After *Brown*

The *Brown* decision determined that separate was not equal. However, federal desegregation efforts, though powerful, did not begin to dismantle the prejudice or social norms associated with segregated education. Though educational institutions were integrated by law, there were no policies created that addressed systems of oppression or the prejudice perpetuated by social attitudes within the educational systems; bigotry, separation, and hate still persisted. Though the academy was supposed to be open to all, it did not mean everyone was, or felt, welcomed on campus as informal segregation was still practiced.

EXCLUSION BEYOND RACE AND ETHNICITY

Practices of educational exclusion touched other social groups beyond race and ethnicity. Admission policies, student conduct codes, and architectural design all supported the exclusion of communities based on religion, sexual orientation, ability, and social class.

Jewish Students

In the 1920s and 1930s, elite institutions, specifically Harvard, Yale, and Princeton, intentionally excluded Jewish students from their admission processes. At the core of their strategies was the use of discretion and vagueness in the admission process and criteria (Karabel, 2005). Measures for admission included culturally biased understandings of merit such as knowledge of languages like Latin and Greek, demonstrated athletic prowess, and particular character traits (Karabel, 2005). These standards were tested by the rising numbers of academically able Jewish applicants in the 1920s. Excluding Jews was deemed necessary to preserve the White Anglo-Saxon Protestant social climate of the colleges and to safeguard the institutions' status and desirability among the sons of the Protestant elite (Karabel, 2005). Colleges admitted students according to internally determined criteria, including emphasis on "character," the preference for alumni sons and athletes, the widespread use of interviews and photos in application files, the reliance on personal letters of recommendation, and the denigration of applicants whose sole strength was academic brilliance. Though Jewish students are no longer systematically excluded from higher education, these practices continue today through selective admissions defined by some scholars as the ability of private (and "privatizing" public) colleges, acting for the supposed public good, to choose the next generation of leaders (Karabel, 2005).

Gay, Lesbian, Bisexual, and Transgender Students

The climate for gay, lesbian, bisexual, and transgender (GLBT) students has been hostile at best. Allyn (2000) noted, "It was typical for colleges up through the 1960s to expel students suspected of having homosexual relations" (p. 151). However, removal from the institution did not rely only on evidence of participation in a sexual act with a same-sex partner. Some institutions instituted and enforced policies that prohibited nonheterosexual behavior, which was often hidden behind seemingly neutral language like "conduct unbecoming a student" (Dilley, 2002, p. 413). Discussing non-normative sexuality was not an option for students (Dilley, 2002). Essentially, these students were silenced and, despite their presence on college campuses, their experiences and perspectives were excluded from college norms and popular culture depictions of the American college student. Although nonheterosexuality is not typically a cause for expulsion at public colleges and universities, GLBT students at private, church-affiliated institutions are still kept in the closet by campus conduct codes that forbid nonheterosexual romantic relationships. Moreover, the university climate for many GLBT students is still oppressive and non-welcoming, including at public campuses, specifically when registration services, housing policies, health care policies, and restroom availability are examined.

Students With Physical Disabilities

It was not until the passage of the Education for All Handicapped Children Act (since renamed the Individuals with Disabilities Act) in 1975 that children with disabilities were guaranteed the right to attend public schools in the United States (Byrom, 2001; Longmore & Umansky, 2001), which in turn impacted access to higher education. Through the 19th century, it was common for people with disabilities to be institutionalized and treated as patients in need of a cure. This practice had the effect of excluding people with disabilities from the larger society and indicated that something was intrinsically and permanently wrong with them (VSA, n.d.). In addition, this practice denied opportunity for integration into society, particularly into schools, and perpetuated myths of inequality and inferiority. Around the turn of the 20th century, a new definition of disability emerged. "Hospital-schools" were developed in the 1890s, and through the "opening of the first programs for the vocational training of 'cripples,' [*sic*] an approach to the problem of disability emerged that became known as rehabilitation" (Byrom, 2001, p. 133). The hospital-school was a combination of education (moral, vocational, academic), socialization, and medical practice. "They were not purely medical institutions and were created to act as a temporary haven for crippled [*sic*] children from an outside world seemingly hostile to their very existence" (Byrom, 2001, p. 145). However, as the years progressed, the hospital-school model gradually changed to a medical model, and education was no longer a focus.

A study of the landscapes of our college campuses also teaches about the history of excluding those who are not able-bodied. The physical layout of college campuses and their buildings clearly demonstrate that most campuses were not designed to accommodate students with physical disabilities. The iconic campus landscape includes hills, buildings with elaborate entrance steps, and brick walkways. For institutions with older buildings, historical preservation efforts prevent the renovation of multistory buildings to include elevators. Again, federal legislation such as Section 504 of the 1973 Rehabilitation Act and the 1990 Americans with Disabilities Act intervened to require that colleges and universities ensure greater access to academic facilities for students with disabilities. However, students with disabilities are often still marginalized on campus as decisions to participate in out-of-class activities require much forethought and planning, and student organizations are often not trained to be aware of making their events accessible to all students, not just in location but also the very activities planned.

Socioeconomic Background

Little attention has been paid to the complexities of social class in U.S. educational settings (Brown, 1998; Duffy, 2008). Discussions of class have been, and continue to be, limited to the social conditions of the urban poor (Van Galen, 2000). According to bell hooks (1994), "nowhere is there a more intense silence about the reality of class differences than in educational settings" (p. 177). Until the 1960s, schools, specifically K–12, were seen as the most important means for the development of a democratic and egalitarian society (Duffy, 2008). The beginning of tuition-free schooling in the late 19th century afforded those lacking wealth the opportunity to attain social mobility and full participation in political and financial institutions through higher education (Brubacher & Rudy, 1999). Schooling was thought to serve a democratizing function, a vehicle in which one's talents and abilities determined academic success, regardless of race, gender, or social class. However, this democratic vision often was not realized owing to inequities in resources and the class-based campus norms that marginalized those who came from the poor and working classes.

The evolution of higher education from colonial times to contemporary U.S. society can be defined by the tensions between education for the elite, as supported by Thomas Jefferson, and equal access, as supported by Andrew Jackson (Brubacher & Rudy, 1999; hooks, 1994; Hurtado, 1992). In the context of higher education, the American academy originated as an elite system for the purpose of training financially privileged, White Protestant men for the clergy. Under President Jefferson, universities operated as a refuge maintained and funded by the federal government for the sons of the elite. It was not until the early 19th century, under the leadership of President Jackson that a more egalitarian model of higher education was created with the belief that higher education should be a public enterprise and all citizens, rich and poor, should have access (Allen & Jewell, 2002; Brubacher & Rudy, 1999).

HISTORY'S IMPACT TODAY

Historical discrimination and segregation in U.S. education has contributed to current inequalities in educational attainment (Valencia et al., 2004). Although there have been legal successes, such as *Mendez* and *Tape*, these cases have had little lasting impact overall. Moreover, though the *Brown* decision had a major impact on desegregating schools and creating a gateway for equity in education, social norms and attitudes have not been altered to shift the power dynamic on college campuses. Until the 1960s, college campuses were still spaces designed for White, Christian men of privilege (Thelin, 2004). It was not until the tumultuous times of the 1960s and the Civil Rights Movement that university spaces and communities began to open up for many more student populations, particularly women and people of color.

Education played a key role in helping people of color and other subordinated groups assimilate to the dominant culture. Boarding schools, such as those for Mexican and American Indian students, were designed to assimilate and teach students to fit into the dominant U.S. society, while forcing them to abandon their cultural identities (Benham, 2003; Valencia et al., 2004). The educational environment became hostile and unwelcoming for students who had to learn how to become more like White society. Regardless of what laws and policies were established to create equity in education, only part of the system was changed. The U.S. legal system, composed of federal, state, and local laws, was changed to protect the rights of U.S. citizens. Universities responded by creating policies and procedures in line with federal and state mandates, yet the invisible systems of privilege, prejudice, and oppression were not addressed, manifesting themselves through professional practices, attitudes, and curriculum and perpetuated through campus culture and traditions. Though laws had changed and campuses were desegregated and coeducational, the environment on college campuses was still hostile and unwelcoming. It is for these reasons, and many more, that multicultural student services were necessary and essential on college and university campuses.

The intersections of shared histories of oppression must be acknowledged at the outset of a conversation about the development of services meant to redress that oppressive history. One can argue that oppression is about race and ethnicity or that it is about gender or another subordinated identity. In actuality, oppression is about power. It is about the power to grant or deny access to resources that promote and/or support educational success. It is about the power to place or remove roadblocks to make educational attainment possible or impossible. The work of student affairs professionals and university officials reaches beyond supporting students who identify with marginalized communities to knowing and understanding the work of those who came before and building on that foundation. It is this legacy of resistance that will teach us, direct us, and help us better understand why multicultural student services are necessary. As the proverb shared at the beginning of this chapter teaches, knowledge comes from multiple sources. Knowledge about the work of multicultural student services on college campuses requires education in the schoolhouse of resistance. Doing so honors those who have resisted oppression in the past, acknowledges their struggles, and helps in the effort to establish spaces that contribute to the development of campus communities and environments that welcome, affirm, and support all students.

REFERENCES

Allen, W. R., & Jewell, J. O. (2002). A backward glance forward: Past, present, and future perspectives on historically Black colleges and universities. *The Review of Higher Education, 25,* 241–261.

Allyn, D. (2000). *Make love, not war: The sexual revolution, an unfettered history.* New York, NY: Little, Brown.

Benham, M. K. P. (2003). The journey of Native American higher education initiative and tribal colleges and universities. In M. K. P. Benham & W. J. Stein (Eds.), *The renaissance of American Indian higher education: Capturing the dream* (pp. 3–23). Mahwah, NJ: Lawrence Erlbaum.

Braddock, J. H. (1980). The perpetuation of segregation across levels of education: A behavioral assessment of contact hypothesis. *Sociology of Education, 53,* 178–186.

Braddock, J. H. (1985). School desegregation and Black assimilation. *Journal of Social Issues, 41*(3), 9–22.

Braddock, J. H., Crain, R. L., & McPartland, J. M. (1984, December). A long-term view of school desegregation: Some recent studies of graduates as adults. *Phi Delta Kappan,* 178–186.

Braddock, J. H., & Dawkins, M. (1981). Predicting achievement in higher education. *Journal of Negro Education, 50,* 319–327.

Braddock, J. H., & McPartland, J. M. (1982). Assessing school desegregation effects: New directions in research. In A. C. Kerckhoff (Ed.) & R. C. Corwin (Guest Ed.), *Research in sociology of education and socialization,* Vol. 3 (pp. 259–292). Greenwich, CT: JAI.

Brown, L. M. (1998). *Raising their voices: The politics of girls' anger.* Cambridge, MA: Harvard University Press.

Brown v. Board of Education of Topeka, 347 U.S. 483 (1954).

Brubacher, J., & Rudy, W. (1999). *Higher education in transition.* New Brunswick, NJ: Transaction Publishers.

Byrom, B. (2001). Hospital-schools in progressive America. In P. K. Longmore & L. Umansky (Eds.), *The new disability history: American perspectives* (pp. 133–156). New York: New York University Press.

Dilley, P. (2002). Twentieth century postsecondary practices and policies to control gay students. *The Review of Higher Education, 25,* 403–431.

Duffy, J. O. (2008). *Working-class students at Radcliffe College, 1940–1970: The intersection of gender, social class, and historical context*. Lewiston, NY: The Edwin Mellon Press.

Duster, T. (1993). The diversity of California at Berkeley: An emerging reformulation of "competence" in an increasingly multicultural world. In B. W. Thompson & S. Tyagi (Eds.), *Beyond a dream deferred: Multicultural education and the politics of excellence* (pp. 231–255). Minneapolis: University of Minnesota Press.

Ginsberg, R. B. (2004, October 21). *Brown v. Board of Education in international context*. Speech presented at Columbia University School of Law, New York City, NY. Retrieved from http://www.supremecourt.gov/publicinfo/speeches/

Goodell, W. (1968). *The American Slave Code in theory and practice: Its distinctive features shown by its statutes, judicial decision, and illustrative facts*. New York, NY: Negro Universities Press. (Original work published 1853)

hooks, b. (1994). *Teaching to transgress: Education as the practice of freedom*. New York, NY: Routledge.

Hurtado, S. (1992). The campus racial climate: Contexts for conflict. *The Journal of Higher Education, 63*, 539–569.

Hurtado, S., Milem, J. F., Clayton-Pedersen, A. R., & Allen, W. R. (1998). Enhancing campus climates for racial/ethnic diversity: Educational policy and practice. *The Review of Higher Education, 21*, 279–302.

Juneau, S. (2001). *Indian education for all: A history and foundation of American Indian education policy*. Helena: Montana Office of Public Instruction. Retrieved from http://opi.mt.gov/Programs/IndianEd/IEFAResources.html#gpm1_2

Karabel, J. (2005). *The chosen: The hidden history of admission and exclusion at Harvard, Yale, and Princeton*. Boston, MA: Houghton Mifflin.

Longmore, P. K., & Umansky, L. (2001). Introduction: Disability history: From the margins to the mainstream. In P. K. Longmore & L. Umansky (Eds.), *The new disability history: American perspectives* (pp. 1–29). New York: New York University Press.

Mendez v. Westminster School District of Orange County, 64 F. Supp. 544 Decision (1946).

Peterson, M. W., Blackburn, R. T., Gamson, Z. F., Arce, C. H., Davenport, R. W., & Mingle, J. R. (1978). *Black students on White campuses: The impacts of increased Black enrollments*. Ann Arbor: Institute for Social Research, University of Michigan.

Plessy v. Ferguson, 163 U.S. 537 (1896).

Soo, J. D. (2006, August 26). Back to school for integration: Catch-22 of excellence and diversity with race. *Asian Week* [electronic]. Retrieved from http://news.new americamedia.org/news/view_article.html?article_id = 0b132aaf51dd1f6e6a877 f8335b4aa8f

Tape v. Hurley, 66 Cal. 473 (Supreme Court of California, 1885).

Thelin, J. R. (2004). *A history of American higher education*. Baltimore, MD: The Johns Hopkins University Press.

Thompson, D. (2004). *The Tapes of Russell Street: An accomplished family of school desegregation pioneers*. Retrieved from http://www.berkeleyheritage.com/essays/tape_family.html

Valencia, R. A., Garcia, S. R., Flores, H., & Juarez, J. R., Jr. (2004). *Mexican Americans and the law*. Tucson: The University of Arizona Press.

Van Galen, J. A. (2000). Education and class. *Multicultural Education, 2*–11.

VSA. (n.d.). *A brief history of the disability movement*. Retrieved from http://www.vsarts.org/x537.xml

2

Historical and Philosophical Development of Multicultural Student Services

Bettina C. Shuford

Chris, a master's student in a student affairs graduate program, notices that the unit responsible for providing services to underrepresented students is called something different than the office that did this at hir[1] undergraduate school. Ze asks one of hir peers after class one day, "Why are all these offices called different things: Minority Student Services, Office of Ethnicity and Diversity, Multicultural Affairs, Office of Pluralism and Inclusion? What's the difference anyway? Why can't everyone just agree on one label and stick with it?"

MULTICULTURAL STUDENT SERVICES (MSS) offices have played a significant role in supporting underrepresented populations on campus and in developing systemic change around multicultural issues within institutions. The literature on multicultural affairs offices is quite sparse. However, one can glean from the available literature that most multicultural affairs offices were established to serve specific underrepresented racial and ethnic populations. As Chris's exasperated question reflects,

---

[1] Readers are encouraged to review the discussion in the Introduction regarding the use of gender-neutral pronouns in this chapter's vignette.

over time the nomenclature used to describe these offices has changed, as have the purposes and the populations they served. This chapter provides a historical overview of the creation of multicultural affairs offices on college campuses. A distinction between multicultural affairs offices and cultural centers will also be discussed.

UNDERREPRESENTED RACIAL AND ETHNIC STUDENTS IN HIGHER EDUCATION

Leilani Kupo (Chapter 1) gives a cogent summary of the history of inclusion and exclusion of racial and ethnic minorities within U.S. higher education, using a framework of privilege and marginalization. As Kupo discusses, a number of factors influenced the access of African Americans, Asian/Pacific Americans, Hispanic/Latino Americans, and Native Americans into higher education, the most significant influence being court mandates stemming from the civil rights movement and other government-sanctioned initiatives. Prior to the civil rights and La Raza movements, historically Black colleges, Hispanic-serving institutions, and tribal colleges played a significant role in providing access for underrepresented groups to higher education.

These social movements and attending climate shifts throughout history were major forces influencing the educational movement for diverse student populations. The social climate dictated the debate over vocational versus liberal education for African Americans and Native Americans, mandatory English in the classroom for Hispanics, and separate but equal schools for ethnically diverse students (Anderson, 1988). The tide for greater access into predominantly White institutions (PWIs) and mainstream academic programs began when targeted racial groups in the United States began to challenge the status quo. Such challenges gave way to greater opportunities for inclusion in the academy. Although some ethnic groups continue to be underrepresented in higher education, enrollment and graduation rates have significantly improved within the last decade.

HISTORICAL CONTEXT OF MULTICULTURAL AFFAIRS OFFICES

Very little documentation appears in the literature on the history of multicultural affairs offices. To obtain greater confirmation on when multicultural affairs offices were established and for what purpose, I developed a survey and sent it electronically in spring 2001 to 120 multicultural offices/centers across the country. Invitations to complete the survey were also distributed at a national student affairs conference, a national institute, and through a national association electronic listserv. Additional information was obtained from institutional websites and through personal interviews. The data gathering process yielded information on the history of 39 multicultural affairs offices and cultural centers. The information presented here is from those survey results as well as information found in the literature. Dafina Lazarus Stewart and Brian Bridges (Chapter 3) present more recent data that also support the same trends identified nearly 10 years ago.

The establishment of multicultural affairs offices began in the early- to mid-1960s and continues into the 21st century. Diverse student populations arrived at PWIs because of legal challenges that paved the way for legal equality and greater access into higher education. As these students arrived at predominantly White campuses, they were met with neutral policies and color-blind programs and services (Young, 1995). No special provisions were made to accommodate the new mix of diverse students on campuses. Students were expected to assimilate into the mainstream culture. Institutional leaders used a paradigm for diversity that practiced the "Golden Rule," where everyone was treated the same (Palmer, 1989). Campuses were not prepared for the reactions they received from diverse student populations when they began to enroll in larger numbers.

Many of the initial multicultural affairs offices were established to meet the needs of targeted racial and ethnic groups on campus. Institutional leaders shifted the diversity paradigm away from the Golden Rule model of treating everyone the same to "righting the wrongs" experienced by disadvantaged groups. In most cases, the most disadvantaged group on campus became the target for services (Palmer, 1989). For example, in the South, multicultural affairs offices were initially established to serve African American students, whereas the priority of schools in the Southwest was serving Hispanic and Native American students.

Underrepresented racial and ethnic students encountered issues and concerns related to adjustment to college, academic performance, financial resources, feelings of loneliness and isolation, racial/ethnic identity development, racial hostility, issues of entitlement, and a lack of connection to the college environment (Ponce, 1988). Adjustment issues were faced by all students, but the issues faced by underrepresented ethnic groups were "qualitatively and quantitatively different from those faced by White students" (Ponce, 1988, p. 3). As an example, Ponce (1988) cited that White students did not have to face racial hostility and harassment in the form of individual, cultural, and institutional racism. Asian/Pacific American, African American, Hispanic American, and Native American students did not see the curriculum as culturally relevant, they lacked role models, and programs and services on campus did not reflect their cultural interests (Ponce, 1988). These students were expected to acculturate into the mainstream culture and thus shed their racial and ethnic group identity.

During the period that MSS offices were first established, political activism was very high. The Black Power and La Raza movements galvanized students, and their heightened racial consciousness clashed with the majority culture, leading to racial tensions on campuses. Students of color felt a sense of empowerment and entitlement based on their racial identity. In this context, what made them different on the PWI campus in fact gave them power to demand programs and services to meet their unique needs (Steele, 1995). MSS offices were developed as a result of student protest, from a desire to meet the needs of underrepresented students, and in reaction to court mandate (Wright, 1987). The majority of these offices were developed at PWIs; however, MSS offices were also developed at a few historically Black colleges to meet the needs of White students. The initial purpose of many of these offices at PWIs was to provide students with a safe place on campus, as well as to assist with retention efforts, financial aid, and recruitment. MSS staff served as mediators between students and the institution's administration (Young, 1991). Advising multiethnic student organizations was also an important part of the office's responsibilities. In some cases, academic support and advising were also a major part of the office. A long-term director of the Black Cultural Center at the University of Cincinnati indicated that many of the offices that provided a strong academic purpose were offshoots of TRIO programs that provided similar services for low-income, first-generation, and disabled students and were located in the Midwest (E. Abercrumbie, personal communication, October 15, 2001). According to Thurman (1986), minority services and (academic) support services were sometimes used interchangeably.

As MSS offices evolved in the 1980s and 1990s, the scope of their services broadened. No longer were single groups targeted as in the previous decade; instead support services for a broader range of multicultural students were developed, with particular emphases on students of color; gay, lesbian, bisexual, and transgender students; women; and religious diversity. This widened scope was due, in part, to an increased demand for services from other underrepresented groups and a heightened awareness of these groups in the greater society. The services provided for these underrepresented groups ranged from advising, providing mentoring programs, and focusing on personal and social development, such as coming-out support groups, to providing academic support. MSS offices also provided multicultural programming and education for all students on campus. In this latest phase of development, institutional leaders incorporated a diversity paradigm that valued individual and group differences, where everyone was expected to understand and appreciate individuals who were different from oneself. The "valuing differences" approach, as described by Palmer (1989), is still the prevailing paradigm on most campuses based on the scope of services reported both in 2001 and again for this volume.

The nomenclature used to describe offices serving special populations also has evolved over time. In the early years, many MSS offices were identified as "minority affairs" or "minority student services." As the mission of the office began to expand to include a more diverse audience and people began to react negatively to the connotations of the term *minority*, the name changed to titles such as "multicultural affairs," "diversity affairs," "intercultural services," "AHANA" (African, Hispanic, Asian, Native American) office, "ALANA" (African, Latino, Asian, Native American) office, and "multicultural/cultural center." Staff who served as directors of previously "minority affairs" offices in the 1960s and 1970s were later "promoted to mainstream positions in the 1980s" that did not have a specific diversity focus (E. Abercrumbie, personal communication, October 15, 2001). Some MSS offices were cut back or eliminated during this period, and the services were absorbed into other student affairs offices.

In terms of organizational structure, most of the offices that responded to the survey in 2001 indicated that the MSS office was in the student affairs division's reporting line. This trend continues, according to the data reported by Stewart and Bridges in Chapter 3. However, several of the offices established within the previous five years reported having a much different focus. Newer offices were usually headed by a senior-level administrator who reported to a provost or president and provided oversight for campus-wide approaches to diversity that included planning and development, assessment, campus culture, recruitment of diverse faculty and staff, and curriculum development. A number of campuses also reported having developed cultural centers rather than MSS offices at their institutions. The distinction between MSS offices and cultural centers is discussed in the next section.

MULTICULTURAL/CULTURAL CENTERS

The timeline for the development of cultural centers on campuses is similar to the progression made by MSS offices. For example, Black cultural centers and Black Studies programs first developed in the late sixties (Hefner, 2002). In some cases, cultural centers evolved from Black houses (a designated facility for African American students to congregate) and later broadened their missions to serve students from other ethnic groups (Stennis-Williams, Terrell, & Haynes, 1988). The catalyst for developing cultural centers was usually student protest. Some centers were developed to meet the needs of a specific ethnic group, whereas others were developed to serve all students of color. A number of campuses in the survey had separate centers for each ethnic group. The only regional differences found in the survey data were from the California schools. The development of cultural centers was much more prevalent throughout that state. A number of centers within the state of California belong to the California Council of Cultural Centers in Higher Education (CaCCCHE), founded in 1997. The CaCCCHE is a forum for reaffirming the work of centers, programs, and individuals committed to the work of diversity. The Association for Black Cultural Centers (ABCC) is another organization that promotes networking among centers. Founded in 1987 by Dr. Fred Hord, the organization has more than 700 colleges and universities that are members or affiliates in 49 states.

As multicultural affairs offices have evolved, the distinction in mission and programmatic thrust between MSS offices and cultural centers has become less evident. What makes cultural centers unique from MSS offices is most cultural centers have a discrete space for programming, which most MSS offices lack (Young, 1991). Cultural centers and MSS offices both provide support for a variety of multicultural groups and multicultural programming for all constituents within the campus community. Cultural centers, on the other hand, have a broader mission that includes academic, social, and cultural activities (Stennis-Williams et al., 1988). In some cases, cultural center staff members hold faculty status and collaborate with academic programs in offering credited courses and noncredit programs related to multicultural perspectives (Stennis-Williams et al., 1988). Cultural centers also serve a variety of other functions, including providing academic and counseling resources, electronic resources, leadership training, cultural programming, art exhibits, literary publications, community programs and services, lectures, research, and grant writing (Bankole, 2005; Young, 1991). Associations such as CaCCCHE and ABCC provide support and guidance for cultural centers. The ABCC has developed an accreditation process for Black and multicultural centers that provides some standardization among cultural centers across the country (Hord, 2005).

CONCLUSION

MSS offices and cultural centers have played a significant role in the retention of underrepresented racial and ethnic minoritized students. These offices/centers fulfilled a special role on campus that could not be provided within the mainstream campus climate. The mission in their nascent years was to provide support to a new influx of students who had been historically disenfranchised from attending PWIs by providing personal, social, and academic support to aid them in their acclimation to the PWI campus. Multicultural students began to feel as if they mattered on campus and that their needs could be met.

As the affirmative action policies from the previous decades were entrenched in the 1980s and 1990s, MSS offices evolved to meet the changing needs of the campus community. They had adjusted their initial mission of providing direct services to targeted racial and ethnic groups on campus by broadening their scope of services to include other underrepresented groups on campus and expanding program offerings to the entire campus community. These offices and centers now had a three-part mission of providing direct services to targeted populations, providing multicultural programming and education for all students, and promoting systemic change to foster multicultural perspectives across campus (Shuford & Palmer, 2004). There was a greater emphasis on offering educational and cultural programming on campus to educate faculty, staff, and students about diversity. Staff in these offices and centers also made concerted efforts to improve the campus climate for underrepresented groups by working with the administration to develop policies that were more inclusive of diverse perspectives and to train faculty, staff, and students on how to interact more effectively with diverse groups. A major focus of MSS staff was to continue to provide direct support for underrepresented groups, while simultaneously working to foster a campus climate that embraced multiple identity groups on campus.

In some respects, MSS staff were working themselves out of a job. If the campus climate was more embracing of diversity, where all students felt welcomed and included on campus, there would be no need for direct services for underrepresented groups on campus. Even as the population of non-majority students continues to grow and campuses are improving their ability to embrace them and address their needs on campus, racism, sexism, heterosexism, and religious intolerance still exist on campuses and in the greater society. Until campuses truly become multicultural communities where diversity is embraced and valued, multicultural student services offices will always have a role in providing educational programming that will enable all students to live and prosper in a global society.

REFERENCES

Anderson, J. (1988). *The education of Blacks in the south, 1860–1935.* Chapel Hill: University of North Carolina Press.

Bankole, K. (2005). An overview of Black cultural centers in higher education. In F. L. Hord (Ed.), *Black culture centers: Politics of survival and identity* (pp. 164–182). Chicago, IL: Third World Press.

Hefner, D. (2002, February 14). Black cultural centers: Standing on shaky ground? *Black Issues in Higher Education, 18*(26), 22–29.

Hord, F. L. (Ed). (2005). *Black culture centers: Politics of survival and identity.* Chicago, IL: Third World Press.

Palmer, J. D. (1989). Diversity: Three paradigms for change leaders. *OD Practitioner: Journal of the National Organization Development Network, 21*(1), 15–18.

Ponce, F. Q. (1988). Minority student retention: A moral and imperative. In M. C. Terrell & D. J. Wright (Eds.), *From survival to success: Promoting minority student retention* (pp. 1–23). NASPA Monograph Series, no. 9. Washington, DC: National Association of Student Personnel Administrators.

Shuford, B. C., & Palmer, C. L. (2004). Multicultural affairs. In F. MacKinnon (Ed.), *Rentz's student affairs practice in higher education* (3rd ed., pp. 218–238). Springfield, IL: Charles C Thomas.

Steele, S. (1995). The recoloring of campus life: Student racism, academic pluralism, and the end of a dream. In J. Arthur & A. Shapiro (Eds.), *Campus wars: Multiculturalism and the politics of difference* (pp. 176–187). Boulder, CO: Westview Press.

Stennis-Williams, S., Terrell, M. C., & Haynes, A. W. (1988). The emergent role of multicultural education centers on predominantly White campuses. In M. C. Terrell & D. J. Wright (Eds.), *From survival to success: Promoting minority student retention* (pp. 73–98). NASPA Monograph Series, no. 9. Washington, DC: National Association of Student Personnel Administrators.

Thurman, A. (1986). Establishing special services on campus: Factors to consider. In C. Taylor (Ed.), *The handbook of minority student services* (pp. 3–12). Madison, WI: National Minority Campus Chronicle.

Wright, D. J. (1987). Minority students: Developmental beginnings. In D. J. Wright (Ed.), *Responding to the needs of today's minority students* (pp. 5–20). New Directions for Students Services, no. 38. San Francisco, CA: Jossey-Bass.

Young, I. M. (1995). Social movements and the politics of difference. In J. Arthur & A. Shapiro (Eds.), *Campus wars: Multiculturalism and the politics of difference* (pp. 199–225). Boulder, CO: Westview Press.

Young, L. W. (1991). The minority cultural center on a predominantly White campus. In H. E. Cheatham (Ed.), *Cultural pluralism on campus* (pp. 41–53). Lanham, MD: American College Personnel Association.

3

A Demographic Profile of Multicultural Student Services

Dafina Lazarus Stewart
Brian K. Bridges

María, the director of Multicultural Affairs, has been asked by her dean of students to produce some benchmarking data for staffing, range of services, and budgeting at other multicultural student services offices nationally, as well as for their peer institutions. María's contacts in the area help her to easily compile the requested information regarding peer institutions, but she is at a loss as to where to find current national data on these units.

INTRODUCTION

MULTICULTURAL STUDENT SERVICES first came into existence as an organizational unit in U.S. colleges and universities in the 1960s during the student activism that accompanied the civil rights movement. Bettina Shuford (Chapter 2) gives a thorough review of the historical development of multicultural student services units and presents data she collected in 2001 regarding these offices. Since that time, however, there has been no national empirical study of these units, including the number of such units, how they are defined, what services they provide, or other information that would shed light on how these units enhance the academic and social experiences of undergraduate students. Charles Taylor's edited volume, *The Handbook of Minority Student Services*, published in 1986 also provides no such comparative data.

To begin to fill this gap and help professionals like María in the introductory vignette, we developed a questionnaire, "Survey of Multicultural Student Services" (Bridges, Cubarubbia, & Stewart, 2008). The survey's target population was members of the American College Personnel Association (ACPA), College Student Educators International, who identified multicultural student services as their principal job responsibility. A link to the Web-based survey was distributed by electronic mail through ACPA's International Office in the fall of 2008 to 464 members whose membership profiles identified them as professionals working in multicultural affairs. The initial invitation and two reminders yielded 134 respondents who completed the survey anonymously, reflecting a 28.9% response rate.

A PORTRAIT OF MULTICULTURAL STUDENT SERVICES

Missing and unclear data, less than 18% for most items but between 28% and 40% on a handful of items, make the use of cross-tabulations somewhat specious, and readers are urged to review such analyses with caution. For instance, a major variable in the survey was institutional classification, but 30% of the respondents failed to indicate whether they worked at private or public institutions. Such a high rate of missing data makes data permutations highly unreliable and would corrupt cross-tabulations and regressions using this variable. Some other responses were similarly compromised. Therefore the findings reported here should be taken with caution and viewed as indicative of no more than trends among the respondents who did completely respond to the survey items. These complete, correct responses account for 72% or greater of responses in each item.

General Institutional Information

The first three items in the survey asked respondents to describe their institutions in terms of institutional control, composition, size, and classification.

Control and Classification. The first item asked respondents to indicate whether their institution was public or private, as well as whether it was a two-year or four-year institution. Of those respondents who completely answered this item, 97.6% of them were at four-year institutions; only 3 respondents (2.4%) were from two-year colleges. This is reflective of ACPA's membership, which is mostly from four-year institutions. Twenty institutions in ACPA's list of institutional members included the words *community* or *technical* in their names and therefore are likely to be two-year institutions; this is only 4.1% of ACPA's institutional membership, which totaled 482 institutions in January 2010. However, two-year institutions (public and private, nonprofit) number 1,677 (including branch campuses), representing nearly 38.5% of the nation's higher education institutions (National Center for Education Statistics, 2008). Therefore, it is clear that these data represent the nature and characteristics of multicultural student services (MSS) at four-year colleges and universities to the near exclusion of two-year campuses. This lack of representation within ACPA's membership might be expected, given student affairs units' underdeveloped status at community colleges relative to four-year institutions generally and specifically in terms of multicultural student services (see Zamani-Gallaher & Bazile, Chapter 10).

Of the 70.1% of respondents who indicated whether they were at public or private institutions, 40.4% were at public institutions, and 59.6% were from private institutions. Given that four-year, private, nonprofit institutions constitute only 35.2% of the higher education institutions in the United States (National Center for Education Statistics, 2008), private, four-year colleges constituted a larger proportion of these survey respondents than their representation in higher education. Therefore, similar to the case for four-year institutions, the findings reported here may be skewed by the over-representation of respondents from private institutions.

Racial/Ethnic Composition. Respondents were asked whether their institution was a predominantly White institution (PWI), historically Black college (HBCU), or Hispanic-serving institution (HSI). Respondents from PWIs constituted 96.2% of the sample, whereas respondents from HBCUs and HSIs together made up 3.8% of the sample. Professionals working at HSIs were the majority of those respondents ($n = 4$). Only one respondent worked at a an HBCU. Again, these data in part reflect the ACPA membership, also mostly working at PWIs. Cross-referencing of ACPA's institutional membership list as of January 2010 with lists of HSIs (Excelencia in Education, 2006–2007) and HBCUs (White House Initiative, 2010) revealed the following data: Of the 482 institutional members within ACPA, 14 institutions appeared in the list of HSIs (2.9% of ACPA's institutional members), and 15 institutions appeared in the list of HBCUs (3.1% of ACPA's institutional members). This reflects an institutional membership within ACPA that is 94% PWIs (no tribal colleges are represented). As Rome (Chapter 11) and Riding In and Longwell-Grice (Chapter 12) illustrate, multicultural student services are thought of and practiced very differently at HBCUs and tribal colleges, and the critical mass of Latino/a students at HSIs also is likely to alter MSS's character. Unfortunately, these data offer little insight about the nature of MSS at these institutions.

Size. Survey respondents were asked the total size of their full-time undergraduate population (i.e., FTE). Fifty-seven percent of respondents worked at institutions with fewer than 10,000 full-time undergraduate students, with more than a quarter (27.1%) at institutions of between 5,000 and 9,999 students. Fifteen percent of respondents were at institutions of between 10,000 and 19,999 students; 14.3% were at institutions between 20,000 and 30,000; and 13.5% were at institutions with more than 30,000 undergraduate students. Only one respondent did not answer this question. Institutional size was distributed somewhat evenly across the survey respondents, except for smaller midsize colleges (5,000–9,999 students), which constitute more than one-quarter of the sample. Based on these findings, these data may be reflecting trends in multicultural student services at private, four-year, predominantly White colleges and universities across a range of institutional sizes.

General Program Information

Six questions in the survey asked respondents to share additional information about the general character of MSS at their institution. This information included: (a) how multicultural students were defined, (b) whether a centralized office existed, (c) the division in which the office was housed, (d) how long the office had been in existence, (e) under what conditions the office was originally established, and (f) if the focus or population served by the MSS office had changed since its inception. Based on these data, a clearer picture of MSS at these respondents' institutions evolved.

Defining Multicultural Students. An essential question to resolve when planning a unit to provide services to multicultural students and educational programming and services to the broader campus is exactly what populations are being included under the moniker of *multicultural students*. Survey participants were asked to select as many defining characteristics as were applicable from the following list: race and ethnicity, gender, sexual orientation, nationality, faith/religion, disability, social class. Respondents were also given the opportunity to note other identity categories that had not been suggested. Table 3.1 reports the percentage of respondents who indicated that a category was used to define students served by multicultural student services.

Most readers are likely not to be surprised to see that 100% of respondents indicated that race and ethnicity were used to identify multicultural student populations on campus, but the lesbian, gay, bisexual, and transgender (LGBT) student population has not yet been uniformly identified as a student population with needs and issues that are addressed within multicultural student services, nor have issues related to LGBT education or ally development been incorporated under the MSS umbrella. It is also worthy of note that international students (who would be defined as multicultural

Table 3.1
PERCENTAGE OF RESPONDENTS INDICATING
CATEGORY USED TO DEFINE STUDENTS

Identifying Category	% of Respondents
Race & ethnicity	100.0
Sexual orientation	58.2
Gender	54.5
Nationality	51.5
Religion/faith	35.1
Disability	34.3
Social class	23.1
Other	6.0

students by nationality) are also identified as multicultural students by a bare majority of this study's participants. However, it is possible that international students are served by a dedicated international programs and services office that provides educational programming as well as social and academic support services for students. This might also be the case for students with disabilities, identified as a population included within MSS by 34.3% of the respondents. Services and programming for this population could be housed under a separate unit or individual professional charged with the university's ADA compliance or in combination with the college's student counseling services.

Conversely, the small but appreciable reflection of faith/religion and social class to define multicultural populations demonstrates the increasing significance of these identities in the college experiences of students' and institutions' responses to that significance by providing intentional services to these groups. Readers are encouraged to review Chapter 6 for Jenny Small's discussion of the incorporation of religious and faith diversity within MSS on campus.

Regrettably, gender identity and expression were not suggested on the survey, and no respondents included it as a free response under "Other." However, it is possible that gender identity and expression were included with sexual orientation in the minds of respondents as they completed the survey. Moreover, given that 54.5% of respondents to this item did indicate gender as a means by which to identify multicultural students, transgender and gender-nonconforming students could have been included in respondents' minds under this category.

homeless?

Other identity categories given by respondents included identifying multicultural students by differences in language (e.g., English as a Second Language), veteran status, first-generation college students, foster youth, and geographic origin, whether "rural or urban." These other identities that are emerging as significant shapers of student experience represent areas of future work for MSS and a need for more research to inform practice in these areas.

Centralized MSS Office. More than 80% of respondents indicated that their campuses did have a centralized or freestanding office dedicated to the provision of services to multicultural student populations, as defined by the institution. Of those who indicated that their institutions did not have a centralized MSS office, thematic analysis of their free responses indicated that services to multicultural student populations were addressed within the missions of existing student affairs units (e.g., campus activities office or counseling centers), carried out by various academic units (e.g., ethnic studies departments), or operated in a decentralized student affairs model. In the latter case, respondents usually described a scenario where several racial/ethnic groups were each served by an office specifically devoted to their needs (e.g., African American Student Services, Latino Student Services, etc.) or across offices who addressed different constituent identity categories (e.g., Cross-Cultural Center, LGBT Center, Women's Center, Disability Center).

For institutions that did have a centralized MSS office, 79.1% of respondents reported that the office was administered through student affairs. Of the remaining responses, 8.2% indicated that the centralized MSS office was housed in academic affairs, reporting to the president or provost. One respondent indicated a nontraditional reporting line in which the MSS office was situated in the president's office but reported "on the ground" through the vice president of student life. Another respondent replied that the "VP of Academic and Student Affairs supervises all Deans plus [the] Director of Diversity," resulting in a blended reporting line that included both academic and student affairs. There are yet other institutions that have one office that reports to the president or provost on issues related to faculty and staff diversity and campus climate, with another MSS unit situated in student affairs that is responsible for social, cultural, and academic support programming for students. Despite the variety in organizational structures that exists, the dominant trend in these data is that centralized offices for MSS are housed within divisions of student affairs, although their work might include academic support and other academic affairs-related activities (see discussion under "Range of Services Provided" for further elaboration).

Length of Existence. A centralized office for MSS existed at these institutions across a range of time periods. Two-fifths (40.4%) of respondents indicated that their MSS offices were in existence for ten or fewer years. More than two-fifths (44.0%) had offices that existed for 11 to 25 years, and 15.6% of respondents said their offices had existed for 26 or more years. Although the 1970s through 1980s was an active period for the development of MSS units in the aftermath of student activism (Shuford, Chapter 2), it is evident from these data that there remains a considerable number of colleges for whom multicultural student services is a relatively new undertaking in the history of the institution.

Impetus for Creation. Respondents were asked what conditions spurred the creation of the office(s) devoted to multicultural student services. Survey options included student interest/activism, to serve demographic shifts in enrollment, as a result of institutional reorganization, to address retention issues, and other, with a follow-up prompt to explain what that was. More than one-fifth of respondents (23.1%) did not answer this question, which possibly indicates that the development of services for multicultural student populations is not well documented or not included at all in the "organizational saga" (Clark, 1972) of the institution. Table 3.2 gives the percentage of respondents reporting each of the aforementioned stimuli for the creation of MSS at their institutions.

For those who reported other reasons, responses thematically converged around the following six stimuli:

1. To create better synergy and collaboration among offices that were previously addressing these issues in a decentralized manner and "across underrepresented and marginalized groups"
2. To respond to federal mandates for equal opportunity programs and initiatives
3. To respond to "Black faculty and staff activism"
4. To meet voluntary regional accreditation requirements
5. In response to increased multicultural awareness on the part of the campus community
6. In response to a racist incident on campus

Most of these stimuli (both survey and self-defined options) were externally driven or reactive, as opposed to more proactive stimuli, such as institutional

Table 3.2
VARIABLES SPURRING CREATION OF MSS OFFICES

Conditions Under Which Office Was Established	%
Student interest/activism	47.6
Address retention issues	45.6
Serve demographic shifts in enrollment	44.7
Institutional reorganization	17.5
Other	13.6

reorganization to create better synergy and collaboration or increased multi-cultural awareness within the institution. The reactive history of MSS development might hamper unit effectiveness when faculty, staff, or students are less active or institutional priorities are realigned to meet new demands made by external constituents, such as state and federal governments and accreditation agencies.

Evolution. Looking forward from the historical development of the MSS unit, respondents were asked whether the focus of the office or population served had changed since its inception and, if so, how. There were missing responses for this item as well (17.9%). Similar to the previous item, this might indicate that information about how the office had evolved over time is inaccessible and unknown to many professionals currently working in multicultural student services. For those who did respond, 72.7% indicated that either the focus of the office or the population served had changed since the office's inception, and 27.3% reported that these things had not changed.

The survey also asked respondents which explanation provided best reflected how the office had evolved for the 80 respondents who indicated that the focus and/or population served by their institution's MSS office had changed over time. More than three-fifths (62.5%) indicated that the population they now serve has broadened; 36.2% reported that additional services were now being offered; 1.2% of participants described the change as a narrowing of the population being served by their MSS office. These data support Shuford's discussion (Chapter 2) of the ballooning of responsibilities in multicultural student services units.

Personnel Information

The next section of the survey asked participants to describe personnel matters, including titles, reporting lines, required educational level, salary range, primary job responsibilities, total office staff, and total annual budget. Combined, these data paint a picture of MSS personnel.

Title of MSS Leader. For this item, respondents were given a free-response item and asked to provide the title of the person with primary oversight in the MSS office. Usable responses (i.e., a specific individual's name was not given) were supplied by 91% of the sample with all participants supplying a response. The most frequently reported response included the word *director* in the title, followed by *assistant director* or *assistant dean*. *Coordinator* also appeared among the responses. Given the inconsistency in titles and institutional stratification, it is unclear what level in the student affairs division these personnel occupy; the positions could reflect mid-level managers or entry-level professionals. Other responses (13.1%) indicated that the principal MSS professional in the unit had a more senior or upper middle-management position. Such levels might be reflected in titles such as associate dean or associate director, as well as assistant vice chancellor, vice president, or vice provost.

Reporting Line. An earlier survey item sought information about where the MSS office was located within the college or university structure. This item asked respondents to identify the title of the person to whom the MSS office head reported. Response options were supplied for the participants, and only 12 individuals did not answer the question. Twenty-seven percent identified a dean of students as the supervising professional for the MSS head, 25.4% identified the supervisor as a vice president/chancellor for Student Affairs, and 4% chose the president/chancellor as the supervisor. However, 43.4% selected other, and these responses included a mid-level manager at the associate dean level within student affairs or senior level positions in academic affairs, such as a vice provost, vice president, or provost. If the supervising professional was in academic affairs, the title was consistently at the vice or associate provost/president level. Based on these data, albeit limited, it appears that MSS is located higher in the organizational hierarchy when placed under academic affairs than when situated in student affairs. However, this placement is not significantly correlated with student, faculty, or senior administrators' attitudes toward MSS. Bivariate correlations using Spearman's rho, a non-parametric statistical test appropriate for the ordinal level data collected, showed very low associations between the variables of reporting line for the MSS office and student, faculty, and senior administrators' attitudes, as well as between who supervised MSS and the attitudes of these three groups. Moreover, none of the correlations were determined to be statistically significant for these data.

Required Education. The next item on the survey asked respondents the required level of education for the person leading the MSS office. The overwhelming majority of respondents (82.1%) reported that a master's degree was the highest required level of education for the head of the MSS office, 11.2% indicated that a doctoral degree was the highest level of education required, and 6.7% reported that a bachelor's degree was the highest level. It is not clear from this finding whether these master's degrees were from a student affairs graduate preparation program or another field. Other disciplines that might provide personnel for MSS are counseling, social work, ethnic studies, and sociology. Graduate preparation in student affairs would be a valuable asset for professionals in MSS to navigate working within student affairs and academic affairs (see discussions by Kimbrough & Cooke in Chapter 14 and by Kodama & Takesue in Chapter 15), as well as understanding institutional context and environment (see Petitt & McIntosh, Chapter 13).

Salary Range. Reported salaries for chief MSS officers varied widely. Only 4% of respondents said that the salary was between $30,000 and $39,000. The remaining responses were spread somewhat evenly across the other salary ranges: 32% between $40,000 and $49,000; 24% between $50,000 and $59,000; 22.4% between $60,000 and $69,000; and 17.6% reporting a salary more than $70,000.

Primary Responsibilities. Survey participants were asked the primary responsibilities for the chief MSS officer. Respondents were asked to select as many as applied from a list of responses and to add other responsibilities that were not represented. The highest reported job responsibility was programming (83.3%). Student advising and consulting with senior level administrators on multicultural student issues followed as primary responsibilities for 62.9% of respondents for each category. Conducting professional development for faculty, staff, and other constituents was another common primary responsibility selected by 58.3% of survey respondents. Much less frequently reported was developing research related to multicultural issues. Less than one-quarter of respondents selected this as a primary job responsibility.

Other responses given by respondents included the following activities: academic enrichment and support; student organization advising; creating institution-wide diversity plans; overseeing scholarship programs and funds for multicultural students; campus climate and other assessments; fundraising; multicultural student recruitment; precollege programs; and MSS staff supervision. These data together present a picture of head MSS officers with a broad and extensive range of responsibilities. On many campuses, it appears that MSS has been organized to function almost as a college within a college, specifically for multicultural student populations, offering a one-stop shop for almost every aspect of a student's life. Manning and Muñoz (Chapter 19) critique the viability of this continued role for MSS in the future. Additionally, MSS officers often are viewed as the campus experts on issues of multicultural issues and student populations.

Full-Time, Professional Office Staff. Respondents were next asked to indicate whether and how many full-time professional employees were on staff and dedicated to the MSS unit. More than three-fourths of respondents (76.9%) indicated that the head MSS officer did have staff reporting to them. However, this left 27.6% reporting no staff in the MSS unit other than the lead staff member. For those who did answer "yes," staff numbers were commonly low, with typically no more than four total full-time staff reported, and most of these offices functioning with only two full-time professional staff. Many respondents also added student staff and volunteers in their total numbers. It is also not clear whether respondents inadvertently included the head of the office in their response. A small number of respondents reported MSS offices with much larger staff numbers, such as 12, 18, 19, and even 35 at one institution. Another 14 respondents reported staff sizes between 5 and 8 full-time professionals. After cleaning the data, the mean staff size was 4 full-time professionals, but with a standard deviation of 4.

Institutional size could be a factor influencing available resources to hire larger numbers of staff and larger student populations to serve. Bivariate correlations to test the strength of the association between institutional size and the size of the MSS office staff revealed a somewhat weak but statistically significant relationship (Pearson's $r = .210$, $p < .05$). This indicates that although larger institutions are somewhat more likely to have larger MSS staffs, this is weakly correlated and even institutions with larger student populations might have relatively small numbers of staff in the MSS office. This might be indicative of the small proportion of the multicultural student population at most predominantly White institutions relative to the entire student body and a philosophy of MSS as only necessary to provide direct student support to targeted groups. However, given that nearly three-fifths of respondents indicated that they had responsibilities to provide training to faculty, staff, and other constituents (see "Primary Responsibilities" above), there is a danger that MSS offices are understaffed relative to the extensive duties they are expected to perform.

Annual Operating Budget. When asked about the annual budget for multicultural student services, 31.3% of survey respondents did not answer, so these findings are based on 92 responses. It is possible that those who chose not to respond may not have had budget oversight for the office. For those who did respond, 80.4% of respondents indicated annual budgets of less than $499,000, but responses varied widely with no more than 30% of respondents selecting any of the budget categories. A very small number of respondents ($n = 5$) reported annual budgets of less than $10,000 and a similarly small number ($n = 4$) reported an annual budget of more than $1.5 million. Between these extremes, the following budget ranges were reported: $10,000 to $49,999 (13.0%); $50,000 to $99,999 (15.2%); $100,000 to $249,999 (30.4%); $250,000 to $499,999 (16.3%); $500,000 to $749,999 (4.3%); $750,000 to $999,999 (3.3%); $1 million to $1.5 million (7.6%). The extent to which these responses include personnel-related expenses (e.g., salary, work-study, professional development allocations, etc.) as part of the budget figure is unclear. This is another variable that institutional size might play an influential role in determining; however, bivariate correlations revealed a very weak and statistically insignificant relationship (Spearman's rho = .084, p = .430) between institutional size and MSS budget. Therefore, it would be spurious to assume that MSS offices at larger institutions necessarily have more generous budget allotments. Therefore, given the extensive range of responsibilities charged to these offices, a good number of them might be underbudgeted.

Facilities

The next section of the survey focused on the physical space occupied by MSS offices, and for what purposes the facilities were used. Respondents were queried about the physical location of the MSS office and how that space was used.

Location. Two-fifths of valid survey responses (39.1%) reported that the MSS office was located in the campus student union building. The next most frequently reported responses were in an administrative building (30.5%) and as a stand-alone facility (13.3%). Much less common was for the MSS office to be located in an academic building (6.2%) or residence hall (2.3%). Respondents were also allowed to identify other facilities that did not appear on the list. One respondent indicated that the MSS unit was housed in an area of the university library as a "separate tenant." Another respondent stated that their MSS unit was housed in a "mixed-use building" that served as classroom space, the library, dining area, and some student affairs offices. Three participants replied "we have none," indicating that multicultural student services was without a home on these campuses.

Space Utilization. Next, participants selected and reported how the space was used. Office space (86.4%), library/resource center/personal study space (53.8%), and programming space (47.0%) were the three most frequently selected responses. A small number of respondents also indicated that their facilities were used as classroom space ($n = 8$). Some respondents provided additional information and indicated that their facilities also were locations for advising, socializing, meetings and storage for student organizations, and, in one case, an art gallery. A number of responses also used the phrase *safe place* to describe the purpose of their facilities. Truly, the picture reflected here is of a multifunctional space serving a variety of needs and purposes for both office staff and multicultural student populations.

Range of Services Provided

Section five in the survey addressed the range of programming and services provided by multicultural student services targeted toward students. Respondents were asked to describe the academic, cultural, and social programming offered through multicultural student services. However, it is important to remember differences in student population composition. Four respondents did indicate that they were at an HSI or HBCU, and one respondent commented at the end of the survey that "I am on a campus where our 'minority' is the 'majority.' I think this has impacted the way we program." The chapters by Rome (Chapter 11) and Riding In and Longwell-Grice (Chapter 12), in this volume, help to elucidate these differences.

Academic Programming. Forty-five percent of respondents indicated that their MSS units offered academic programming for students. Examples of such programming included study skills workshops, tutoring in math, science, and/or writing, peer mentoring, academic advising, collaboration with faculty on course development, credit-bearing courses, a first-year seminar section for multicultural students, summer bridge programs for multicultural students, and guest lecturing in classes.

Cultural Programming. Cultural programming was much more frequently selected by respondents. Among respondents, 92.5% indicated that their MSS office did offer cultural programming. Examples of cultural programming included a wide array of heritage month celebrations, ally training (e.g., Safe Zone), and other diversity awareness-raising events (e.g., Tunnel of Oppression), hosting symposia, inviting performers and speakers to campus, and planning and facilitating retreats and dialogue sessions both on and off campus.

Social Programming. Social programming was a close second to cultural programming, with 91.9% of respondents indicating that they offered students opportunities for social interaction. Examples of social programming covered the gamut from casual, fun events like parties, dances, mixers, game and movie nights, and tailgates to more cerebral activities such as book clubs, discussion groups, and poetry nights. Also, fellowship opportunities were created through hosting meals, receptions, and coffee hours. Opportunities to celebrate achievements were achieved through events like multicultural graduation ceremonies. Finally, perhaps in recognition of the lack of culturally relevant personal care services offered in the locales of many predominantly White universities, a number of respondents reported sponsoring barbershop or haircut nights for students.

Adequacy of Services. In this section of the survey, respondents were asked whether their MSS office was able to provide adequate programming, advising, and support to all underserved students enrolled at the institution. More than 80% of survey respondents answered "no." When asked which groups were particularly underserved by their MSS office, a number of groups were most commonly identified: multiple and intersecting identity groups, women students, Asian Pacific Islanders, and American Indian students (one respondent specifically identified Hmong, Cambodian, and non-Chicano students), Arab and Muslim students and faith-based communities in general, LGBT students, first-generation students, students with disabilities, commuter and nontraditional-age students, and as one respondent said, "students of color who are not Black, Latino or White." A number of respondents offered explanations along with their answers; all who did so said lack of funding and staff contributed to these deficiencies. This theme came up again in responses toward the end of the survey.

These responses suggest that most MSS offices remain centered on issues of racism and exist primarily for the support of racial and ethnic groups, particularly African Americans and Latinos. In many cases, MSS's historic origins in student activism (as illustrated by earlier findings in this survey and Shuford's chapter in this volume), particularly by African American students (see Patton, Ranero, & Everett, Chapter 4), have perhaps led to this continued narrow terrain. Yet, it should be noted that professionals in MSS recognize the need for expanded programs and services and desire to serve a wider range of multicultural student populations.

Assessment. Accountability has become a necessary part of the duties of all professionals in higher education. MSS and other student affairs offices must be able to demonstrate their effectiveness through careful and regular assessment that is used to inform, revise, and design practice for the attainment of student learning outcomes. Toward that end, we asked respondents several questions about assessment and evaluation: whether it was done, what methods of assessment or evaluation were used, and how often these assessments or evaluations were conducted.

A great majority of respondents (79.9%) indicated that they did assess or evaluate the programs and activities offered in MSS. One respondent indicated that their MSS unit was "just instituting an official assessment process." Among this group, surveys provided the dominant mode of assessment, with 92.4% of respondents indicating that they used them to conduct assessments or evaluations. Focus groups were also somewhat popular among these respondents, netting 43.8% of responses. Only 34.3% of respondents who conducted assessments or evaluations did so by individual interviews with office constituents. Other modes of assessment offered by respondents included examining GPA and retention rates for students who participated in special, targeted programs (e.g., summer bridge programs), assessing participation ratios for events, reports from and conversations with student leaders, student-written reflections, and informal conversations with students. Respondents reported that most often these assessments or evaluations occurred immediately after a program or event (85.4%). However, periodic assessments and evaluations (e.g., a five-year review) were also reported by 46.6% of respondents. Respondents also indicated that evaluations were carried out at the end of the academic year (42.7%) and at the conclusion of each academic term (25.2%). Other respondents also reported doing evaluations or assessments "during programs," "within a week of a program," and in the "middle of the semester."

Campus Attitudes Toward Multicultural Student Services

Respondents next considered how MSS was viewed by students, faculty, and senior administrators on campus. Student attitudes were described mostly as being "somewhat supportive and interested" (60.4%), with "barely supportive and interested" (15.7%), and "very supportive and interested" (14.9%) rounding out the three most frequently selected responses for this item. Faculty attitudes toward MSS were perceived as somewhat less positive, with just over half (50.7%) of respondents indicating "somewhat supportive and interested feelings" and 30.6% indicating that they perceived faculty to be "barely supportive and interested." Only 9.0% of respondents perceived faculty on their campus to be "very supportive and interested." Regarding senior administrators, the perception on the part of MSS professionals who completed this survey was also lukewarm. Almost three-fifths (58.2%) of respondents did perceive their senior administrators to be "somewhat supportive and interested," whereas 25.4% described their senior administrators as "barely supportive and interested," and 11.9% described this group as "very supportive and interested."

Additionally, these MSS professionals reported their perception that students and faculty were "unaware we exist" (7.5% and 5.2% of respondents, respectively). An anecdotal account of a recent experience seems to lend credence to the problem posed even when small numbers of students or faculty are uninformed and unaware of the existence of MSS on campus. Recently, a graduate student visited a small, private, liberal arts, predominantly White college to learn more about its services to multicultural students. The student was unable to locate the office for quite some time, even with the help of two White student tour guides, a pair of students of color encountered along the way, and the White student working at the campus information desk. Finally, the office was found when the student desk worker called the office and asked where in the building it was located. If a campus visitor had trouble getting to the office, imagine the difficulty students who are not connected to the office already must have obtaining services and support. Together with the fairly lukewarm reception that these professionals perceive they are getting from faculty and senior administrative staff, it appears that MSS may operate in an institutional climate at many campuses that might not be openly hostile, but neither is it truly encouraging and supportive. Navigating such a complex institutional climate is vital, and Petitt and McIntosh (Chapter 13) address such issues in this volume.

Improving MSS Organizational Effectiveness

At the end of the survey, respondents were asked to reflect on what they would need to improve the effectiveness of their MSS office. Respondents were given a set of responses from which they could select all that applied and were allowed to write in additional improvements. Of the selected responses, "more human resources" (i.e., more staff) was selected most often by these MSS professionals (81.7%). "More financial resources" was the next most frequently selected response (73.3%), followed closely by "more involvement from majority students" (71.0%) and "more involvement from targeted multicultural students" (68.7%). Most respondents also felt that "more support from faculty" (55.7%) and "more support from senior administrators" (53.4%) would help them improve their effectiveness in serving the campus. Other responses given included leadership (a couple of respondents indicated that their MSS office was without a director, one had been without a director for more than two years), more physical space, greater multicultural alumni involvement, better marketing of programs and services, a move in the organizational chart, and a seat at the academic table.

When asked how these improvements would help MSS be more effective on their campus, respondents were quite thoughtful, and their replies mostly indicated that they would simply be able to help more students and do a better job if they had these things and "more knowledge of [our] existence." For example, one respondent wrote, "[We would be] able to grow the department and do more than just cultural programming." Another respondent said, "Additional staff and funding could provide [a] broader range of services and events." Yet another wrote, "Caseloads could be reduced, allowing for more meaningful relationships with advisees"; another indicated that "comprehensive, strategic, infused support from all directions [would be] essential for sustainability and growth." Finally, one respondent stated, "it [would] reveal more of a concrete commitment to diversity and social justice education on campus." Every single respondent provided a response to this item. Reading their words and sensing their almost tangible desperation for more help to do what they were expected to do was powerful. It is clear that these professionals are passionate about their work and the students they serve. But it is also apparent that they are passionate about the students they cannot reach because the funds do not stretch far enough and there are not enough hours in the day, week, and year for one or two people to do it all.

IMPLICATIONS AND RECOMMENDATIONS

Several implications for multicultural centers emerge from these data. These implications include: (a) the need to expand populations served, (b) reviewing the limitations of fiscal resources, (c) examining the hierarchical and physical placement of these offices and centers for greatest impact, and (d) cultivating greater connections with faculty and building support from them through more academic-oriented programming. One conclusion we offer from our review of the survey data is that the effectiveness of multicultural centers is hindered, in part, by perceptions that they serve a limited population based on race or that they are solely programming offices and by a lack of visibility with faculty. Given the data presented here, these perceptions are largely inaccurate. A robust discussion with relevant stakeholders of how these implications can be addressed on campus can provide increased visibility and effectiveness for multicultural centers.

The need for multicultural student services to expand the groups they serve beyond racial and ethnic categories is important, given the continuing diversification of college campuses. As emerging group identities become more highly represented within higher education, an increased demand for services from these groups will likely follow. Survey results indicate that MSS offices have expanded their services and broadened the scope of groups they assist, which indicates an attempt to address the needs of emerging groups on campus. In addition, the differentiation of service offices, such as offices for disability services and LGBT concerns, have diverted the need for these groups to rely heavily on MSS offices. However, as the academy is looked to as a potential source for addressing societal conflicts that occasionally emerge from different perspectives, MSS offices can perform a pivotal role by facilitating cross-cultural interactions and programming.

The proper allocation of fiscal resources is often a concern within the academy, especially for student services offices. More than 60% of the institutions that responded to our survey have less than $250,000 allocated for their annual operating budgets. The extent to which this figure might include allotments for salary and other personnel-related expenses is unclear. However, if it does, it paints an even more meager picture of limited funding for programming and initiatives. The implications of inadequate funding for MSS offices as service demands increase, the costs of programming increase, and institutions reduce funding to what are viewed as supplemental (i.e., not essential) programming offices is that the quantity, quality, depth, breadth, and scope of these offices will certainly suffer and institutional diversity initiatives could be hampered. Colleges and universities that are committed to programs and activities that engage students, faculty, and staff should take steps to ensure successful funding levels for their respective MSS offices. Assessing program effectiveness and understanding the return on funding investments becomes more critical as resources remain scarce. This indicates that assessment has to be more central to the daily operations of MSS offices, as well as finding ways to collaborate on services and programming. Both these issues are central ideas for many of the chapter authors in this text.

The hierarchical and physical placement of MSS needs to be strategically considered on each campus for maximum impact and to infuse diversity effectively throughout the institution. Where MSS is located within the organizational hierarchy, specifically whether it is located in academic or student affairs, can be important for connections with faculty and introducing more academically oriented programming with targeted learning outcomes. Therefore, placement within academic affairs might afford MSS offices greater access to senior administrators as well as to faculty (see Kodama & Takesue, Chapter 15, for further discussion of collaborations between MSS and academic affairs). These offices must also be centrally located on campus to reinforce their importance to an institution's diversity agenda. Placing these offices within buildings on the campus fringes or providing inadequate space marginalizes MSS and sends a subliminal message to identity groups that low priority has been placed on them and their needs. A central campus location and placement within the academic hierarchy sends a valuable message to campus stakeholders, particularly faculty, about the imperative nature of MSS, which can promote its effectiveness.

Multicultural student services must establish greater connections with faculty and garner their support through more academic programming. This has potentially significant implications for the way these offices conduct their business, especially if they are housed in student affairs. Connecting and collaborating with faculty more effectively can lead to increased programming, attendance, service utilization, visibility, and respect. Faculty often make up the largest block of employees on campus and certainly shape its academic culture. Survey results indicate that fewer than 10% of faculty are perceived to be very concerned about and supportive of MSS. If this is an accurate perception, it can be rectified through faculty advisory groups, creating faculty research and discussion series, and promoting programming in line with curricular needs and desired outcomes; however, without adjustments to the faculty reward system for participating in these sorts of activities, many are likely to shun this level of involvement. Despite this reality of modern higher education, facilitating and furthering these collaborations are essential to the future success of MSS.

The recommendations that emerge from these implications can change considerably the way MSS conducts its work. Although many campuses will not have the ability to implement these recommendations in total, even addressing one or two can have a lasting impact.

CONCLUSION

Multicultural student services is a complex functional area, and a deeper understanding of its nature, structure, and service within campus communities is desperately needed. This chapter contributes to our knowledge and understanding of MSS by providing some empirical data about these offices, their personnel, and the services they perform for students, faculty, and staff. Much more research needs to be done. Conducting this survey revealed the highly disparate ways in which multicultural student services are practiced even within this small, albeit national, sample. Further, lack of explicit knowledge about the origins of these units and how they have evolved affects our ability to gather good data about these questions. It is vitally important that current professionals in multicultural student services search out this history at their institutions and be willing to share it with researchers and fellow practitioners.

Finally, the complex and varied structure and character of these offices might exceed the capacity of survey research. Although several questions could have been refined to garner more reliable data, it was clear that there are more questions that simply cannot be effectively posed or answered in a questionnaire. Moreover, as researchers, we must practice multicultural competence in our research methods. Although it cannot be supported in these data, as Washington points out in Chapter 16, multicultural student services professionals are most often members of the multicultural populations served by their offices. In light of this, researchers must be aware of different cultural attitudes toward research methods. For many people of color, surveys are not effective data-collection tools, because they are too impersonal and restrictive, and participants are unable to build rapport and trust with the researcher, which is critical to gathering reliable and authentic data from these populations (Pope, Reynolds, & Mueller, 2004; Scheurich & Young, 1997). Therefore, it is likely that qualitative research would enhance the findings generated by survey research on this population.

The voices of the respondents and their own dedication, commitment, and sometimes frustration with this work speak most clearly about the need for multicultural student services. So, finally, here is a sampling of additional comments offered at the conclusion of the survey:

> "As higher education starts to welcome more students of color—we need to continue our efforts."
>
> "It's comprehensive, specialized, difficult—but rewarding work."
>
> "[We are] moving away from surface heritage celebrations toward a greater focus on identity/cultural competency."
>
> "MSS/Cultural center work needs more publications and studies to support the practice."
>
> "My work with students has opened my eyes to the type of student affairs professional I want to be."
>
> "Senior administrators focus recruitment on assimilated diverse students who don't see the value of our work."

These statements point toward the current and future challenges that confront multicultural student services as it continues to evolve. Some of these challenges open up controversial perspectives about assimilation, integration, and what should be the mission of these offices. Later chapters in this volume speak to these issues and further expose the debates and complex realities that inform them.

REFERENCES

Bridges, B. K., Cubarubbia, A., & Stewart, D. L. (2008). *Survey of multicultural student services*. Available from the authors.

Clark, B. R. (1972). The organizational saga in higher education. *Administrative Science Quarterly, 17,* 178–184.

Excelencia in Education. (2006–2007). *Hispanic-serving institutions list: 2006–07.* Retrieved from www.EdExcelencia.org

National Center for Education Statistics. (2008). *Degree-granting institutions, by control and type of institution: Selected years, 1949–50–2007–08* [table 265]. Retrieved from http://nces.ed.gov/programs/digest/d08/tables/dt08_265.asp

Pope, R. L., Reynolds, A. L., & Mueller, J. A. (2004). *Multicultural competence in student affairs*. San Francisco, CA: Jossey-Bass.

Scheurich, J. J., & Young, M. D. (1997). Coloring epistemologies: Are our research epistemologies racially biased? *Educational Researcher, 26*(4), 4–16.

Taylor, C. A. (Ed.). (1986). *The handbook of minority student services*. Madison, WI: National Minority Campus Chronicle.

White House Initiative on Historically Black Colleges and Universities. (2010). *List of HBCUs*. Retrieved from http://www2.ed.gov/about/inits/list/whhbcu/edlite-list.html#list

Part Two

Multicultural Student Services Affirming and Integrating Diversity

THE CHAPTERS IN THIS SECTION discuss race/ethnicity, sexual orientation and gender identity, as well as religious/spiritual identity. These are three of the most common aspects of MSS work on campus. The authors offer compelling arguments for integrating MSS services, given the multiple and intersecting identities of college students.

4

Engaging Race in Multicultural Student Services

Lori D. Patton
Jessica Ranero
Kimberly Everett

Student leaders from the Black Student Union, Latino Caucus, Indigenous Tribal Council, and Asian Americans United came together in a retreat to discuss their concerns with the expansion of services recently announced by the campus office for multicultural affairs. Primarily, they feared that more services to groups not defined by race and ethnicity signaled a lack of awareness by the college's administration that racism and racial exclusion were still negatively affecting student recruitment and retention. The students also acknowledged that racism impacted the perceptions of the multicultural affairs office by other people on campus.

As DISCUSSED IN EARLIER CHAPTERS, the establishment of multicultural student services (MSS) dates back to the Black student movement of the 1960s and its precursor, the civil rights movement. Further, as Shuford illustrated, African American student protest resulted in demands that predominantly White institutions (PWIs) meet their academic and cultural needs through several changes in curriculum, faculty and staff representation, and student services (see also Patton, 2005, 2006b; Williamson, 1999). Over the years, colleges and universities have established MSS

63

units to deal with issues of multiculturalism, affirm diversity on campus, and provide support for students from historically and racially underrepresented populations (Patton & Hannon, 2007).

In this chapter, we reconsider the presence of MSS through a different lens, focusing on the role of racism in maintaining the challenges and perpet-uating the myths and misconceptions associated with these units, as the student leaders in the opening vignette also called for. As Taylor (2000) noted, "For multiculturalism to reassert its relevancy, it must openly identify oppression and struggle against it more explicitly. How? By keeping *race* at the center of its agenda" (p. 540). Thus, we use critical race theory (CRT) as a framework to identify underlying issues and challenges of MSS, address the ways racism affects the presence of MSS at colleges and universities, and suggest how MSS can remain culturally relevant.

CRITICAL RACE THEORY

Critical race theory is a movement comprising scholars committed to chal-lenging racism and disrupting its social, legal, political, and educational con-sequences. Ladson-Billings (1995) indicated CRT "is about deploying race and racial theory as a challenge to traditional notions of diversity and social hierarchy" (p. 57). Although critical race perspectives have existed for more than a century (see the work of W.E.B. DuBois, for example), the CRT movement emerged during the latter 1970s (Lawrence, Matsuda, Del-gado, & Crenshaw, 1993). A number of salient events brought rise to this movement, three of which we highlight in this chapter.

The first set of circumstances that served as an impetus for CRT occurred following the civil rights movement. Much of the intended racial reform was mediocre at best and failed to fulfill the promise of racial equality. Moreover, efforts toward racial reform were insufficient in addressing covert forms of racism that were deeply entrenched in the social fabric of the United States (Delgado, 1995; Delgado & Stefancic, 2001; Lawrence et al., 1993; Lynn & Parker, 2006).

In addition to the failed reforms of the civil rights movement, legal schol-ars of color were increasingly disconcerted with the critical legal studies agenda, which paid little attention to issues of racism in legal jurisprudence (Crenshaw, Gotanda, Peller, & Thomas, 1995; Lawrence, 2002; Lawrence et al., 1993). Although critical legal studies was viewed as a more progressive movement, it was composed largely of White liberal scholars who failed to respond to the racial marginalization experienced by people of color. According to Lawrence (2002), legal scholars of color sought a space where their experiences of racial subordination could be acknowledged. They also envisioned an alternative agenda that centered the importance of challenging racism and revolutionizing the way law was interpreted and critiqued. Finally, they hoped to engage White scholars in a way that allowed them to examine their own racial privileges (Crenshaw, 2002; Lawrence, 2002; Lawrence et al., 1993).

The CRT movement was also influenced by student protests that took place in the 1980s at the Harvard Law School. Derrick Bell, the school's first Black professor, had been teaching a course entitled "Race, Racism and American Law" (Crenshaw, 2002). Following his exit, law students galvanized a boycott in an effort to encourage the hiring of more faculty of color, particularly a person who could teach Bell's course. However, the student demands were not met, prompting them to create their own course on racism and the law (Crenshaw, 2002). Many of the most prominent critical race scholars were trained in this course and went on to contribute scholarship grounded in what has come to be known as CRT. Clearly, parallels exist between the establishment of MSS and CRT, namely, through the agency of people of color to assert their voices to enact social change, challenge the status quo, and hold institutions accountable for becoming more culturally relevant.

Although CRT as a movement began with a small group of legal scholars, these individuals are largely responsible for developing an oppositional scholarship that has contributed significantly to contemporary knowledge and understanding about racism in its overt and insidious forms. Because of their contributions, CRT exists as both a movement and a body of knowledge. According to Crenshaw et al. (1995), "The task of Critical Race Theory is to remind its readers how deeply issues of racial ideology and power continue to matter in American life" (p. xxxii). Crenshaw and her colleagues identified two core themes that resonate throughout CRT in its attempt to address racism. The first theme is that White supremacy has been and remains central to the continued subordination of people of color. The second theme addresses the importance of moving beyond mere acknowledgment of the connection between the law and racism and fervently working toward challenging and disrupting this relationship.

Although these themes clearly resonate throughout much of the existing CRT scholarship, Lawrence et al. (1993) have identified other major tenets to create a more unified framework of CRT. Rather than outline these common themes, we present them specifically in relation to higher education and MSS.

First, CRT acknowledges the endemic nature of racism and explores how racism is transmitted through American ideals and values (e.g., property rights, democracy, individual rights; Lawrence et al., 1993). Moreover, CRT scholars contend that racism is a permanent fixture embedded within the very fabric of society influencing politics, law, and education (Ladson-Billings, 2000). Given the firmly established nature of racism, CRT recognizes that racism's largest project has been the social construction of race, ensuring that clear lines are drawn between the resources and privileges afforded White people in contrast to people of color. Race and racism are also deeply entrenched in the structures, policies, procedures, and daily happenings in higher education. Thus, MSS must operate in the inherently racist framework that shapes much of higher education. However, neither race nor racism should be viewed as existing in isolation; instead, they intersect with other types of oppression and coexist as part of a larger system of power that exploits and disenfranchises people of color as well as other marginalized groups based upon gender, sexual orientation, religion, ability, and class.

The second feature is that CRT critiques, questions, and challenges notions of equal opportunity that are framed through the concepts of color blindness, objectivity, neutrality, and meritocracy (Lawrence et al., 1993). Moreover, these ideas when collectively engaged produce a dominant ideology rooted in the premise that race is a concrete and stable attribute void of any historical or contemporary context. Solórzano and Yosso (2001) noted that color blindness serves as a "camouflage" to maintain White privilege and self-interests. In higher education, affirmative action policies, particularly with regard to admissions, are often met with contention. Opponents of these policies purport that such measures are unnecessary because "everyone" has equal opportunity and should be rewarded based upon hard work. Similarly, MSS offices have received criticism for promoting separation among individuals who contend that we live in a color-blind, post-racial society.

Third, CRT scholars insist that present day racial inequities be situated historically and contextually. They suggest that to understand the complex realities and consequences of racism, it is necessary to connect them within a historical framework that disrupts dominant, ahistoric viewpoints. "A critical race theory in education challenges ahistoricism and the unidisciplinary focus of most analyses and insists on analyzing race and racism in education by placing them in both a historical and contemporary context using interdisciplinary methods" (Solórzano, 1998, p. 123). Similarly, the discourse surrounding MSS must always be connected to its historical establishment, which is deeply connected to the civil rights and Black student movements.

Fourth, in an effort to empower marginalized groups, CRT also insists on the validation of their experiential knowledge (Delgado & Stefancic, 2001; Lawrence et al., 1993). The experiential knowledge of people of color is transmitted through storytelling, counter narratives, biographies, and qualitative interviews. Such stories, when told from the perspective of people of color, can be liberating for the storyteller, while simultaneously serving as an educational tool to bring understanding about the unique experiences of racially subordinated groups (Delgado, 1998; Solórzano & Yosso, 2001, 2002). Any examination of MSS would be incomplete without acknowledging the role these entities have played (and continue to play) in serving as a venue through which the voices of students of color can be heard and validated; inarguably, MSS were established to do just that.

Finally, at its core, CRT represents a transdisciplinary framework rooted in post-structural, Marxist, and feminist (to name a few) epistemologies (Lawrence et al., 1993; Lynn & Adams, 2002). As a result, CRT scholars integrate and use a host of perspectives that not only produce new knowledge, but also move their social justice agenda forward. Thus, CRT is aimed at challenging racism and eliminating it along with other forms of oppression within the larger context of social justice (Solórzano & Yosso, 2001, 2002).

Although CRT is firmly connected to legal scholarship, its influence has spanned across various disciplines and fields of study, including political science, ethnic studies, and philosophy (Delgado & Stefancic, 1995). To date, CRT has had the strongest impact on education (Ladson-Billings, 1995; Ladson-Billings & Tate, 1995; Tate, 1997). Ladson-Billings and Tate (1995) are credited with writing the seminal work that situated CRT in education. In "Toward a Critical Race Theory of Education," Ladson-Billings and Tate offered a critical analysis of educational inequities in the United States. Through the use of several propositions, their analysis not only links racism to the historical construction of property rights in America, but also reveals how whiteness functions to ensure the maintenance of systemic inequities in schools. Other educational scholars have also drawn attention to issues (e.g., curriculum, teacher education, funding, access, retention) affecting the educational pipeline and devoted further analysis to various populations. These "spin-off movements," including LatCrit (Delgado Bernal, 2002; Solórzano & Yosso, 2001; Villalpando, 2004), AsianCrit (Buenavista, Jayakumar, & Misa-Escalante, 2009; Teranishi, Behringer, Grey, & Parker, 2009), and TribalCrit (Brayboy, 2005), have ushered a wide range of perspectives into the CRT discourse, contributed significantly to understanding the inequities that diverse peoples of color experience, and drawn specific attention to issues and policies regarding language, immigration, and ethnicity. Overall, CRT serves as a useful analytical framework for examining a host of inequities that permeate education. Its utility is evident in moving beyond simple discussions about race toward embracing interdisciplinary perspectives that yield a more robust and enriching examination. As West (1995) noted, "Critical Race Theorists put forward novel readings of a hidden past that disclose the flagrant shortcomings of the treacherous present in the light of unrealized—though not unrealizable—possibilities for human freedom and equality" (pp. xi–xii).

USING CRT TO EXAMINE ISSUES OF
RACE AND RACISM WITHIN MSS

A full critical race analysis is beyond the scope of this chapter; however, in this section we introduce aspects of CRT's lexicon and highlight ways CRT can facilitate a greater understanding of how race and racism affect MSS at PWIs. Using constructs of CRT—including (a) microaggressions, (b) racial realism, (c) interest convergence, (d) the Black/White binary, and (e) color blindness—we discuss how a critical race perspective can inform contemporary understandings of race and MSS. Manning and Muñoz, in Chapter 19, illustrate the principles of CRT by applying them to particular issues and challenges faced by MSS offices. We encourage readers to review their discussion for a more complete application of CRT's framework to the structure, function, and services provided by multicultural student services in higher education.

Racial Realism and Multicultural Student Services

As previously mentioned, the functional area of MSS was born out of the protests of Black students in the late 1960s. This era marked a time of heightened racial conflict in the United States, and that conflict was also present on college campuses across the nation. Fast-forward to the 21st century, and many would argue that much progress has been made in the elimination of racism in this country. Laws abolishing overt acts of racism, as well as those designed to ensure greater inclusion of people of color, have been enacted. Because institutions of higher education reflect the broader society in which they exist, it is fair to assume that there must have been progress on campuses as well. For example, the demography of PWIs has changed drastically (also discussed in a later section). Students representing a range of diverse characteristics attend PWIs, which suggests that some important changes have occurred over the past 35 years.

Although some steps have been taken to address racism in the United States, including its college campuses, racism is still a pervasive issue that has been internalized and institutionalized to the point of being an essential and inherently functioning component of everyday life. In other words, critical race scholars contend that racism is normal (Delgado & Stefancic, 2001; Ladson-Billings & Tate, 1995; Lynn & Parker, 2006; Villalpando, 2004). Individual overt racist acts are deplored by U.S. society, yet racial microaggressions, or unconscious and subtle attacks directed toward people of color, are a regular occurrence on campuses (Smith, Allen, & Danley, 2007; Solórzano, 1998; Solórzano, Ceja, & Yosso, 2000).

Microaggressions take on numerous forms, such as the consistently low numbers of faculty, staff, and students of color at PWIs, despite the creation of strategic diversity plans and institutional missions that espouse diversity. A tall African American male who is presumed to be on the basketball team by his White academic advisor, the Latina who is singled out by her professor to give the "Latino perspective" in class, and the experiences of Native American populations that remain unacknowledged in a U.S. History course are all examples of racial microaggressions. Key to understanding microaggressions is recognizing that those who commit them may do so consciously or unconsciously, they have a cumulative impact on those who experience them, and they stem from racist assumptions that "inform our public, civic institutions—government, schools, churches—and our private, personal, and corporate lives" (Delgado & Stefancic, 2001, p. 2).

For four decades, MSS administrators have worked to address the needs of students of color, educated the campus on those needs, and dealt with numerous other duties. This complex and multifaceted role remains essential in promoting the success of students of color and any promise of a diverse learning community. However, PWIs are still often perceived as environments embedded in whiteness by students of color attending them (Brown, 2000; Cabrera, Nora, Terenzini, Pascarella, & Hagedorn, 1999; Feagin, Vera, & Imani, 1996; Hinderlie & Kenny, 2002). Although the demography of higher education has changed, the same structures and everyday inner workings of many campuses that are deemed "normal" remain laden with unspoken rules and processes that are racist and oppressive and that produce microaggressions. For example, several campus events and programs that are considered "tradition" (such as Homecoming and Greek Week) are often perceived as overwhelmingly White, racist, and exclusionary by students of color (Patton, 2006a, 2006b; Patton & Hannon, 2007). As a result, students of color are less likely to participate or feel a sense of connection with the campus community through such events. More often than not, MSS units bear the responsibility of organizing programs and events that attract students of color, encouraging their involvement and fostering a sense of connection to the campus.

Because racism and oppression exist in the broader society, White students, as well as students of color, continue to come to campus with attitudes of racial subordination, privilege, and internalized racism (Harvey, 1998). Barring a revolution that eliminates racism, predominantly White colleges and universities are likely to reflect and maintain such systems, perpetuating a persistent racial reality. The reality is that as long as racism exists at PWIs, the need for MSS and professionals at PWIs to serve and advocate for racially marginalized students will remain intact. We support Bell's (2005) paradox: "On the one hand, I urge you to give up the dream of real, permanent racial equality in this country. On the other hand, I urge you to continue the fight against racism" (p. 90). In our assessment, racism is not likely to end soon, yet the desire to challenge racism and work toward its elimination is worth the effort. One way to do this is through the continued existence of MSS on college campuses.

Interest Convergence and Multicultural Student Services

Using a critical race lens, one could argue that from their inception MSS were founded under the principle of interest convergence. According to Bell (1995), interest convergence suggests "the interest of blacks in achieving racial equality will be accommodated only when it converges with the interests of whites" (p. 22). Furthermore, interest convergence proposes that although the interests of White people and people of color converge, White people stand to gain the greatest benefit, and the interests of people of color are often sacrificed. As a result, the structures and systems that promote White dominance are reinforced. Despite the historical understanding that MSS units were established to support Black students and other students of color, a critical race analysis of the current role of MSS on college campuses makes it clear that these offices were established to serve the interests of White people over people of color.

As Black students began to enter institutions that were previously only accessible to White students, a national movement for overall equality began to develop. We noted earlier that in addition to demanding societal changes, students protested for reform through admissions policies, additional monetary resources to support Black student groups, hiring more Black faculty, culturally based programming, and the establishment of ethnic studies programs (Patton, 2006a; Wolf-Wendel, Twombly, Tuttle, Ward, & Gaston-Gayles, 2004; Yamane, 2001). In response to student demands and unrest, initiatives such as Black culture centers and MSS were established because PWIs were not prepared to meet the needs of the increased number of students of color on their campuses (Council for the Advancement of Standards [CAS], 2006; Hefner, 2002; Patton, 2006b; Yamane, 2001). Offices of multicultural student services and cultural centers were established to restore campus order and calm the unrest created by the student protests (Sutton & Kimbrough, 2001). Using CRT as an analytical framework, we argue that the interests of PWIs to restore and maintain order superseded the needs for support and advocacy of students of color. In other words, the concessions that many PWIs offered during the student protests resulted more from their desire to reestablish normalcy and silence dissent rather than from a sincere desire to ensure that students of color felt welcomed and supported.

Other examples of interest convergence can be identified in the purposes and goals of many MSS units today. According to the CAS Professional Standards for Higher Education (2006), the four main goals of multicultural student programs are: (a) to promote academic and personal growth of underserved students; (b) to work with the entire campus to create an inclusive climate; (c) to promote access and equity; and (d) to offer diversity education programs for the entire campus. A CRT analysis of the CAS goals for multicultural student programs makes it evident that PWIs have much to gain from the presence of MSS. Stage and Hamrick (1994) stated that the presence of multicultural student services "absolves other institutional agents of responsibility for even basic individual awareness of diversity or change" (p. 331). As a result, other members of the campus community are relinquished of any responsibility to promote diversity education and advocacy for students of color. A prime example of this occurs when historically Black sororities and fraternities are either housed in MSS or advised through MSS, begging the question of why the Greek Affairs office is not providing advisory support for these groups. The underlying assumption is that these organizations exist on the fringes of the Greek community, when they should be benefiting from resources in the Greek Affairs office. This example illustrates the expectation that MSS offices serve as a self-contained student affairs division because other departments feel no sense of obligation for assisting students of color, nor is there sufficient accountability to encourage them to do so. Furthermore, because most administrators who work in MSS are people of color, the role of diversity education and working with students of color becomes the tokenized responsibility of administrators of color (Banning, 2003). The role of MSS in many ways is structured to serve the interests of PWIs over the interests of people of color.

The Black–White Binary in Multicultural Student Services

In the late 1960s, as MSS offices proliferated on college campuses, issues of race were treated as a binary relationship between Blacks and Whites. At that point, Whites comprised nearly 90% of the U.S. population and, with African Americans accounting for approximately 10% of the population, other people of color did not constitute the critical mass required to garner the attention of the nation's lawmakers (Ramirez, 1995). Attempts to redress past and present discrimination in higher education and in the society as a whole focused on the needs of African Americans, with little to no attention given to other racially minoritized groups.

More than forty years later, the demographics of higher education have changed with an increase in students of color and an increasing number of students of color who are not African American (Ramirez, 1995; Tienda & Simonelli, 2001). Despite these changes, a Black–White binary persists. The Black–White binary frames the racial subordination of all people of color through referencing the subordination of African Americans (Delgado, 1998; Delgado & Stefancic, 2001; Martinez, 1998). This binary is rooted in historical conditions, including (a) the long-held status of African Americans as the largest minority group in the country and (b) the existing model for racism, precipitated by the enslavement of African Americans (Delgado, 1998; Martinez, 1998). In addition to the historical context of the Black–White binary, many members of the campus community, including some individuals in MSS, ascribe to stereotypical images of other students of color. The notion of Latino/a students as the emerging minority group, Asian American students as a model minority with no need for services, or Native American students as historical and no longer relevant continues to keep African Americans at the center of issues facing all students of color (Brayboy, 2005; Iverson, 2007; Ramirez, 1995; Tienda & Simonelli, 2001).

Some would argue that the legacy of slavery in the United States and the legal segregation of the Jim Crow era entitle African Americans to occupy the center of the discourse on racial issues on campus and throughout the country (Delgado & Stefancic, 2001). After all, the very existence of MSS stemmed largely from the struggles of students who were African American. This attitude of exceptionalism does little to benefit students of color as a whole and works counter to the pursuit of any meaningful advancement of students of color on campus. Operating within a Black–White binary serves to fragment the communities of color that use MSS. It creates greater problems by validating African American students' experiences as most important and vital, while delegitimizing the lived experiences and needs of Latinos/as, Native Americans, Asian Americans, multiracial students, and other students of color. Moreover, it creates a spirit of competition among diverse student populations and prevents the establishment of coalitions across racial lines. One factor that maintains the Black–White binary is the overwhelming perception that equates "anything multicultural" with "everything Black." This poorly conceived assumption can hinder the work of MSS if the perception is that this office exists to serve African American students *only* or *first*. If this perception continues, it can further marginalize other students of color and contradict the true mission of MSS, which includes services to other marginalized populations.

Color Blindness and Multicultural Student Services

Color blindness has also affected the role of MSS on predominantly White campuses. Taylor (2000) argued that color blindness is senseless, given that people's experiences and how they are treated is rooted in the color of their skin. As race-based programs are called into question both on individual campuses and nationally, MSS administrators are often in a predicament that requires them to justify their existence. One aspect of color blindness is the call for race neutrality in student programs and services. Race neutrality or the implementation of programs and initiatives that do not account for race are placing MSS in danger, given that a large part of their mission is working to provide education toward the eradication of racism.

One consequence of race neutrality is the adoption of a "one size fits all" model for MSS. According to Patton (2006b), this model "assumes that underrepresented populations have needs that should be met in the same way" (p. 642). In this model, the definition of multicultural student programs is expanded and, some would argue, diluted, in an effort to include students of color as well as other identity groups, such as women and LGBT students (CAS, 2006). Such identities are treated as discrete rather than recognizing the ways students' experiences are fluid and intersecting. Despite well-conceived intentions of creating campus environments that promote inclusiveness, expanded services often threaten the ability of MSS to effectively carry out its original mission of providing support to students of color, particularly when such efforts lack intentionality. Furthermore, efforts stemming from a one size fits all model are unlikely to have long-term success, because the model fails to provide an appropriate format from which expanded services might emerge. Without such a format, they run the risk of essentializing the experiences of nondominant student populations. In other words, commonalities are considered, while failing to account for the various ways oppression manifests and the differential impact that oppression might have on individuals and groups. Readers are encouraged to review

Almandrez and Lee (Chapter 7) for further discussion of the need for integrated services for multiple student constituencies within MSS by using an intersectional framework.

Taylor (2000) contended that multiculturalism guided by an activist agenda is shifting toward color blindness. As a result, rather than addressing the needs of students of color, the role of MSS is being diminished to "cultural tourism." Thus, MSS becomes responsible for planning monthly ethnic celebrations and events to "educate" the campus, rather than focusing on the real needs of students of color. The color blindness of administrators, students, and faculty contributes to dismissing targeted services for students of color because many people, some in MSS areas, believe that racism no longer exists. They often rely on evidence such as the increased enrollment of students of color to justify their beliefs. Holding on to color-blind beliefs allows individuals to disregard the impact of racism on the experiences of students of color at PWIs—experiences that often impact and in some cases impede their social and academic success. Moreover, color blindness reifies White racism, which is equated with the "norm" and reinforces White dominance and privilege (Taylor, 2000).

MSS must move toward a broader mission that acknowledges higher education as a location for the performance and perpetuation of multiple forms of oppression, including racism, but also envisions serving a larger group of students and addressing intra- and intergroup differences and commonalities among its diverse constituents. As Almandrez and Lee more fully discuss later in this volume, MSS might do well to consider a framework that embraces intersectionality, "the examination of race, sex, class, national origin, and sexual orientation, and how their combination plays out in various settings" (Delgado & Stefancic, 2001, p. 51). One aspect of adopting this particular paradigm involves redefining what the "multicultural" in MSS means. More specifically, to avoid the desire to create broad categories of individuals who are served by MSS, professionals within this functional area will need to participate in what Delgado and Stefancic (2001) described as "perspectivalism, [or] the insistence on examining how things look from the perspective of individual actors" (p. 55). Perspective-taking provides a more in-depth understanding of multiple, intersecting identities and allows for the generation of strategies to serve a larger population of students through MSS. A more expanded vision promoted through MSS would demonstrate that the original mission (race) cannot be fully understood without acknowledging the interlocking nature of social identities of both the privileged and the oppressed.

CONCLUSION

In this chapter we have attempted to provide a critique of MSS's focus on issues of race and ethnicity through the lens of CRT. A preliminary critical race analysis was central to illuminating ways in which the racism embedded in higher education affects the presence of MSS, as well as how MSS are perceived. Our analysis clearly suggests that there is a continuing need for MSS, as long as racism remains a defining feature of the structures and processes of higher education. Thus, we recommend that colleges and universities that do not have MSS conduct a diversity audit to ascertain the needs of various student populations on campus (see Petitt and McIntosh, Chapter 13, for further discussion of this). This audit should help determine how MSS would be beneficial toward eliminating racism, while also advocating for a wide range of populations on campus. For campuses where MSS currently exist, we encourage an honest assessment of how MSS are perceived on campus, which groups use this functional area, the extent to which the mission is met, and the resources that are allocated to ensure the success of this office. The survey data reported by Stewart and Bridges (Chapter 3) might provide a helpful starting place for benchmarking MSS on campus.

Our analysis also identified a need for PWIs to assess the ultimate value of and the context in which MSS exist. We suggest that institutions spend intentional time focusing on MSS to: (a) reassess its role, (b) prioritize the responsibilities of the office, (c) identify key constituent groups, and (d) ensure that MSS is valued because of the services provided to students rather than the benefits garnered by the institution.

Finally, our discussion addressed the need for MSS to acknowledge its original mission while embracing a paradigm of intersectionality. To do so, addressing race and racism should remain a significant aspect of the services provided. We are not suggesting that MSS be separatist in nature, nor are we suggesting that the needs of other student populations cannot be met through MSS. To remain relevant, MSS must embrace a paradigm that accounts for "the intersectional complexity of social power while also comprehending the fluid, dynamic, and contested character of representational categories" (Crenshaw et al., 1995, p. 354) related to race, gender, nationality, ethnicity, and age (among others). However, we urge MSS to remain mindful of their original mission to ensure that the history and struggles of the past that were instrumental in the success of students of color are not forgotten. On the same note, we contend that MSS must consciously and intentionally promote a mission and vision, services, and programming that reflect an awareness of identities existing at the intersection of multiple sites of oppression (Delgado & Stefancic, 2001) and engage the campus community in a way that disrupts the institutionalized attitudes, behaviors, and beliefs that perpetuate oppression.

REFERENCES

Banning, J. H. (2003). The institution's commitment to diversity: An aid or hindrance to teachers of diversity. In W. Timpson, S. Canetto, E. Borrayo, & R. Yang (Eds.), *Teaching diversity: Challenges and complexities, identities and integrity* (pp. 207–216). Madison, WI: Atwood Publishing.

Bell, D. (1995). *Brown v. Board of Education* and the interest convergence dilemma. In K. Crenshaw, N. Gotanda, G. Peller, & K. Thomas (Eds.), *Critical race theory: Key writings that formed the movement* (pp. 20–29). New York, NY: The New Press.

Bell, D. (2005). Racism is here to stay: Now what? In J. Stefancic & R. Delgado (Eds.), *The Derrick Bell reader* (pp. 85–90). New York: New York University Press.

Brayboy, B. M. J. (2005). Toward a tribal critical race theory in education. *The Urban Review, 37,* 425–446.

Brown, T. (2000). Gender differences in African American students' satisfaction with college. *Journal of College Student Development, 41,* 479–487.

Buenavista, T. L., Jayakumar, U. M., & Misa-Escalante, K. (2009). Contextualizing Asian American education through critical race theory: An example of U.S. Pilipino college student experiences. In S. D. Museus (Ed.), *Conducting research on Asian Americans in higher education* (pp. 69–81). New Directions in Institutional Research, no. 142. San Francisco, CA: Jossey-Bass. doi: 10.1002/ir.297

Cabrera, A. F., Nora, A., Terenzini, P. T., Pascarella, E., & Hagedorn, L. S. (1999). Campus racial climate and the adjustment of students to college: A comparison between White students and African-American students. *The Journal of Higher Education, 70,* 134–160.

Council for the Advancement of Standards in Higher Education. (2006). *CAS professional standards for higher education* (6th ed.). Washington, DC: Author.

Crenshaw, K. (2002). The first decade: Critical reflections or a "foot in the closing door." In F. Valdes, J. M. Culp, & A. P. Harris (Eds.), *Crossroads, directions, and a new critical race theory* (pp. 9–31). Philadelphia, PA: Temple University Press.

Crenshaw, K., Gotanda, N., Peller, G., & Thomas, K. (Eds.). (1995). *Critical race theory: Key writings that formed the movement.* New York, NY: The New Press.

Delgado, R. (1995). *Critical race theory: The cutting edge.* Philadelphia, PA: Temple University Press.

Delgado, R. (1998). The black/white binary: How does it work? In R. Delgado & J. Stefancic (Eds.), *The Latino/a condition: A critical reader* (pp. 369–375). New York: New York University Press.

Delgado, R., & Stefancic, J. (1995). Why do we tell the same stories? Law reform, critical librarianship, and triple helix dilemma. In R. Delgado (Ed.), *Critical race theory: The cutting edge* (pp. 206–216). Philadelphia, PA: Temple University Press.

Delgado, R., & Stefancic, J. (2001). *Critical race theory: An introduction.* New York: New York University Press.

Delgado Bernal, D. (2002). Critical race theory, LatCrit theory, and critical raced-gendered epistemologies: Recognizing students of color as holders and creators of knowledge. *Qualitative Inquiry, 8*(1), 105–126.

Feagin, J. R., Vera, H., & Imani, N. (1996). *The agony of education: Black students at White colleges and universities.* New York, NY: Routledge.

Harvey, W. B. (1998). When silence is not golden: University initiated conversations on racism and race relations. *College Student Affairs Journal, 18*(1), 18–24.

Hefner, D. (2002). Black cultural centers: Standing on shaky ground? *Black Issues in Higher Education, 18*(26), 22–29.

Hinderlie, H. H., & Kenny, M. (2002). Attachment, social support, and college adjustment among Black students at predominantly White universities. *Journal of College Student Development, 43,* 327–340.

Iverson, S. V. (2007). Camouflaging power and privilege: A critical race analysis of university diversity policies. *Education Administration Quarterly, 43,* 586–611.

Ladson-Billings, G. (1995). New directions in multicultural education: Complexities, boundaries, and critical race theory. In J. A. Banks & C. A. McGee Banks (Eds.), *Handbook of research on multicultural education* (2nd ed., pp. 50–65). San Francisco, CA: Jossey-Bass.

Ladson-Billings, G. (2000). Racialized discourses and ethnic epistemologies. In N. Denzin & Y. Lincoln (Eds.), *Handbook of qualitative research* (2nd ed., pp. 257–277). Thousand Oaks, CA: Sage Publications.

Ladson-Billings, G., & Tate, W. F. (1995). Toward a critical race theory of education. *Teachers College Record, 97*(1), 47–68.

Lawrence, C. R., III. (2002). Foreword: Who are we? and why are we here? Doing critical race theory in hard times. In F. Valdes, J. M. Culp, & A. P. Harris (Eds.), *Crossroads, directions, and a new critical race theory* (pp. xi–xxi). Philadelphia, PA: Temple University Press.

Lawrence, C. R., III, Matsuda, M. J., Delgado, R., & Crenshaw, K. W. (1993). Introduction. In M. J. Matsuda, C. R. Lawrence III, R. Delgado, & K. W. Crenshaw (Eds.), *Words that wound: Critical race theory, assaultive speech, and the first amendment* (pp. 1–16). Boulder, CO: Westview Press.

Lynn, M. & Adams, M. (2002). Critical race theory and education: Recent developments in the field. *Equity & Excellence in Education, 35,* 87–92.

Lynn, M., & Parker, L. (2006). Critical race studies in education: Examining a decade of research on U.S. schools. *The Urban Review, 38,* 257–290.

Martinez, E. (1998). Beyond black/white: The racism of our time. In R. Delgado & J. Stefancic (Eds.), *The Latino/a condition: A critical reader* (pp. 466–477). New York: New York University Press.

Patton, L. D. (2005). Power to the people! A literature review of the impact of Black student protest on the emergence of Black culture centers. In F. Hord (Ed.), *Black culture centers and political identities* (pp. 151–163). Chicago, IL: Third World Press.

Patton, L. D. (2006a). Black culture centers: Still central to student learning. *About Campus, 11*(2), 2–8.

Patton, L. D. (2006b). The voice of reason: A qualitative examination of Black student perceptions of Black culture centers. *Journal of College Student Development, 47,* 628–646.

Patton, L. D., & Hannon, M. D. (2007). Collaborating with cultural centers and multicultural affairs offices. In S. Harper (Ed.), *Creating inclusive campus environments for cross cultural learning and engagement* (pp. 139–154). Washington, DC: National Association of Student Personnel Administrators.

Ramirez, D. (1995). Multicultural empowerment: It's not just black and white anymore. *Stanford Law Review, 47,* 957–992.

Smith, W. A., Allen, W. R., & Danley, L. L. (2007). "Assume the position . . . you fit the description:" Psychosocial experiences and racial battle fatigue among African American male college students. *American Behavioral Scientist, 51,* 551–578.

Solórzano, D. (1998). Critical race theory, race and gender microaggressions and the experience of Chicana and Chicano scholars. *International Journal of Qualitative Studies in Education, 11,* 121–136.

Solórzano, D., Ceja, M., & Yosso, T. (2000). Critical race theory, racial microaggressions, and campus racial climate: The experiences of African American college students. *The Journal of Negro Education, 69,* 60–73.

Solórzano, D., & Yosso, T. (2001). Critical race and LatCrit theory and method: Counter-storytelling Chicana and Chicano graduate school experiences. *International Journal of Qualitative Studies in Education, 14,* 471–495.

Solórzano, D., & Yosso, T. (2002). Critical race methodology: Counter-storytelling as an analytical framework for education research. *Qualitative Inquiry, 8*(1), 23–44.

Stage, F. K., & Hamrick, F. A. (1994). Diversity issues: Fostering campuswide development of multiculturalism. *Journal of College Student Development, 35,* 331–336.

Sutton, E. M., & Kimbrough, W. M. (2001). Trends in Black student involvement. *NASPA Journal, 38*(1), 30–40.

Tate, W. F., IV. (1997). Critical race theory and education: History, theory, and implications. *Review of Research in Education, 22,* 195–247.

Taylor, E. (2000). Critical race theory and interest convergence in the backlash against affirmative action: Washington State and Initiative 200. *Teachers College Record, 102,* 539–560.

Teranishi, R. T., Behringer, L. B., Grey, E. A., & Parker, T. L. (2009). Critical race theory and research on Asian American and Pacific Islanders in higher education. In S. D. Museus (Ed.), *Conducting research on Asian Americans in higher education* (pp. 57–68). New Directions in Institutional Research, no. 142. San Francisco, CA: Jossey-Bass. doi: 10.1002/ir.296

Tienda, M., & Simonelli, S. (2001). Hispanic students are missing from diversity debates. *Chronicle of Higher Education, 47*(38), p. B13.

Villalpando, O. (2004). Practical considerations of critical race theory and Latino critical theory for Latino college students. In A. Ortiz (Ed.), *Addressing the unique needs of Latino American students* (pp. 41–50). New Directions for Student Services, no. 105. doi: 10.1002/ss.115

West, C. (1995). Foreword. In K. Crenshaw, N. Gotanda, G. Peller, & K. Thomas (Eds.), *Critical race theory: The key writings that formed the movement* (pp. xi–xii). New York, NY: The New Press.

Williamson, J. A. (1999). In defense of themselves: The Black struggle for success and recognition at predominantly white colleges and universities. *Journal of Negro Education, 68*(1), 92–105.

Wolf-Wendel, L. E., Twombly, S. B., Tuttle, K. N., Ward, K., & Gaston-Gayles, J. L. (2004). *Reflecting back, looking forward: Civil rights and student affairs.* Washington, DC: National Association of Student Personnel Administrators.

Yamane, D. (2001). *Student movements for multiculturalism: Challenging the curricular color line in higher education.* Baltimore, MD: Johns Hopkins University Press.

5

Engaging Sexual Orientation and Gender Diversity in Multicultural Student Services

Nicholas A. Negrete
Christopher Purcell

Amar, a junior from India who identifies as gay to his friends, talks openly about applying to graduate school, in part to avoid having to go home to India. He fears if he does go home he will have to enter into the marriage that has been arranged for him. Jamie, a bisexual Asian American woman, must now pay her own way through school. She was disowned when her mother found out about her girlfriend. Rita, a senior, who is Latina and identifies as transgender, wonders if she'll ever find a job. She is currently in the process of transitioning.

THESE ARE SOME of the real struggles of today's students. These are students with narratives so rich that no single developmental model could ever define their experience. They struggle for autonomy while still attempting to honor their heritage, culture, and families. When rights for lesbian, gay, bisexual, and transgender (LGBT) individuals are discussed in popular media, it is often in the context of whether or not same-sex couples could and should be married. However, those who work with LGBT college students know that the questions our students have are far more fundamental. Among many concerns, these students want to know if

81

their friends and families will still love them if they "come out" and if they will be safe from harm and discrimination. It is the responsibility of all of those working in higher education to transform these concerns into policies and practices that make a difference in LGBT students' lives. We must transform questions into affirmation and fear into hope.

Although many universities are now recognizing the needs of LGBT college students, many continue to be satisfied with silence. Unfortunately, their silence, although sometimes politically convenient, can be personally devastating to students. Sanlo (2000) wrote:

> As LGBT students come to campuses—some still secretive and some quite open about their sexual orientations and gender identities—they expect their worldviews to be embraced. They expect their voices heard, their concerns acknowledged, their needs met, and their educational environments welcoming. (p. 486)

As student affairs educators, we must use our leadership, institutional positions, and the impact and institutional power that may come with such positions to speak on behalf of those who are marginalized and educate our colleagues to embrace these identities.

SEXUAL ORIENTATION AND GENDER IDENTITY: THE NEW CHALLENGES

As visibility, awareness, and activism surrounding LGBT college students has come to the attention of administrators in institutions of higher learning, specific support services and staff are being dedicated to serve such populations. The first known LGBT Campus Center was established in 1971 at the University of Michigan (Sanlo, 2000). Since then, some 140 colleges and universities have specific centers and staff dedicated for this purpose. Most of these services and centers came to fruition in the late 1990s and early 2000s and more are being added each year. Many other institutions are expanding the purview of multicultural centers to address the concerns of LGBT students. The types and extent of programs vary, inevitably, from institution to institution. Most provide avenues of support and affirmation, social and leadership development, education, advocacy work, and programming. Organizations such as the Consortium of Higher Education LGBT

Resource Professionals, NASPA's GLBT Issues Knowledge Community, and the ACPA Standing Committee on LGBT Awareness disseminate best practices and new knowledge among their memberships to aid administrators in promoting LGBT campus equality.

The landscape for LGBT student services is changing quickly; so, too, are the students. Many argue that as acceptance of the fluidity of sexual orientation and gender becomes more prominent, the need for specific labeling of identity will become less important to today's youth. Savin-Williams (2005) found:

> The new gay teenager is in many respects the non-gay teenager. . . . For these young people, being labeled as gay or even being gay matter little. They have same-sex desires and attractions, but unlike earlier generations, new gay teens have much less interest to name these feelings or behaviors as gay. (p. 1)

Should this assertion be true, it would certainly have an effect on how we serve students. Will students of the future even consider their sexual orientation or gender identity to be an important enough marker to warrant targeted programs and services? Does a broader acceptance of LGBT individuals mean that administrators' efforts to provide more inclusive environments are unnecessary?

Certainly, systematic discrimination against LGBT individuals still exists. Our politics and policies have yet to catch up with the prevailing attitudes of today's youth. Still, although many students are finding affirmation at younger ages, many continue to struggle with issues of sexual orientation and gender identity, particularly but not exclusively as these identities intersect with gender, race, religion, class, and nationality, among other identities. In addition, as individuals across the continuum of sexual orientation and gender identity continue to gain acceptance in society through increased visibility, they face a more covert kind of discrimination. According to some, those who identify as gay, lesbian, or bisexual are finding some acceptance, as long as they do not "act" gay, just as African Americans, Asian/Pacific Islanders, and Latino/a individuals may gain acceptance only by performing in ways that are consistent with assumptions shaped by the dominant culture. Yoshino (2006) refers to this as "covering."

Arguably, there has been significantly less progress when it comes to addressing the needs of transgender students on campus. Some universities are adding "gender identity" or "gender identity and expression" to their nondiscrimination policies in support of the transgender community. When surveyed, however, most administrators at these universities indicated that few changes had occurred as a result of the nondiscrimination policy (Beemyn & Pettitt, 2006). There are many areas of concern for transgender students entering higher education, from residence hall living to health and safety, which must be addressed to ensure a quality educational experience for transgender students.

Still, even while there is continued progress for LGBT students, navigating the world of partial acceptance (Yoshino, 2006) can be difficult. Students report being "out" as LGBT to some groups (maybe friends or extended family) while feeling great shame or anxiety about being "out" in other venues (perhaps in religious environments or with immediate family). Although students might not require quite as much guidance on how to combat outward instances of homophobia and transphobia as would have been necessary in past decades, helping students navigate heterosexism and more covert forms of homophobia and transphobia is the new role of the supportive mentor or ally (Yoshino, 2007). The question is whether administrators in multicultural student services (MSS) are examining issues such as these and properly responding to the emerging needs of all LGBT students.

INTERSECTING MULTIPLE IDENTITIES: HONORING THE WHOLE STUDENT

MSS offices that house multiple identity groups have the unique opportunity to address intersections of various identities under one roof. If resourced well, both human and fiscal, a multicultural student center has the capacity to impact the greater campus community, using tools such as educational dialogue, awareness programs, and student ambassadors to educate on specific issues affecting marginalized communities. According to Stewart and Bridges (Chapter 3), it is becoming more common to find MSS centers that serve people of color as well as LGBT and women's communities rather than stand-alone identity centers with one specific target audience, such as an LGBT Student Resource Center.

However, establishing a safe space for LGBT students can be difficult in a center where multiple identities exist, including, for example, the intersections of racial and ethnic identities with sexual orientation and gender identities. Many communities of color are tightly connected to religious or cultural views and philosophies, which might affect the perspectives and opinions of students who use centers that strive to be inclusive to all. Historically, some religious faiths have been less inclusive or accepting to those who identify as LGBT. Dumas (1998) highlighted the struggle some nonheterosexual people of color face, specifically stating that the Black church "has never been simply a religious body. It is also a space in which black people form supportive community structures and develop spiritual and material tools for survival in an anti-black world" (p. 81). What then should a student do if his or her church is openly hostile to LGBT individuals but serves as the student's only source of spiritual and community support? How then, do students navigate their multiple identities that might often conflict? Do they feel they must piece apart their own identities to participate and benefit from those separate services?

Arguably, nonheterosexual students of color find it just as difficult to find validation within the LGBT communities on their campuses, because many are predominantly White organizations with limited knowledge of the cultural factors that might affect the experiences of students of color (Stevens, 2004). In response to this reality, there are student organizations on a handful of college campuses to address some of the unique experiences students of color who identify as LGBT encounter. This begs the question of the need for a safe space within multicultural student services, not only for LGBT students as a whole, but also for LGBT students of color within their own communities.

Many LGBT students of color are torn by the need to straddle both of their identities, often feeling compelled to choose one identity as primary at any given time. In fact, the experiences of ethnic minorities who identify as LGBT can be described as straddling three different worlds (Chan, 1989; Icard, 1986; Morales, 1990) identified in this quote from Newman (1998):

> First, [ethnic minorities] face the homophobia and discrimination of the dominant heterosexual culture, compounded with racism. Second, as opposed to heterosexual minority youth . . . LGBT youth may feel a sense of alienation

from their own ethnic community due to homophobia. Third, ethnic minority youth frequently do not experience the larger LGBT community as home,
due to the racism that exists in this often European American-dominated
culture. (p. 162)

Newman's assertions hold true even today, as queer students of color continue to fight predominant homophobic and heterosexist views that could
make living their lives as openly LGBT difficult. More specifically, in
Latino/a communities heterosexism and homophobia often permeate the
culture, reinforcing what it means to be "authentically Latino" (Misa, 2001).
It is the concept of *la familia*, that Misa (2001) described as feeling the
pressure to uphold the heterosexual family unit. The romanticized aspiration
of the heterosexual family unit is not only specific to Latino/a communities
but can also be found in Asian communities where "what is commonly
considered 'traditional Asian values' dictates 'getting married, having children, and passing down the family name'" (Kumashiro, 2001, p. 6). These
examples are not to imply that homophobia and heterosexism only exist in
communities of color, but rather they depict how deeply rooted homophobia
and heterosexism are in the larger cultural context and how different communities of color respond to such privileges through their own cultural
framework. This is one of many challenges that student affairs educators
must consider as they strategize how to best serve the diversity within the
LGBT community and how to address intersecting identities in a way that
allows students to express their whole and authentic selves.

THE COMMON THREAD: MARGINALIZATION,
STRENGTH, AND RESILIENCY

Student affairs educators are often witness to the common experience of
marginalization and challenges that historically oppressed groups encounter
throughout their college experiences. These challenges might take the form
of the struggle to secure safe space, visibility and validation, and the sense of
belonging to a community. Although the experience of marginalization is a
common one among oppressed groups within the United States (whether
that marginalization is by race, sexuality, gender identity, or other sources),
it continues to be a struggle to find solidarity across multiple identities. "Too

often, oppressions are discussed as if they exist individually, as constructs of domination occupying completely separate spaces than other forms of domination" (Dumas, 1998, p. 83).

Unfortunately, a similar struggle is happening within higher education student service units, particularly concerning LGBT issues in the context of this discussion, where various identity centers and student groups compete for scarce resources. Often the conversation around diversity and inclusion is unbalanced, where race and ethnicity are highlighted and the LGBT conversation continues to fall by the wayside (Evans & Wall, 1991; Sanlo, 2000; Stevens, 2004). The competition for scarce resources can often be seen in the form of institutional "cultural" or "diversity" funds that are to be divided among programs or services that meet the criteria as a "diversity need." Although the intent may be to provide programs and services that pertain to diversity and inclusion, programming officers requesting funds for both LGBT and racial/ethnic awareness and advocacy can feel the impact of this fiscal limitation as competitive and inequitable.

In this common struggle to find adequate and equitable resources, LGBT and racial/ethnic identity centers have the opportunity to work together and serve as allies to each other to increase their likelihood of securing such resources. Administrators must serve as role models to students on building coalitions and working across multiple identities for one common purpose. They also must work to establish a strong network of community members and allies that will aid in students' retention and resiliency when their identities are challenged both personally and institutionally. Student affairs educators, and particularly those working in MSS, must guide students in solidarity with each other, while also allowing them to establish strong separate spaces for their own identity development.

Bauder (1998) described a community where specific identity groups worked across perspectives and established "community synergy." He described a campus where the Hillel organization worked closely with the LGBT student group during their remembrance of the Holocaust, mindfully addressing the pink triangle and the persecution of gays and lesbians during this horrific time. Additionally, he highlighted the university's Black Cultural Center organizing a film series honoring the lives and success of notable nonheterosexual Black artists, writers, and activists. These are two examples of the ways student affairs educators should begin to envision what it means to work across the multiple identities that coexist on our campuses.

Following are suggestions for establishing connections across the experience of marginalization for LGBT and other oppressed groups on campus:

- Hone in on specific identity groups, providing the opportunity to explore their self-awareness, and empower them in their personal identity development. This can be done through programs focused on different aspects of identity development and empowerment, such as racial identity, sexuality, or even immigrant identity. One example can be found at the University of Vermont, where they have developed a retreat focusing on racial identity known as *Racial Aikido*.

- Understand that students are not in any one place in regard to identity development. As we address multiple intersecting identities, there might be some identity negotiation occurring, where one might be challenged to address certain aspects of his or her identity, while suspending attention to other parts. This can be better understood through the Multiple Identity Development Model (Jones & McEwen, 2000), where the backdrop of context impacts the saliency of certain identities. This identity negotiation is sometimes experienced by LGBT students of color.

- Identify student leaders who are able to successfully build coalitions and connect across both the LGBT and the various students of color communities on campus.

- Use the leadership and spheres of influence of these student leaders to begin a larger movement to communicate and engage across multiple identity groups.

- Continue to focus adequate energy toward students who are still processing in their immersion experience, with hopes they can make a similar transition into identifying the larger vision around multiple identities and the common experience of oppression and marginalization. Supporting students for whom their sexual orientation or racial/ethnic identity is the most significant aspect of how they make meaning of themselves is critical to their further development.

Almandrez and Lee (Chapter 7) further discuss the need to provide integrated services that acknowledge students' multiple and intersecting identities and offer suggestions for implementing integrative policy and practice in MSS.

FORGING OUR FUTURE: EXPANDING AND ENHANCING SERVICES FOR LGBT STUDENTS

Compared to other functional areas of student affairs, addressing LGBT student needs institutionally is a relatively new venture that is ever changing and expanding. By providing multifaceted services, working toward positive institutional change, and preparing professionals for working with LGBT students, the student affairs profession can reach positive outcomes for LGBT students.

Provide Multifaceted Services, Programs, and Resources

LGBT college students need to be engaged in a variety of ways to ensure their retention and success in higher education. Professionals should seek to provide social and academic support services to LGBT students. Programmatic efforts within MSS should be internally audited for inclusiveness of LGBT students. Moreover, a specific focus on the interconnectedness of oppression should be ingrained in the fabric of MSS's programmatic efforts and into individual discussions with students. For resistant administrations, a coalition of academic and administrative units, LGBT and ally alumni networks, and community partners is vital to ensuring an effective and supportive response to LGBT student needs.

Some MSS offices and cultural centers have begun to meet these challenges. Although we know not all students are ready or willing to walk through the doors of particular cultural centers, administrators might serve these students by providing comprehensive lists of institutional and community resources for LGBT students on their websites and in their publications. Topics might include information on student groups, coming out to family and/or in places of worship, health and safety topics, healthy social opportunities, and avenues for activism.

For students who do seek meaningful interaction with peers, providing opportunities for fostering healthy relationships with fellow students is pivotal. This is done through both social programming and providing avenues for in-depth discussion of LGBT identity that allows students to find affirmation within a community.

For students who are seeking support services or counseling, several MSS offices and centers provide peer discussion groups or identity-focused counseling or build strong relationships with institutional and community counseling centers. Positive mentoring relationships with LGBT faculty and staff are also powerful tools for building community and affirming identity.

Raising awareness and ally development are two other critical roles MSS offices can play. Formal and informal conversations and "trainings" provide an avenue to educate students, faculty, and staff about LGBT issues and concerns. These trainings go by many names (Safe Zones, Ally Trainings, etc.) but the aims are similar: to provide much needed education and awareness to faculty, staff, and students and build allies in the fight for equity. These programs also increase visibility of LGBT concerns and often spark important conversations (Evans, 2002). However, far too many universities provide a variation of safe zone trainings but have no visible Internet presence or actual programs to promote community for LGBT students. Such examples of universities acknowledging LGBT students in theory (through safe zone programs), but ignoring them in practice (support services), show that, although we have come far, we have far to go toward providing adequate services for LGBT students.

Become Catalysts for Change

Although programmatic efforts to serve LGBT students are important, so, too, are the institutional policies and structures that have threatened equity and justice for these students. Some universities have established LGBT task forces or commissions to address such concerns. Often, these committees report directly to the university president or provost.

Many universities protect sexual orientation in their nondiscrimination policies, whereas others are beginning to add "gender identity" or "gender identity and expression" to show support for transgender faculty, staff, and students. Other policies, such as establishing social justice–themed living communities and establishing or refining bias incident protocols, serve many varying and intersecting communities. In addition, working with community nonprofit and advocacy organizations that work on social justice initiatives can result in students learning to be more effective community advocates long after their college experience is completed.

Prepare Professionals for the Work

Sanlo (2000) noted that professionals might be underprepared to address LGBT student concerns. Few if any graduate preparation programs for student affairs professionals have a course specifically related to addressing issues of sexual orientation or gender identity or even specific academic coursework designated for how to run identity-based centers (Sanlo, 2000). Moreover, some professionals might be averse to learning about or providing services for LGBT students owing to personal moral conflicts or in anticipation of political backlash. These professionals might choose to ignore the unique needs of LGBT students. Unfortunately, these students typically do not have the ability to ignore these issues themselves.

We must acknowledge that many of the students and administrators with whom we work vocalize feelings of heterosexism and homophobia. It is important for these individuals to understand that no matter their political affiliation or beliefs, the decisions made in opposition of equality for LGBT individuals have real implications for LGBT lives. Adequately preparing professionals to delve into these discussions with a sense of comfort and responsibility is essential. Expanding knowledge of accepted LGBT-related terminology, LGBT student concerns, and current trends in support services is essential to the ability of professionals, within and beyond MSS, to serve LGBT students and students with LGBT friends or family members.

CONCLUSION

LGBT student services on college campuses would not have come to existence if it were not for fellow students, administrators, and community members who had the courage to break the silence about LGBT student needs. Now, administrators must have the courage to dismantle those policies, philosophies, and ideologies that continue to plague institutions of higher education with homophobia and heterosexism. We must build campus climates where a student like Amar, in the opening vignette, feels his identity as a gay Indian man is validated and not silenced. We must work to help students like Rita feel proud that the Career Development Center is well equipped to guide transgender students and provide them with adequate knowledge on how to navigate a career search during transition. This is a call for MSS and all student service units to think critically about how they are inclusive to their LGBT student population and what they can do to ensure that their staffs are knowledgeable and well equipped to work with these students. We must continue to learn from our students and our colleagues at the forefront of addressing these needs to provide campuses where LGBT students not only survive, but thrive, ultimately creating brighter futures and stronger, more inclusive communities.

REFERENCES

Bauder, D. (1998). Establishing a visible presence on campus. In R. L. Sanlo (Ed.), *Working with lesbian, gay, bisexual, and transgender college students: A handbook for faculty and administrators* (pp. 95–103). Westport, CT: Greenwood Press.

Beemyn, B. G., & Pettitt, J. (2006). How have trans-inclusive non-discrimination policies changed institutions? *GLBT Campus Matters, 3*(1), 6–7.

Chan, C. S. (1989). Issues of identity development among Asian-American lesbians and gay men. *Journal of Counseling and Development, 68,* 16–20.

Dumas, M. J. (1998). Coming out/coming home: Black gay men on campus. In R. L. Sanlo (Ed.), *Working with lesbian, gay, bisexual, and transgender college students: A handbook for faculty and administrators* (pp. 79–85). Westport, CT: Greenwood Press.

Evans, N. J. (2002). The impact of an LGBT Safe Zone project on campus climate. *Journal of College Student Development, 43*(4), 522–539.

Evans, N. J., & Wall, V. A. (Eds.). (1991). *Beyond tolerance: Gays, lesbians, and bisexuals on campus.* Alexandria, VA: American College Personnel Association.

Icard, L. (1986). Black gay men and conflicting social identities: Sexual orientation versus racial identity. In J. Gripton & M. Valentich (Eds.), *Social work practice in sexual problems* [Special issue]. *Journal of Social Work and Human Sexuality, 4*(1–2), 83–93.

Jones, S. R., & McEwen, M. K. (2000). A conceptual model of multiple dimensions of identity. *Journal of College Student Development, 41,* 405–414.

Kumashiro, K. K. (Ed.). (2001). *Troubling intersections of race and sexuality.* Lanham, MD: Rowman & Littlefield.

Misa, C. M. (2001). Where have all the queer students of color gone? Negotiated identity of queer Chicana/o students. In K. K. Kumashiro (Ed.), *Troubling intersections of race and sexuality* (pp. 67–78). Lanham, MD: Rowman & Littlefield.

Morales, E. S. (1990). HIV infection and Hispanic gay and bisexual men. *Hispanic Journal of Behavioral Sciences, 12*(2), 212–222.

Newman, P. A. (1998). Coming out in the age of AIDS: HIV prevention on campus. In R. L. Sanlo (Ed.), *Working with lesbian, gay, bisexual, and transgender college students: A handbook for faculty and administrators* (pp. 159–170). Westport, CT: Greenwood Press.

Sanlo, R. (2000). The LGBT campus resource center director: The new profession in student affairs. *NASPA Journal, 37,* 485–495.

Savin-Williams, R. (2005). *The new gay teenager.* Cambridge, MA: Harvard University Press.

Stevens, R. A. (2004).Understanding gay identity development within the college environment. *Journal of College Student Development, 45,* 185–206.

Yoshino, K. (2006). *Covering: The hidden assault on our civil rights.* New York, NY: Random House.

Yoshino, K. (2007). They're here, they're queer, and they don't need us . . . or do they? *The Advocate,* no. 1009. Retrieved from http://www.advocate.com/issue_story_ektid53767.asp

6

Engaging Religious and Faith Diversity in Multicultural Student Services

Jenny L. Small

Zachary considers himself a cultural Jew and does not participate in the Hillel on campus, which he finds too religious. He seeks an organization that will allow him to express himself culturally, without religious pressures. Samah, a second generation American Muslim, remains connected to her Middle Eastern heritage through practicing a traditional belly dance. She wishes there were a place on campus that would allow her to connect to dancers promoting other traditional cultures. Eric, a secular humanist, feels that atheists do not receive many of the privileges that benefit religious students on campus, especially Christians. He seeks the support of a staff member who can take his case to the administration, advocating for students not to have to hear prayers during convocation and graduation.

LTHOUGH THE SCENARIOS about Zachary, Samah, and Eric are fictional, they represent the struggles and concerns of many students in higher education, those for whom religious beliefs (or lack thereof) and related cultural values and ideologies are at the forefront of their identities. In fact, for some students, it is religion, more than other identity elements, that is their most salient lens for self-understanding (Garza & Herringer, 1987; Markstrom-Adams, Hofstra, & Dougher, 1994;

Peek, 2005). As two Muslim authors explained, "religion not only defines us in terms of our participation in practices and membership in certain communities within the context of our societies, but it also defines us in relation to God and the universe" (Nasir & Al-Amin, 2006, p. 23). Religion, faith, and spirituality matter significantly during the college years, and higher education institutions could do much to facilitate students' development in these areas.

Given the centrality of the search for greater meaning in students' lives, this chapter poses the question of whether these elements of students' identities should be included in the mission of multicultural student services (MSS) offices. Is it appropriate to give attention to students' inner lives within this particular forum? If so, how would MSS staff conduct such an undertaking? What would be the particular point of entry into students' religious, faith, and spiritual identities for MSS, and what could MSS offer in addressing these topics that is not already being addressed by other campus offices?

To answer these questions, it is first important to know that students are highly interested in discussing their spiritual lives, but are not necessarily supported through the curriculum in doing so (Higher Education Research Institution, 2005). This mismatch exists despite evidence on the positive outcomes related to spirituality, such as taking leadership roles (Posner, Slater, & Boone, 2006) and being more engaged in campus life (Kuh & Gonyea, 2005). Second, the presence of Christian privilege, much like the White racial privilege commonly addressed by MSS, can be an obstacle for some students' learning and development (Seifert, 2007). Third, minority religions often have accompanying lifestyle differences that can be readily understood within MSS, with its focus on cultural distinctions (see Shuford, Chapter 2). As well, given the negative implications of religious misunderstandings in educational settings (Uphoff, 2001), avoidance might have particularly bad consequences on diverse campuses. MSS, uniquely positioned to address a multiplicity of diversities and related complications within higher education, can help to ensure that these negatives are avoided, while the positive consequences of religious diversity are fully engaged and explored.

Despite the apparent match between the interests of MSS and the needs catalyzed by campus religious diversity, religion has not been given the same level of attention by practitioners and researchers as has been given to racial diversity in the past 30 years. In 2007, Eboo Patel's article entitled "Religious Diversity and Cooperation on Campus," challenged college educators to rectify this and asked us to consider why religion has been left out of the diversity question:

> I think the time is right for college campuses to engage religious diversity in a serious way. This engagement of religious identity makes sense for the central mission of higher education—which is to educate students and to create an environment conducive to that end. Moreover, I think that if the American campus engaged religious diversity seriously, it could have a powerful and positive impact on pressing social issues, both in our country and abroad. (p. 4)

This critical timing exists for historical as well as academic reasons. One explanation for the exclusion of religion/spirituality from discussions of diversity is the trend toward separating faith from the academy (Stamm, 2003). Additionally, Pope (1993) described a fundamental reason why there might be discrepancies among institutions as to whether the mission of MSS includes diversities beyond race/ethnicity:

> At times the word "multicultural" is used synonymously with the word "multiracial"—referring only to racial and/or ethnicity diversity. Other times the term "multicultural" is used more inclusively to cover such diverse groups as students of color, gay, lesbian, and bisexual students, international students, students with disabilities, and students with a variety of religious beliefs, denominations, or preferences. Although the same term "multicultural" is used in these two different situations, in actuality, these two meanings are very different. Confusion, misunderstanding, and exclusion often are the results of different uses of the term "multicultural." (p. 201)

MSS offices, which have been at the forefront of the movement to embrace higher education's racial diversity, are uniquely positioned to respond to Patel's call and to assist in the productive reintegration of religion within academic settings. Unlike campus ministries, which are targeted toward specific religious groups, MSS offices have the mission to provide "support to underrepresented cultural groups" (Shuford & Palmer, 2004, p. 227) of all types. This can be interpreted to include adherents of minority religions and nonbelievers. Although it is rare for the term *diversity* to truly have implications beyond race (Schlosser, 2003), the presence of Christian privilege, both in society and on college campuses, demands that religion be included in institutional diversity considerations, and particularly by MSS, a mainstay of inclusion and support for minority college students.

Bringing religion into the conversation within MSS is not an entirely new proposition. For many students, particularly racial and religious minorities, these two factors of identity might be inseparable. When society's notions of how race and religion operate are in conflict, however, students might be forced to choose between their identities (Nasir & Al-Amin, 2006). Stewart and Lozano (2009) discussed the intersections of race, culture, and religion, noting that "religious and spiritual traditions may provide language for resistance and affirmation for students of color" (p. 30)—some of the same students who might already be involved with MSS. As latent racism might be disguised as traditional religious practices (Stewart & Lozano, 2009), MSS can help deconstruct the intersections of race and religion and work with students to understand how they might inadvertently be oppressing others. These intersections are certainly an area in which MSS has an advantage in knowing how to address students' needs.

RELIGION AND HIGHER EDUCATION: HISTORY AND CURRENT STATUS

The historical relationship between religion and higher education is long, complicated, and ever changing. Though this chapter is not the appropriate venue for recounting the whole of this history, it is important to note the many decades of oppression and discrimination faced by religious minorities on college campuses. Jewish students were subjected to admissions quotas (Wechsler, 1977) and limitations on their involvement in campus activities (Greenberg & Zenchelsky, 1993). Evangelical Christian students were shocked by the overt secularism at many schools and the way others looked down on their literalist beliefs (Hunt & Hunt, 1991). Muslim women who wear the *hijab* (veil) continue to experience "social and academic alienation, isolation, and sometimes-visible discrimination" (Cole & Ahmadi, 2003, p. 62). Regarding all of those religious groups that have faced overt discrimination or the subtle labeling of out-group status, Marsden (1994) said:

> Groups were underrepresented in the leading institutions of the dominant culture for two major reasons. At one end of the spectrum were those who

chose to maintain their own cultural identity, usually supported by strong religious convictions. At the other end were those who, while cultivating cultural identities with religious roots, nonetheless aspired to become part of the mainstream. Most religious groups, however, fell somewhere in between, exhibiting various mixes of both tendencies. (p. 357)

Even now, as higher education has long ended religious quotas in admissions and institutional mission statements purport to be fully embracing of all religious diversities, research into the lives of minority students and practical supports for their daily needs lag behind that which is provided for the religious mainstream. Recently, numerous leaders, scholars, and practitioners in higher education have called for a movement to address this research and practice gap (e.g., Cherry, DeBerg, & Porterfield, 2001; Chickering, Dalton, & Stamm, 2005; Higher Education Research Institution, 2005; Mayrl & Oeur, 2009).

In 2009, members of the American College Personnel Association (ACPA) formed a group that would become a commission-level entity focused on spirituality, faith, religion, and meaning in higher education and student affairs (ACPA, 2009). The founding members of the commission saw the need for ACPA to give attention to the inner lives of students and the association's members. The commission joined the already existing Spirituality and Religion in Higher Education Knowledge Community, which is part of the National Association of Student Personnel Administrators (NASPA, 2009). These two groups represent the perspective that student affairs professionals should "facilitate student learning, growth, and development in the areas of spirituality, faith, and religion" (Small, Hoefle, & Stewart, 2009, para. 3). Neither group, however, specifically discusses the potential links with MSS, which both Shuford (Chapter 2) and Stewart and Bridges (Chapter 3) indicate to be a necessary area for growth.

As these efforts move forward, researchers have begun to provide some noteworthy attention to students who do not claim a religious identity, but who define themselves as atheists, humanists, or other types of non-God believers (Goodman & Mueller, 2009; Nash, 2003). Within the practice arena, nonreligious students have been drawing attention to their need to have support for their spiritual searches. At Tufts University, a student organization called the Tufts Freethought Society requested that the administration hire a humanist chaplain to serve them (Kolowich, 2009). The Campus

Freethought Alliance provides an "affirmation of a life philosophy, offering moral direction, an intellectual toolkit, and a call to political action" (Nussbaum, 1999, p. 30) for humanist students around North America.

It is not just nonbelievers who diverge from the mainstream, though their uniqueness is perhaps most obvious to others. In my own research, I have focused on the differing worldviews and on-campus experiences of students from majority and minority faiths. I have found that students' religious backgrounds do impact the ways they view the world, as well as their perspectives on religious marginalization in society (Small, in press). This suggests that any current educational practices that attempt to address students' inner lives without attending to their important faith-based distinctions are missing an important developmental reality—that religious diversity does matter in educational settings. Importantly for the work of MSS, a colleague and I have also determined that religious minority students have reduced well-being during the college years (Bowman & Small, in press), adding further urgency to the point that these students rely on knowledgeable educators to support them.

Regarding the latter finding, it has been established that campus racial climate is related to the adjustment and sense of belonging of both students of color and White students (e.g., Locks, Hurtado, Bowman, & Oseguera, 2008). By extension, then, an inclusive religious and spiritual climate might also benefit a variety of students. MSS, with its expertise in promoting tolerant and embracing campus climates can take an important role in promoting this type of change. Practitioners can also use texts addressing other forms of diversity with which they have familiarity and translate them to illustrate the impacts of religious diversity. For example, Nasir and Al-Amin (2006) have discussed how stereotype threat, originally conceived by Steele (1997) in regards to racial stereotyping, has a negative influence on Muslim students.

Religion, faith, and spirituality—elements of students' inner lives and identities—might be less visible, however, than the forms of diversity educators are used to encountering in MSS. Clues toward individuals' race, physical ability, and gender are often readily apparent and might give an educator a starting point in working with students. Unless a religious student is wearing the symbols and clothing of his or her group, the reason for his or her presence at MSS might initially be mysterious.

Fortunately, the missions of some MSS offices have begun to expand beyond race to "include programs and services for lesbian, gay, bisexual, and transgender (LGBT) students, international students, and religious diversity" (Shuford & Palmer, 2004, p. 226), providing instruction on how others in higher education can update services. For example, the University of South Carolina provides a thorough list of religious resources on the website for its Multicultural Student Affairs office (University of South Carolina, n.d.), making it clear that religious needs are one aspect of students' lives the office does address. The website for Multicultural Student Services at Lewis University, in Romeoville, Illinois, lists religion as one of the topics about which students can engage during a dialogue series and includes the Muslim Student Association as one of its affiliated student groups (Lewis University, 2009). Resources and dialogue—these are but two basic steps all MSS offices can readily take.

NEXT STEPS FOR SERVING STUDENTS' INNER LIVES WITHIN MULTICULTURAL STUDENT SERVICES

The work of MSS in addressing students' religious, faith, and spiritual identities is not meant to replace that being done by an institution's Office of Spiritual Life, or the myriad student organizations—such as Hillel for Jewish students, Newman for Roman Catholic students, the Campus Freethought Alliance, or the Muslim Students Association—that directly serve students. Complementarily, the MSS can be supportive of the cultural manifestations of these elements of students' lives. For example, Judaism is considered more than just a religion; it "encompasses religion, history, language, culture" (Einstein & Kukoff, 1991, p. xii), aspects of which might be easily embraced through the MSS lens. This might take the form of an event featuring traditional Jewish foods, a movie on Jewish history, or perhaps a dance class featuring Israeli-style dancing. Indeed, the MSS might be freer in its examination of the connections between religion and culture, because it can legitimately avoid the more contentious elements of ideology and ritual practice, which must be addressed in student religious organizations and the offices serving them.

At the intergroup level, MSS offices can begin to develop programming to help students understand one another's religious identities. MSS staff can also use their existing expertise in facilitating dialogues among students of diverse backgrounds to bring religion into campus conversations. Being practiced in the skill of helping students talk through and engage in their differences, MSS educators might have an advantage over professionals who more regularly associate with students from only one religious background, such as clergy or program professionals serving one faith group. Models for this type of work exist on college campuses, such as the Spiritual Pathways Series at the University of Minnesota–Morris (Hodges, 1999). In addition, practitioners can use guidelines from experts on conducting moral conversations (Nash & Strong, 2008). Topics of learning can include "religious holidays and celebrations; comparing and contrasting religions; and the influence of religion in politics, education, and health care" (Shuford & Palmer, 2004, p. 230) and whatever else might be pressing to the participating students.

As MSS offices become more attentive to students' religious, spiritual, and faith diversity, staff members having this added to their portfolios will need training on how to attend to creating an inclusive, supportive environment around these elements of identity. The following are some suggestions for this training, plus ideas about how educators' new skills can be applied on campus:

1. MSS practitioners will need to be become proficient in their knowledge about the diversity of their students' religious practices and beliefs, developing what Nash (2007) calls religious "literacy." Temkin and Evans (1998) pointed out that "a general knowledge and understanding of the ideology and ritual of Christianity, Judaism, Islam, Hinduism, and Buddhism is important for a well-prepared student services practitioner" (pp. 3–4); this list should also include a basic understanding of the various forms of students' nonbelief. Moreover, those religions and ideologies have implications for students' specific advocacy needs. Practitioners will need to become more aware of particular sensitivities, such as the importance for a female staff member to leave the door open with a conservative Muslim man, even during a private conversation.

2. MSS staff will need to "factor in their own biases and beliefs and understand the privilege that comes with being a Christian, or even a religious practitioner, in the United States" (Fairchild, 2009, p. 9). People who are intensely familiar with how racism and White privilege

operate in the United States might, after some exposure, be able to understand religious marginalization and Christian privilege. After building understanding, the MSS itself can be assessed to ensure an absence of any overt or covert Christian privilege.

3. Just as in their work with students characterizing other forms of diversity, MSS educators will need to offer direct advice and support in students' quests to fully express their diverse religious, faith, and spiritual perspectives. As students engage in the development of these elements of their identities, it is critical that they interact with members of a "mentoring community" (Parks, 2000, p. 93) that offers both nurture and challenge. Knowledgeable MSS staff members can become these mentors, just as they are for students exploring their racial and ethnic identities. Also, the physical space operated by the MSS can be offered for students' religious needs, such as being opened for Muslims to use as a prayer space during the day or for a meal after sundown during Ramadan (Nasir & Al-Amin, 2006).

4. MSS offices will not be engaging in this work in isolation and therefore should reach out to other campus organizations and units serving students in their searches for meaning. These are likely to include the offices of the dean of students and spiritual life, chaplaincies and student clubs, and faculty in programs such as religious studies and philosophy. The classroom in particular has been noted as an area that holds great untapped potential for fostering students' spiritual growth (Bonderud & Fleischer, 2003), and faculty members may be open to capitalizing upon a new working relationship with MSS.

5. MSS staff members are, by virtue of their jobs, positional leaders in institutional efforts at advancing diversity causes, what Shuford and Palmer (2004) call "[promoting] systemic change" (p. 227). This provides them with the critical opportunity to be proponents of broader change at the campus level and to speak to faculty, upper level administrators, and even student leaders on the needs of religiously diverse students. They can provide educational information on intersections between types of identities as well as advocate for broader notions of what "diversity" can mean for an institution.

6. To ensure that these practices are effective, MSS offices should engage in evaluation and assessment of their efforts to support students of all religions and all forms of nonbelief. At the basic level, this could take

the form of a survey to the students already participating in MSS programs, to ascertain if their religious and spiritual needs are being appropriately served by the organization. A more intricate assessment would need to include other stakeholders, such as administrators, faculty members, professionals in offices also serving students' religious and spiritual needs, and the broader student body. Important questions of what more could be done, why students might not approach MSS for interfaith programming, etc., would need to be addressed at this point.

CONCLUSION

Educators within MSS currently have the timely opportunity to get involved in a growing movement to support students' spiritual growth, for those from all religious backgrounds and faith identities. As the research literature on this topic continues to grow, and as associations such as ACPA and NASPA give more focus to this area of need, now is the time to develop the natural synergy in missions between MSS and other educators focused on the spiritual needs of college students. The unique niche of MSS, with its mission to serve all students and all of their diversities, positions these organizations to propel forward the work of fully addressing students' religious, spiritual, and faith identities.

Although it is not the responsibility of MSS to be the sole provider of support for students' spiritual explorations during the college years, MSS can certainly engage the cultural components of students' religious identities and act as a conduit for inter-faith conversations. In addition, the interaction between students whose faith is the strongest element of their sense of self and those for whom a different element, such as race or ethnicity, supersedes faith can also be an important form of dialogue. Finally, MSS can become advocates within their campus settings to ensure that religion, spirituality, and faith are truly considered within larger efforts to promote diversity, helping to catch up with the 30-year head start that Patel (2007) says has been given to addressing racial diversity. Now is the time to fully integrate students' quest for meaning during the college years into MSS offices and, by extension, more broadly into the higher education arena.

REFERENCES

ACPA: College Student Educators International. (2009). *Commission for spirituality, faith, religion, and meaning.* Retrieved January 4, 2010, from http://www.myacpa.org/comm/spirituality/

Bonderud, K., & Fleischer, M. (2003). *College students show high levels of spiritual and religious engagement: But new study finds colleges provide little support.* Los Angeles: University of California, Los Angeles, Higher Education Research Institute.

Bowman, N. A., & Small, J. L. (in press). Exploring a hidden form of minority status: College students' religious affiliation and well-being. *Journal of College Student Development.*

Cherry, C., DeBerg, B. A., & Porterfield, A. (2001). *Religion on campus.* Chapel Hill: University of North Carolina Press.

Chickering, A. W., Dalton, J. C., & Stamm, L. (2005). *Encouraging authenticity & spirituality in higher education.* San Francisco, CA: Jossey-Bass.

Cole, D., & Ahmadi, S. (2003). Perspectives and experiences of Muslim women who veil on college campuses. *Journal of College Student Development, 44,* 47–66.

Einstein, S. J., & Kukoff, L. (1991). *Every person's guide to Judaism.* Northvale, NJ: Jason Aronson.

Fairchild, E. E. (2009). Christian privilege, history and trends in U.S. religion. In S. K. Watt, E. E. Fairchild, & K. M. Goodman (Eds.), *Intersections of religious privilege: Difficult dialogues and student affairs practice* (pp. 5–11). New Directions for Student Services, no. 125. San Francisco, CA: Jossey-Bass.

Garza, R. T., & Herringer, L. G. (1987). Social identity: A multidimensional approach. *Journal of Social Psychology, 127,* 299–308.

Goodman, K. M., & Mueller, J. A. (2009). Invisible, marginalized, and stigmatized: Understanding and addressing the needs of atheist students. In S. K. Watt, E. E. Fairchild, & K. M. Goodman (Eds.), *Intersections of religious privilege: Difficult dialogues and student affairs practice* (pp. 55–63). New Directions for Student Services, no. 125. San Francisco, CA: Jossey-Bass.

Greenberg, M., & Zenchelsky, S. (1993). Private bias and public responsibility: Anti-Semitism at Rutgers in the 1920s and 1930s. *History of Education Quarterly, 33,* 295–319.

Higher Education Research Institution. (2005). *The spiritual life of college students: A national study of college students' search for meaning and purpose.* Los Angeles: University of California, Higher Education Research Institution.

Hodges, S. (1999). Making room for religious diversity on campus: The Spiritual Pathways Series at the University of Minnesota-Morris. *About Campus, 4*(1), 25–27.

Hunt, K., & Hunt, G. (1991). *For Christ and the university: The story of the InterVarsity Christian Fellowship of the U.S.A./1940–1990.* Downers Grove, IL: InterVarsity Press.

Kolowich, S. (2009). Humanist chaplains [Electronic Version]. *Inside Higher Ed.* Retrieved from http://www.insidehighered.com/news/2009/11/12/chaplain

Kuh, G. D., & Gonyea, R. M. (2005). *Exploring the relationships between spirituality, liberal learning, and college student engagement.* Bloomington: Indiana University. Retrieved from http://www.nsse.iub.edu/pdf/research_papers/teagle.pdf

Lewis University. (2009). *Diversity enrichment programs.* Retrieved from http://www.lewisu.edu/studentservices/multicultural/enrichment.htm

Locks, A. M., Hurtado, S., Bowman, N. A., & Oseguera, L. (2008). Extending notions of campus climate and diversity to students' transition to college. *The Review of Higher Education, 31,* 257–285.

Markstrom-Adams, C., Hofstra, G., & Dougher, K. (1994). The ego-virtue of fidelity: A case for the study of religion and identity formation in adolescence. *Journal of Youth and Adolescence, 23,* 453–469.

Marsden, G. M. (1994). *The soul of the American university: From Protestant establishment to established nonbelief.* New York, NY: Oxford University Press.

Mayrl, D., & Oeur, F. (2009). Religion and higher education: Current knowledge and directions for future research. *Journal for the Scientific Study of Religion, 48,* 260–275.

Nash, R. J. (2003). Inviting atheists to the table: A modest proposal for higher education. *Religion and Education, 30*(1), 1–23.

Nash, R. J. (2007). Understanding and promoting religious pluralism on college campuses [Electronic Version]. *Spirituality and Higher Education Newsletter, 3*(4), 1–9.

Nash, R. J., & Strong, A. B. (2008). A step-by-step how-to guide for facilitators and participants when doing moral conversation. In R. J. Nash, D. L. Bradley, & A. W. Chickering (Eds.), *How to talk about hot topics on campus: From polarization to moral conversation* (pp. 205–217). San Francisco, CA: Jossey-Bass.

Nasir, N. S., & Al-Amin, J. (2006). Creating identity-safe spaces on college campuses for Muslim students. *Change, 38*(2), 22–27.

NASPA: Student Affairs Administrators in Higher Education. (2009). *Spirituality and religion in higher education.* Retrieved from http://www.naspa.org/kc/srhe/

Nussbaum, E. (1999). Faith no more: The campus crusade for Secular Humanism. *Lingua Franca, 9*(7), 30–37.

Parks, S. D. (2000). *Big questions, worthy dreams: Mentoring young adults in their search for meaning, purpose and faith.* San Francisco, CA: Jossey-Bass.

Patel, E. (2007). Religious diversity and cooperation on campus. *Journal of College and Character, 9*(2), 1–8.

Peek, L. (2005). Becoming Muslim: The development of a religious identity. *Sociology of Religion, 66,* 215–242.

Pope, R. L. (1993). Multicultural-organization development in student affairs: An introduction. *Journal of College Student Development, 34,* 201–205.

Posner, B., Slater, C., & Boone, M. (2006). Spirituality and leadership among college freshmen. *The International Journal of Servant-Leadership, 2,* 165–180.

Schlosser, L. Z. (2003). Christian privilege: Breaking a sacred taboo. *Journal of Multicultural Counseling and Development, 31,* 44–51.

Seifert, T. (2007). Understanding Christian privilege: Managing the tensions of spiritual plurality. *About Campus, 12*(2), 10–18.

Shuford, B. C., & Palmer, C. L. (2004). Multicultural affairs. In F. MacKinnon (Ed.), *Rentz's student affairs practice in higher education* (3rd ed., pp. 218–238). Springfield, IL: Charles C Thomas.

Small, J. L. (in press). *Understanding college students' spiritual identities: Different faiths, varied worldviews.* Cresskill, NJ: Hampton Press.

Small, J. L., Hoefle, S. N., & Stewart, D. L. (2009, Fall). Answering the call to look within: Presenting ACPA's Task Force for Spirituality, Faith, and Religion [electronic version]. *ACPA Developments.* Retrieved from http://www.myacpa.org/pub/developments/

Stamm, L. (2003). Can we bring spirituality back to campus? Higher education's re-engagement with values and spirituality. *Journal of College and Character, 4*(5), Art. 1. Retrieved from http://journals.naspa.org/jcc/vol4/iss5/

Steele, C. M. (1997). A threat in the air: How stereotypes shape intellectual identity and performance. *American Psychologist, 52,* 613–629.

Stewart, D. L., & Lozano, A. (2009). Difficult dialogues at the intersections of race, culture, and religion. In S. K. Watt, E. E. Fairchild, & K. M. Goodman (Eds.), *Intersections of religious privilege: Difficult dialogues and student affairs practice* (pp. 23–31). New Directions for Student Services, no. 125. San Francisco, CA: Jossey-Bass.

Temkin, L., & Evans, N. (1998). Religion on campus: Suggestions for cooperation between student affairs and campus-based religious organizations. *NASPA Journal, 36,* 1–6.

University of South Carolina. (n.d.). *Religious resources.* Retrieved from http://www.sa.sc.edu/omsa/bsr.htm

Uphoff, J. K. (2001). Religious diversity and education. In J. A. Banks & C. A. M. Banks (Eds.), *Multicultural education: Issues and perspectives* (4th ed., pp. 103–121). New York, NY: Wiley.

Wechsler, H. S. (1977). *The qualified student: A history of selective college admissions in America.* New York, NY: Wiley.

7

Bridging Integrated Identities
to Integrated Services

Mary Grace A. Almandrez
Felicia J. Lee

The multicultural student services unit has nine assistant directors: one for each of four racial/ethnic groups (African American, Latino, Asian American, and Native American) and one each for LGBT students, women students, Muslim students, Jewish students, and international students. Although sharing a common reporting line under the MSS director, the nine assistant directors rarely collaborate on programming, are highly secretive about their budgets, and sometimes engage in not-so-subtle competition for students who are drawn to programs offered by multiple departments within the unit. The MSS unit director knows this is a problem, but is unsure how to address or resolve it.

U NFORTUNATELY, THIS SCENARIO is not that uncommon in colleges and universities across the United States. Moreover, the call for recognizing multiple and intersecting identities saturates the authors' prose in the previous three chapters. The need for individuals to seek the integration of multiple and seemingly disparate identities and experiences has been asserted in other contexts, as well. Chicana, lesbian, feminist

107

poet Gloria Anzaldúa (1999) posited that a mestiza, or woman of both Spanish and indigenous lineage, could potentially be the best equipped to navigate the tension of her simultaneous positions of power and oppression. She could do this if she acknowledged her multiple identities, negotiated the conflicts associated with her privilege and oppression, and engaged the intersections of her identities in meaningful ways. This framework moves away from an either/or to a both/and understanding. She called this negotiation of identities mestiza consciousness. *Mestiza consciousness* requires an ability to apply critical lenses to see multiple perspectives, a deep understanding of historical struggles and their sociopolitical contexts, and the capacity to reflect upon the tensions and connections between various identities.

The incredible complexity of this consciousness is a new and emerging consideration for the work of multicultural student services (MSS). Educators should create environments where students, as complete and multifaceted individuals, can explore and express their various identities. It is not enough to have ethnic-specific, lesbian, gay, bisexual, transgender, queer/questioning (LGBTQ)-focused, women-centered programs as isolated learning experiences. MSS can promote and facilitate learning that connects the issues related to race and ethnicity, sexual orientation, gender, religion, and other identity variables. Furthermore, how they operate and who they serve needs to address the realities of the Millennial Generation, whose perspectives about inclusive multicultural environments is different from those of the generation to which many seasoned practitioners belong (Howe & Strauss, 2007).

Similar to how dorms became residence halls then living-learning communities and volunteerism shifted to service-learning, minority affairs have also transformed into multicultural student services and cross-cultural centers. How might student affairs re-envision how MSS, born in an era rife with racial tension and in response to the historical fight for civil rights, meet students where they are now, in the 21st century with uniquely generational-specific needs in the context of a global world? Innovative thinking begins with dismantling prescribed roles, responsibilities, and organizational charts while embracing a philosophical shift that students, as complex and layered human beings, are no longer satisfied with examining one aspect of their selves in a linear, building-block manner. Students of the Millennial Generation view ethnicity as "more often a question of mixed identity than of racial polarization" (Howe & Strauss, 2007, p. 39). If this is the world that our students already inhabit, MSS professionals need to rethink the ways they outreach, program, and educate. As the other authors in Part Two of this volume also acknowledge, higher education does students a disservice by approaching their development as disparate parts of a whole.

The task of integrating services to best serve and educate our diverse student body presents certain challenges and a call to action for student affairs practitioners and institutions of higher education. We believe that colleges and universities must create integrated, intentionally formed services that educate students as whole persons individually and in relationship with diverse others. In other words, MSS can and should promote mestiza consciousness in their programs, services, and guiding principles. This chapter begins by highlighting two contemporary and theoretically based frameworks regarding identity development and their applicability for MSS. A case analysis of the structural and philosophical tensions multicultural centers in the state of California face when attempting to adopt this new model of integration will be presented. Finally, we will conclude with implications for MSS to partner across campus to provide transformative educational experiences for their students.

IDENTITY DEVELOPMENT

Erik Erickson's research on identity development emphasizing the process of gaining clarity on both *who one is* as well as *who one is not* is a commonly cited framework from which other theories have been developed (Torres, Howard-Hamilton, & Cooper, 2003). The most well-known and commonly referenced framework is Chickering and Reisser's (1993) seven vectors of student development: developing competence, managing emotions, moving through autonomy toward interdependence, developing mature interpersonal relationships, establishing identity, developing purpose, and developing integrity. These vectors refer to the psychosocial areas in which traditional-aged college students develop and grow.

Although these theories served as informative templates for practitioners to understand a student's psychosocial maturity, the desire to move beyond a one-dimensional view of identity has prompted scholars to consider not only psychosocial but sociological or environmental factors that shape an individual's understanding of self and others (Taylor, 2008). For example, researchers recognize that students are not only trying to make meaning of who they are but who they are with others and who they are in a particular place or context. Yet universities and colleges readily default to a one-dimensional approach in addressing student development. This unitary and isolated treatment of the diversity on college campuses is not only expressed philosophically through institutional mission statements but is manifested structurally through offices designed to address specific needs (e.g., departmental units that support first-generation students or students with disabilities or LGBTQ students). If MSS adopted a paradigm where the intersections of identity was a primary consideration in the design, delivery, and evaluation of their programs rather than as isolated components of identity development and negotiation, the work might look fundamentally different from how they operate currently.

INTERSECTIONALITY THEORY

Sociologists such as Leslie McCall and womanists such as Patricia Hill Collins and Audre Lorde are credited with developing and expanding the theory of intersectionality. Beginning in the 1960s, increasing numbers of women critiqued existing notions of feminism, arguing that gender was not the only factor that influenced women's lives and that the narratives of women other than heterosexual, White, middle-class women (e.g., women of color, lesbians) were essential contributions to the discourse. Intersectionality theorists recognized that dynamics of privilege, power, and oppression could not be examined through purely gendered lenses. In other words, one identity alone does not determine an individual's lived experiences. Rather, the intersection of various identities makes up a person's fate.

According to Patricia Hill Collins (2000), these dynamics also have to address the matrix of domination that is formed through the interlocking of gender, race, ethnicity, class, sexual orientation, and other social group memberships. In her comments regarding the experiences of Black women in the United States, Collins described the interwoven nature of this web, which makes the separation of oppressions as distinct experiences difficult to discern. One form of oppression alone cannot account for all of an individual's personal experiences. Furthermore, Allan Johnson (2006) stated that specific forms of oppression (e.g., racism, sexism) are part of an overarching, intricate web of oppression. An individual, then, can be in both dominant and subordinated positions at the same time. For instance, a wealthy Hmong American woman might experience privilege as a member of a particular socioeconomic status as well as oppression because of her ethnicity and gender. This both/and model is similar to Anzaldúa's notions of borderlands and mestiza consciousness.

Awareness of this matrix, then, results in important questions for multicultural educators. How can one department or multicultural center meet the needs of poor, first-generation honors students as well as middle-class, second-generation students of mixed ethnic descent? Is it possible for a gay man of color to find a home in the same place as an undocumented immigrant student leader? Do educators encourage students to explore their identities through one specific "label" at a time or challenge them to understand their personhood as complex beings composed of multiple, changing, and interconnected components? Given the lack of financial and human resources that many campuses face, all of these can be extremely difficult tasks. In addition, the push for student learning outcomes and assessment lead to added pressure to ground MSS work in theory while measuring learning and progress in systematic ways.

If done with intentionality and thoughtful planning, MSS staff can implement intersectionality theory in their work with students. MSS offices, whether ethnic-specific or intercultural by design, are likely to focus specifically on race and the racialized experiences of their students. Occasionally, gender, class, or sexual orientation is considered. The challenge, then, is constructing and reconstructing programs and events that make intersectionality explicit and provide consistent learning experiences.

The Multicultural Center at Humboldt State University, for instance, sponsors an annual Qross Qultural Queer Festival (Q-Fest) that features first-run movies and film discussions. The Q-Fest student planning committee makes intentional efforts to include films that speak to the intersections of sexuality, ethnicity, and race. In 2008, the two-day Q-Fest featured seven films, including *Jumping the Broom*, *Johnny Greyeyes*, and *A Jihad for Love*. Intersectionality was at the center of all aspects of the planning, publicity, and implementation efforts.

"Parallels and Intersections" (P&I), organized by Student Diversity Programs at Mills College, is another example of programming for intersectionality. Each workshop in the P&I series allows targeted groups to engage in conversations concerning internalized oppression, agency, and liberation while nontargeted groups raise their awareness of specific forms of oppression as well as discuss the behaviors of allies. Immediately following the workshops are opportunities to focus on the intersectionality of their various identities. Organizers of the series understand the value of having both dominant and subordinated groups explore their specific identities with others who are like them while building bridges for mutual understanding with those who might be different.

When MSS provide programs that address the intersections of identity, their students are afforded rich opportunities for learning and exploration. Another campus, the University of California, San Diego (UCSD), is highlighted in the next section as an exemplary model of practitioners attempting to address intersectionality in services and programs for students.

INTERSECTIONS OF IDENTITY AND INTEGRATED SERVICES: A CASE STUDY OF CAMPUS COMMUNITY CENTERS AT THE UNIVERSITY OF CALIFORNIA, SAN DIEGO

Campus Community Centers at UCSD comprise three distinct yet interrelated centers: the Cross-Cultural Center (established in 1995), the Women's Center (established in 1996), and the LGBT Resource Center (established in 1999). Similar to many centers, all three were individually developed in response to campus community demands for increased visibility of specific marginalized communities as well as institutional commitment to inclusion and social justice.

After many informal conversations regarding their experiences as members of underrepresented and underserved communities, the three directors realized the value of coming together as a united front to work on issues that crossed boundaries, challenged identity politics, and increased collective consciousness. They noticed that all three centers were overtaxed and understaffed. What came from these discussions was a re-envisioning of diversity and social justice work that had at its core individual development and community connections. Although inequities still existed between them in regard to resource allocation, facilities, and visibility, the centers were able to reframe campus ideas around diversity and community-building. Relying on their personal friendships and collegial relationships with one another, the directors shifted from individual collaboration to organizational collaboration to strategize around the ways in which their centers could come together to address intersectionality through integrated approaches to community building that included cross-training, event planning, and collaborative work with student leadership development.

To formalize this collaborative effort, a number of initiatives were implemented. First, the staff for each center began meeting on a monthly basis. In addition to planning collaborative projects and events, these meetings included heartfelt and honest conversations regarding their individual experiences in both their personal and professional lives. Discussion topics ranged from values and behavior congruence, to expectations of collaboration and working together across and with intersectionality. Although emotionally draining and psychologically difficult, the staffs were committed to the conversations as a process to continue developing trust and open communication among the three centers. This initial step of risking vulnerability, managing conflict, and modeling alliance building helped create the foundation for integrated services.

Second, a new reporting structure was created so that all three center directors were under the supervision of the chancellor. This proved to be beneficial in several ways. For example, the configuration positioned the centers' work as campus-wide (i.e., for students, staff, faculty, and external constituents) rather than "extracurricular," which might have been the perception had the centers been housed under student affairs. This in turn opened up access to various campus constituents to work with the centers. In addition, having the same reporting line facilitated communication. Joint staff meetings, as well as individual meetings with the chancellor, afforded each center time to plan and develop shared programs.

Third, the three centers renamed themselves as a collective entity under the name Campus Community Centers (CCC) in 2004. The formation of CCC demonstrated the directors' commitment to their individual centers while also promoting solidarity across their centers. They grounded their work in the belief that ending one form of oppression requires ending all forms of oppression. As Campus Community Centers, they wanted to support interactive learning, self-awareness, leadership development, and intercultural dialogue. The directors also hoped that this symbolic gesture would demonstrate what inclusion might look like. Soon thereafter, they released

CCC marketing materials to the campus community and solidified their integrated programs and services.

One of the clearest examples of the Campus Community Centers' integrated services is their joint programs and trainings. Diversity workshops for staff, student outreach campaigns, and educational and social programs are done as united Campus Community Centers. Therefore, students are continuously and consistently exposed to ideas of intersectionality, whether it is made explicit or not. In December 2007, the staff of CCC participated in a two-day retreat to reflect on their progress as well as share their concerns. In their conversations, they confirmed that some of the strengths of CCC were shared values and purpose, sense of connection to social justice issues, and groundbreaking work that incorporated intersectionality. Their challenges included lack of time and energy to accomplish all their goals, different leadership styles and approaches in their respective centers, and complexities involved with community-building. By the end of the retreat, the joint staff drafted an internal statement of values and began revising their mission statement, vision statement, historical documents, and strategic plan. All voices around the table were honored and valued.

Another example of integrated services within CCC is the student internship program. Although each of the three centers hires, trains, and supervises their respective interns, the recruitment process is a combined effort. Marketing materials, interview timelines, and hiring dates are determined and implemented in collaboration. The internship program features two additional opportunities that reinforce collaboration. First, each center provides a daylong workshop as part of the overall internship training to help the interns cultivate relationships with the other center interns at the beginning of the academic year. Second, each center requires their interns to work together on one collaborative project. Students have the creative license to develop this project with mentorship and support from their respective center director. Their main objectives are to appreciate the interconnectedness and uniqueness of their group identities while embodying the CCC's values of solidarity and social justice.

The Chancellors' Undergraduate Diversity Learning Initiative (CUDLI) is a third example of integrated services spurred by CCC. CUDLI is a quarter-long initiative in which students participate in academic and experiential diversity-related activities related to the Social Change Model of leadership development. In this way, CUDLI functions as a learning laboratory for student leaders. Although all three centers are partners in this initiative, CUDLI operates with a separate budget, work plan, and staff. Therefore, the resources from the centers are not sacrificed and the university administration is accountable for the success of the program.

The work of the Campus Community Centers at UCSD demonstrates what can happen when multiple identities are engaged and this engagement drives the development of integrated services. Additionally, personal commitment, strategic planning, and senior leadership buy-in result in institutionalized change. When personal interactions and organizational initiatives engage intersections of identity, then integrated services become reality.

What follows next are considerations for educators committed to shaping inclusive and holistic campus cultures.

IMPLICATIONS FOR CURRENT PRACTICE IN MSS

The example of UCSD's Campus Community Centers illustrates the depth and breadth of commitment and creativity involved in redefining relationships within and among MSS and their allies. Moreover, it allows student affairs practitioners to reconceptualize the integration of services to address the multifaceted identities of our students. How do practitioners make sure their services and programs address intersectionality? How do they keep current on diversity issues in higher education? As campuses recruit diverse individuals and students seek avenues for inclusion and community, it is essential that educators take time to reflect on their own experiences, participate in personal and professional development opportunities, and develop informed and realistic solutions to institutional problems. Recognizing the inherent challenges in implementing new work models, we offer several ideas for MSS practitioners to consider.

Collaboration

Not surprisingly, the essential element that began the reconceptualization of the Campus Community Centers at UCSD was the solid relationships among the directors of each individual center. Whether in corporate environments or in higher education, the strength of professional ties is often at the heart of creative collaboration. In turn, these partnerships can provide colleagues the permission to make mistakes when sacrifices are requested, or when fatigue and frustration seeps in to quietly derail progress. This permission provides a crucial form of motivation and support that is necessary for creating change of any magnitude and it is often underestimated in its value.

We believe the power of relationships cannot be overstated. It is understood by most practitioners as necessary for achieving outcomes but is not an explicit agenda for discussion and strategic planning in higher education. Often, staff members rely on serendipitous relationship building through committee work, informal daily interactions, or natural friendships formed because of personality commonalities or shared values. Although these variables are valuable in the organic manner by which they materialize, intentionality around initiating, sustaining, and capitalizing on key relationships, internal and external to student affairs, might require a different level of deliberate prioritization and planning.

Though the case study cited focused on the fruits borne from strong relationships among practitioners, how might relationships form among staff and faculty members across institutional divisions? It would be shortsighted of us to believe that work intended to foster intersectionality does not extend into academic borders. For example, a recent effort at Trinity University in San Antonio involves establishing personal connections with tenure-track faculty by hosting a session during new faculty orientation on student life outside the classroom, followed by a lunch inviting the entire student affairs divisional staff to meet new professors. As a follow-up, each new faculty member is invited to coffee with a director-level student affairs professional later in the semester. Although there is no guarantee of future collaboration, planting those seeds (while simultaneously educating others about student development) requires thoughtful planning.

Many campuses have seen that when efforts to reconcile and partner with critical allies to achieve a common purpose are made, tremendous success has followed (e.g., living-learning communities, first-year experience programs, service-learning). These examples foretell the power of strategic collaborative work. Allies from academic and student affairs committed to issues of justice, power, privilege, and oppression, which are at the heart of identity development (Torres et al., 2003), can unite philosophically in goals and behaviorally in spirit. Ally development starts with relationships, and it is at the heart of true systemic change.

We encourage MSS to envision learning spaces that gather campus experts represented in the faculty, staff, and students to work communally such that the work is born intentionally and organically, guided by the philosophy that one's research or program is strengthened by the interconnectedness of multiple identity variables, and where research is supported by practice and practice is informed by research. Clearly, such a conceptual shift of creating new learning centers (notwithstanding the dearth of fiscal and human capital) is contingent on overcoming the historical arguments of validity, legitimacy, and territoriality by both academic scholars and student affairs educators. However, integrated services require intentional relationships.

Institutional Infrastructure

The UCSD Campus Community Centers relied heavily on the strength of collaborative relationships, but it is apparent that the possible dissolution of these collegial ties (e.g., a staff member could relocate, leave the profession, or get promoted to a different job) would jeopardize their continued progress. The ability to develop institutional structures so that implementation of integrated services is positionally based rather than personality based was another important strategy capitalized upon by the UCSD staff. The creation of an external mission statement, writing into job descriptions various requirements that facilitate a shared vision and collaboration, reporting to the same supervisor, and collaborating on internship responsibilities attempted to put in place solid measures for institutional continuity in support of intersectionality and delivery of integrated services. As important as the impetus was for the directors to deepen their working relationships, integrate their respective roles and responsibilities, and re-envision the scope of their mission, the tenure of this effort would be short-lived if the infrastructure supporting their collective vision was not in place.

We recognize that individuals with enough leverage to institutionalize protocol and policies are primarily in senior management positions, yet creative solutions to reorganize departmental units or rewrite innovative job descriptions can be a collective process, involving constituents from across the institution. Allowing multiple voices, perspectives, and experiences at all levels of staffing to visualize new ways to serve our diverse student populations should generate ideas and solutions to address intersectionality in MSS.

Professional Development and Training

Interestingly, multicultural competence is not always cultivated among student affairs—even MSS practitioners—in explicit and intentional ways. As a first step, senior student affairs officers, as key decision makers, must offer learning opportunities for multicultural educators with the same consistency, accountability, and allocation of training resources that college psychologists are required to have to maintain their licenses. This allows for continual learning, awareness of current trends, and the potential to ward off stagnation and isolation. At the same time, this models a true commitment to social justice work as lifelong learning.

Although MSS educators are tasked with the complex responsibility of creating inclusive campus environments for diverse student populations, the educational preparation and ongoing professional training to manage this role often comes at the expense of the seemingly endless management of administrative tasks. As illustrated by the data provided by Stewart and Bridges (Chapter 3), at a minimum, MSS respond to controversial sociopolitical issues, engage in time-consuming student counseling, advocacy, and support, and train and educate others on the merits of diversity. It is not surprising, then, that professionals struggle with their own learning and development around issues of diversity, inclusion, and equity.

Many MSS educators do not hold advanced degrees in cultural studies, sociology, or psychology, although some student personnel preparatory programs require diversity education courses as part of the curricular load. More often than not, student affairs educators are left on their own to stay current on new theoretical frameworks and research, innovative programs, and best practices. They also have to be mindful of how they connect with colleagues across the nation around best practices. Harper and antonio (2008) stress the intentionality that student affairs educators must have in their approach for cross-cultural learning and student engagement. If we acknowledge that supporting the development of integrated identities is critical to the work of multicultural student services, then how do we prepare our teachers to teach? Strange and Stewart address this important question in Chapter 17.

A practical framework for professionals to consider in the development of their own competencies is offered by Pope, Reynolds, and Mueller's (2004) work on multicultural competence in student affairs (this is also discussed further by Reason and Watson, Chapter 18). Multicultural competence is not merely a checklist of cultural knowledge and facts. Rather, it includes continuous learning around issues of privilege, power, and social justice. It also refers to the process by which individuals and organizations increase their awareness, knowledge, and skills to cultivate meaningful relationships with others who are similar to and different from them (Pope et al., 2004). In addition, a commitment to multicultural competence calls for intense reflection about individual actions, institutional contexts, and real structural consequences.

The functional usability of this framework is based on a list of 33 characteristics presented by Pope, Reynolds, and Mueller (2004) that signal baseline competency for student affairs professionals. Naturally, core competencies essential for program effectiveness and service delivery are also beneficial for students grappling with understanding their own identities and evolution as social, cultural, racial, and gendered beings. We agree with Pope, Reynolds, and Mueller that learning is critical for those in positions responsible for facilitating multicultural education.

How do this and other frameworks, then, inform the work of practitioners? Chickering and Reisser's (1993) theory, although providing a useful paradigm to develop educational programs and services for students, is not consistently used in the day-to-day work of student affairs professionals. Intersectionality provides a theoretical framework that is more realistic, given our changing student demographics and their definitions of identity, but this is also not fully embraced or understood. The clarity provided by Pope and associates' (2004) multicultural competencies simplifies a process for skills development.

In practice, student affairs work relies less on theoretical overlays and more on data gleaned from years of theory used in practice and resulting in trials and tribulations associated with practical experiences working with, and for, students. Although none of the aforementioned frameworks alone provides a perfect "how-to" manual for helping educators respond to the simultaneous development of multiple identities, the confluence of traditional and contemporary frameworks might offer a more holistic understanding of ways to approach increasingly complex questions of identity development.

CONCLUSION

Throughout this chapter we have discussed identity development, intersectionality, and multicultural competence as theoretical frameworks for the work of multicultural student services. A case analysis of UCSD's Campus Community Centers featured the structural and philosophical tensions faced when attempting to address the interrelated issues of identity. We ended with implications for MSS practitioners as they reconfigure programs to educate the whole person.

Similar to mestiza consciousness, multicultural student services need to navigate, negotiate, and engage multiple identities. Given that today's students are likely already familiar with the complexities related to multiple identities, it is important for educators to establish collaborative and strategic relationships across campus so that students can explore their identities in multiple environments in multiple ways. When multicultural student services partners with departments such as athletics, service-learning, and health promotion, students are given opportunities to examine and reflect on their intersectionality in various contexts. It is hoped that the efforts at UCSD can inspire readers to rethink who and how they educate.

REFERENCES

Anzaldúa, G. (1999). *Borderlands/la frontera: The new mestiza*. San Francisco, CA: Aunt Lute Foundation.

Chickering, A. W., & Reisser, L. (1993). *Education and identity* (2nd ed.). San Francisco, CA: Jossey-Bass.

Collins, P. H. (2000). *Black feminist thought: Knowledge, consciousness, and the politics of empowerment* (2nd ed.). New York, NY: Routledge.

Harper, S. R., & antonio, a. l. (2008). Not by accident: Intentionality in diversity, learning, and engagement. In S. R. Harper (Ed.), *Creating inclusive campus environments for cross-cultural learning and student engagement* (pp. 1–18). Washington, DC: NASPA.

Howe, N., & Strauss, W. (2007). *Millennials go to college: Strategies for a new generation on campus* (2nd ed.). Great Falls, VA: Life Course Associates.

Johnson, A. G. (2006). *Privilege, power, and difference* (2nd ed.). New York, NY: McGraw-Hill.

Pope, R. L., Reynolds, A. L., & Mueller, J. A. (2004). *Multicultural competence in student affairs*. San Francisco, CA: Jossey-Bass.

Taylor, K. B. (2008). Mapping the intricacies of young adults' developmental journey from socially prescribed to internally defined identities, relationships, and beliefs. *Journal of College Student Development, 49,* 215–234.

Torres, V., Howard-Hamilton, M. F., & Cooper, D. L. (2003). *Identity development of diverse populations: Implications for teaching and administration in higher education.* ASHE-ERIC Higher Education Report, 29(6). San Francisco, CA: Jossey-Bass.

Part Three

Diverse Contexts, Similar Goals

THE CHAPTERS IN PART THREE review how institutional context influences the design and practice of MSS. Despite the differences, common goals and challenges are made apparent.

8

Multicultural Student Services at Private, Liberal Arts Colleges

Kimberly M. Ferguson
Timeka L. Thomas-Rashid

*Darryl directs the multicultural affairs unit at a small, private, reli-
giously affiliated, liberal arts college and has been in his position for
less than a year. His previous appointment was at a larger, public
institution as a graduate assistant. Quickly, Darryl recognized that
the campus environment was much different than his previous institution, and he struggled with the much smaller population of racial
and ethnic minority students as well as the restrictions communicated
by his dean of students that prevented him from "doing too much"
for the college's increasingly more visible and vocal gay and lesbian
student population.*

THERE ARE 287 COLLEGES with a baccalaureate degree emphasis,
specializing in majors in the arts and sciences, including public,
private, and for-profit institutions (Chronicle, 2009). These colleges
comprise just 6.5% of all institutions and only 3% of total student enrollment; moreover, private colleges constitute 86% of the Baccalaureate, Arts
and Sciences classification (Chronicle, 2009). Despite their small share of
the current college-going market, these institutions, commonly referred to
as liberal arts colleges, represent the earliest organization of higher education

125

in the United States and were responsible for educating the majority of college-going youth until the late 19th century (Thelin, 2004). As Darryl in the opening vignette is realizing, these institutions are unique in their history and character, and this uniqueness influences the students' experiences with college, issues of diversity, and how these two factors intersect. Therefore, this chapter describes the nature and characteristics of multicultural student services (MSS) at private, liberal arts colleges. Issues of location, enrollment, staffing, and governance will be examined to illustrate how MSS operates differently within this institutional type.

HISTORICAL DEVELOPMENT OF PRIVATE, LIBERAL ARTS COLLEGES

The nine colonial colleges—which include Harvard, Yale, Princeton, and Columbia—represent the origins of higher education in the United States. These institutions developed similarly and created a curricular and organizational model stitched together from the English universities of Oxford and Cambridge and the Scottish governance model (Thelin, 2004). These institutions emphasized a generalized knowledge base in broad topics of study. As knowledge expanded following the Enlightenment and the disciplines began to specialize, these institutions also expanded their general curricula to reflect what would be commonly recognized as the arts and sciences, or liberal arts, today (Thelin, 2004). Faculty and student relationships were central, and teaching was the primary role expected of faculty (Thelin, 2004). According to Thelin's (2004) history of higher education, it was common for these institutions, and those that would later emerge, to be located in rural areas, away from the distractions of town life and even at times set on a hilltop. Religious denominations often controlled these first institutions, and their influence over the development of higher education in the United States would balloon during the 19th century (Thelin, 2004).

Religious Affiliation

Many of these institutions were and continue to be residential with enrollments ranging from 800 to 4,000 students and offering small class sizes (Carnegie Foundation, n.d.). According to Brubacher and Rudy (2007), many private liberal arts colleges were founded by a church or religious denomination with governance structures that included clergy. These institutions intended to develop a more literate, college-trained clergy and professional men, who would serve as leaders of society (Brubacher & Rudy, 2007). Although many of today's private liberal arts colleges maintain some form of religious affiliation, some have decidedly limited or abandoned their religious ties to the denomination that founded the institution (Brubacher & Rudy, 2007), and the strength of the affiliation varies (Guthrie, 1992).

Governance and Control

The Dartmouth College case in the early 19th century helped to define the difference between public and private institutions as one that was primarily related to governance and control, whether by a government entity or a private one (Thelin, 2004). At issue was whether the state legislature could dictate changes to the institution's governing board membership. Today, public and private colleges are further differentiated by revenue sources. Unlike public institutions primarily supported by subsidies from the state, private institutions are typically supported by revenues generated from tuition and fees, investments, alumni and private donors, and very little state support (Harcleroad & Eaton, 2005).

Curriculum

Offering a liberal arts curriculum is one of the hallmarks of these institutions. Their primary emphasis on arts and sciences remains one of the defining characteristics for Carnegie classification in the Baccalaureate, Arts and Sciences category. This remains so even as the Carnegie schema has dropped the explicit moniker of "liberal arts" for these institutions to reflect the incorporation of professional and graduate programs of study (Carnegie, n.d.). Michele Tolela Myers (2001), president of Sarah Lawrence College from 1998 to 2007, described a liberal arts education as providing "an education in which students learn how to learn, an education that emphasizes the forming rather than the filling of minds, an education that renders our graduates adaptive to any marketplace, curious about whatever world is around them, and resourceful enough to change with the times" (para. 2). In sum, rather than focusing primarily on job preparation or research activities, private liberal arts colleges and universities are committed to serving students who wish to become educated citizens and productive members of society.

Outcomes

Drawing on data from numerous independent sources, including data from the National Survey of Student Engagement (NSSE), the Council of Independent Colleges (CIC, 2009) identified several advantages of a liberal arts education. Among these advantages were perceived value and financial assistance, access and success for diverse students, greater availability of personal attention, higher graduation rates for students, greater alumni satisfaction, and fostering values education and ethical development. Many of these outcomes are typically connected to the advantages of human scale environments that come with smaller student enrollments (Chickering & Reisser, 1993; Strange & Banning, 2001), which are customary characteristics of liberal arts colleges (National Association of Independent Colleges and Universities [NAICU], 2004).

DIVERSITY AT PRIVATE
LIBERAL ARTS COLLEGES

As Kupo (Chapter 1) discussed, access to a college education was largely denied to women and students of color for most of the first two centuries of higher education's history in the United States. Church-related and independent colleges, which made up the bulk of higher education institutions, were generally no different. Brubacher and Rudy (2007) described the public perception of these institutions as elitist and expensive, out of reach for the common citizen, and generally closed to women and non-White racial/ethnic groups. Many institutions restricted access to non-White students or upon admitting them segregated them in classrooms, residence halls, and student activities (Thelin, 2004).

Despite this, there is a record of magnanimity among private liberal arts colleges and universities as related to women, Blacks, and Native Americans. The period following the Civil War was "dominated by the benevolence, zeal, and humanitarianism of northern Christian churches, especially the

Congregationalist, Presbyterian, Methodist, and Baptist churches" (Brubacher & Rudy, 2007, p. 74). Institutions such as Oberlin College, founded in 1833 by Presbyterian ministers, and Olivet College, affiliated with the United Church of Christ and the Congregational Christian Churches, were the first American institutions of higher learning to admit women, Black students, and other students of color (Brubacher & Rudy, 2007). In fact, Oberlin became the first institution to award a baccalaureate degree to an African American woman (Thelin, 2004). For some church-related colleges, like Oberlin, a religious commitment to equality and fairness demanded that access to an education be extended to all students regardless of gender, race, or nationality (Thelin, 2004).

Yet, these efforts were largely idiosyncratic and inconsistent in the absence of widespread public pressure or federal legislation. However, significant changes to American higher education came after the passage of the Civil Rights Act of 1964 and the Higher Education Act of 1965 (Thelin, 2004). The Civil Rights Act of 1964 prohibited the release of federal funds to segregated institutions, and the Higher Education Act of 1965 made basic opportunity grants and other financial aid funds available to disadvantaged populations, which radically changed the landscape of predominantly White colleges and universities. Many of the legal changes did not address campus climate issues and the need to transform student services to meet the needs of special populations that would later follow (Wolf-Wendel, Twombly, Tuttle, Ward, & Gaston-Gayles, 2004).

The commitment to change enrollment policies and subsequent decision to increase institutional financial and human capital to support new diversity recruitment initiatives brought about many challenges and questions for faculty on private liberal arts campuses, according to interviews with James Lyons, Mark Smith, and Judith Chambers, who were student affairs staff at various liberal arts colleges during the 1960s (Wolf-Wendel et al., 2004). According to Wolf-Wendel and her colleagues' (2004) review of this period, faculty perspectives on whether to increase recruitment of students of color usually came from one of three vantage points: aristocratic/elitist perspectives that a college education should be reserved for the academically gifted and talented students of affluent and prominent members of society; meritocracy perspectives that access should include students who will help meet society's needs; and an egalitarian perspective that everyone has the right to be educated to his or her fullest potential. Wolf-Wendel et al. (2004) also found that although institutions typically did decide to pursue greater structural diversity on their campuses, the institutional commitment to increase access and enrollment to attain a critical mass of students of color came about with little discussion concerning the climate on campus and in the surrounding communities.

Lyons, Smith, and Chambers described the experiences of underrepresented students at their respective institutions as wrestling with their own cultural identity while also trying to conform to dominant cultural values (Wolf-Wendel et al., 2004). The problems confronting these students stemmed far beyond academic preparedness and included the negative self-concepts of being labeled a minority, experiencing racial discrimination both on and off campus, the lack of role models who looked like them and shared their experiences, and the basic personal needs of being understood, accepted, and respected (Wolf-Wendel et al., 2004).

Exacerbating these concerns, faculty dialogues on these campuses focused on students of color as "disadvantaged" and situated diversity in conflict with maintaining a quality student body (Wolf-Wendel et al., 2004). Some faculty believed that African American and other students of color were taking the place of more qualified applicants and students, including the children of alumni. The stories shared by Lyons, Smith, and Chambers revealed that chief student affairs officers, along with the support of sympathetic faculty, advocated for a change in the conversation to focus on improving the overall condition of life on campus for all students, thus improving it for students of color (Wolf-Wendel et al., 2004). This paradigm shift came about in the midst of student protests on campus, including the campus takeover of Denison University in 1971 (discussed by Wolf-Wendel et al., 2004, p. 89), the 1969 demonstrations at the University of the Pacific (see Wolf-Wendel et al., 2004, pp. 104–105), and the 1989 takeover of the Galpin administration building at The College of Wooster ("Black co-eds," 1989).

According to Kuh and Umbach (2005) and our own experiences working in small, private colleges with multicultural student services and shared experiences with other colleagues over the years, many private liberal arts colleges have a difficult time attracting individuals from underrepresented racial and ethnic communities, in addition to those representing a diversity of affectional/sexual orientations, often because of location and perceived lack of affordability. These institutions are also less likely to see large populations of students with disabilities, because the services to support these populations are often limited. Yet, as Harcleroad and Eaton (2005) noted, external and internal forces such as private foundations, institutionally based associations, constituency-based associations, voluntary consortiums, regional compacts, alumni, and other donors contribute to private institutions' ability to create other options for funding diversity initiatives, thereby reducing competing university interests for presidents. This indicates that there are avenues and resources that can overcome the challenges faced by small, private liberal arts colleges to create a more diverse campus community. ✱ finances

MULTICULTURAL STUDENT SERVICES AT PRIVATE, LIBERAL ARTS COLLEGES

Altbach, Lomotey, and Kyle (1999) noted that colleges and universities committed themselves to increasing underrepresented populations and improving student services from the 1960s through the 1990s. Colleges and universities established offices whose missions were to support students of color, promote awareness and understanding of similarities and differences among the campus' racial/ethnic student populations, and/or manage racial/ethnic and cultural centers, activities, and events. Specifically, MSS at private, liberal arts colleges evolved out of student, faculty, staff, and alumni needs to recognize, honor, and respect the diverse ideas and cultural, lifestyle, and religious experiences within the campus community (see Shuford, Chapter 2). During fall 2008, we conducted a case study of multiple institutions to reflect the development and history of MSS offices at private, liberal arts colleges. The study explored the experiences of administrators primarily concerned with providing multicultural programs and services for the campus community and/or special populations and the impact of the programs and services on the institution and its mission.

We used purposeful sampling criteria to select six current and former directors of ethnic/cultural student services and selected deans and vice presidents at Midwestern, private colleges and universities. Of those interviewed, five held positions in Ohio, and the sixth participant worked at a college in Michigan. The research questions focused on the mission and roles of MSS offices and practitioners, how the mission and roles have evolved, and the impact of the office mission and roles on the institutional mission. Both of us conducted the interviews: five by telephone and one in person.

All of the participants were employed at independent, coeducational, residential colleges and universities founded in the 1800s by Brethren, Lutheran, Methodist, or Presbyterian churches. Although these colleges and universities were founded as religious institutions, they were also educational institutions with an expressed commitment to liberal arts education, seeking to prepare men and women for every area of life. Likewise, on the matter of race, each of these institutions endeavored to be a place of intellectual engagement for all. Four of the institutions are located in rural areas and are best described as being very politically and socially conservative. The participants from the four rural institutions noted the locality shaped ethnic minority students' experiences. One participant in particular remarked, "People are not used to seeing and/or experiencing minority students." The other two institutions were located in urban areas with more diverse communities surrounding the campus, although this diversity was not reflected in the student enrollment or among the faculty and staff.

Each institution established an office on campus in the late 1980s or early 1990s whose mission was to support minority students, develop minority student activities, and promote cultural awareness and understanding among students. Individuals in these positions also served as advocates for students, interpreters/liaisons to other offices, and retention specialists responsible for developing programs that complemented the academic curriculum, including academic enrichment services. The terms *minority* and *Black* were used interchangeably in conversations on many of these campuses, indicating the narrowness of the student population served.

The offices at these institutions began with varying levels of staffing, usually one part-time or full-time administrator. The offices had several different names, including Ethnic Minority Student Services, Black Student Services, Minority Affairs, Multicultural Affairs, Minority Student Activities, and Multi-Ethnic Student Affairs. Most administrators who ran these offices were called "directors;" one person held the title of assistant dean. All would be considered mid-level managers, similar to the data reported by Stewart and Bridges (Chapter 3). At least two of the institutions hired alumni to spearhead minority and/or ethnic student services. Some institutions employed recent graduates in administrative intern positions to assist with enhancing the living and learning experience as well as developing campus programs and activities. All positions have reported to a senior student affairs officer, with the exception of two individuals who reported to senior academic administrators.

Moving From Ethnic Student Services to Multicultural Affairs

In the late 1990s three of the institutions expanded the scope of their MSS offices to include services for Asian American/Pacific Islander, Native American, Hispanic/Latino, and biracial and multiracial students. Some offices also expanded to include a focus on religion, gender, (dis)ability, and sexual orientation. As awareness of global interdependence increased in the United States, and, subsequently, Ohio and Michigan, these MSS officers reported that students came to college with more intercultural experiences and expanded relationships with a diverse network of peers. Many of these colleges' perspectives on multicultural programming adapted to expand beyond a mono-racial perspective to one that included an exploration of intercultural communication, pluralism, and inclusion across multiple social identities.

Although many of these institutions were no longer tightly affiliated with their founding church bodies, they continued to maintain an office or position committed to the development of religious life. The religious life offices and chaplains/ministers on these campuses also contributed to increased campus dialogues on multiculturalism and diversity as students with Buddhist, Jewish, Muslim, and other religious affiliations began to request and to demonstrate a need for increased programs and services. The mission of these offices has been to foster religious understanding and a celebration of the diversity of cultural and religious experiences on campus.

Thus, the increasing number of students with diverse experiences, in addition to the increasing religious diversity, was an impetus for change on many of these campuses. The MSS officers we spoke with indicated that faculty, staff, and students began discussions about changing the mission and services of the offices originally created to address the concerns of Black students. However, some faculty and students at these campuses objected to the proposed expansion of services for other diverse populations. They expressed some concern about maintaining adequate support and services for Black students. Nevertheless, recognition of the needs of a more diverse student population triumphed over the concerns of these faculty and students, making room for numerous changes to the mission and objectives of these offices.

Some of these changes resulted in the creation of new reporting lines and/ or units housed in separate areas of the campus. For instance, at one institution, there was an office devoted to multicultural student services, as well as an office for institutional equity and diversity. The participant from that institution explained that MSS addressed student needs, but institutional equity and diversity was a unit within human resources that handled concerns related to fair treatment, hiring procedures, and policies governing faculty and staff. At another institution the MSS officer reported to the director of student activities. The office was known as Multicultural Student Activities and focused on programming, activities, and events for students of color. The position was changed to Multicultural Student Affairs in 1997 and sometime thereafter began to report to the provost. At this campus, along with the change in nomenclature and reporting line, new responsibilities were added. These included oversight of institutional equity and diversity, with a direct impact on hiring procedures, policy, and employment applications. This participant cited the need to maintain faculty as those principally responsible for curriculum development as the motivation for the office's restructuring.

As reflected in the stories shared with Wolf-Wendel and her colleagues (2004), academic deans and faculty at these institutions played a key role in establishing common ground for understanding the academic, residential, personal, and social concerns of multicultural students, faculty, and staff. At the second institution described in the previous paragraph, the adoption of a cultural diversity requirement in the curriculum was made possible by the faculty, with the support of academic deans. Five of the six participants in the study indicated that their institutions had implemented a cultural diversity requirement in the curriculum for all students.

In addition to providing academic enrichment services and cultural celebrations recognizing events and notable persons in African American history (e.g., Dr. Martin Luther King Jr. and Black History Month), these offices sponsored celebrations recognizing important events and figures for other groups, such as months celebrating women's history, Latino heritage, and international festivals. In addition, three of the institutions in our study maintained cultural houses and indicated having some responsibility for working with residence life to select hall staff, make housing assignments, and manage programmatic initiatives in those houses. All participants were charged with taking an active role in helping students find ways to connect and engage with a variety of ethnic, racial, cultural, religious, gender, and sexual orientation learning experiences and educational services.

CHALLENGES FACING MULTICULTURAL STUDENT SERVICES AT LIBERAL ARTS COLLEGES

These diversity initiatives continue to be complicated by the location of private liberal arts institutions. A dominant theme that emerged during the interviews was the location of their campuses and lack of representation of a critical mass of Black and Hispanic students, faculty, and staff. All the administrators interviewed articulated this as a major issue that impacts the retention and graduation of Black and Hispanic students. This was highlighted for MSS administrators at rural institutions with racially homogeneous local communities. As one respondent stated, "They do not see many who look like them." In some cases the institutions in rural areas were more than 60 miles from the nearest metropolitan area. The participants stated they had challenges in providing programs that actively engaged the students. As one put it, "It's overwhelming; you feel that weight on your shoulders to provide something for these students to keep them here, [but] how can you when they feel stuck? And feel isolated!" Being limited to the campus to find others with similar identities and backgrounds because the local community around the campus is almost totally homogeneous is indeed a confining and isolating experience. As Kuh and Umbach (2005) noted,

> Many liberal arts colleges are located for historical reasons in rural settings, which are neither populated nor viewed as desirable collegiate environments by students from historically underrepresented groups. As a result, many liberal arts colleges are not structurally diverse. That is, on average, they enroll relatively small numbers of students from racial and ethnic minority backgrounds. Even so, they seem to leave a distinctive diversity imprint on their students. (p. 16)

According to Kuh and Umbach, liberal arts colleges can address this challenge by intentionally structuring more frequent interactions with peers from diverse backgrounds and encouraging student engagement in diversity-related activities.

Another challenge noted by these MSS administrators was feeling they were "preaching to the choir." As one said, "We are charged with developing programs [to] educate the campus. But yet the only students that come are the students who are the minorities!" The challenge for these administrators was helping the majority to recognize that their programs were not just for underrepresented students. It was clear that these administrators were caught in a unique conundrum: Charged by their divisions and departments to educate the masses, they were also charged to be the advocates for students who felt isolated, misunderstood, and were minimally represented. Given these issues, many of the administrators stated they relied on the mission of the institution and missions of their offices for guidance on where to place their priorities. As noted earlier, the titles of their offices were direct reflections of their office missions. These titles, whether multicultural, ethnic, or diversity programming, dictated their direction and priorities.

RECOMMENDATIONS

Despite these challenges, the participants also gave recommendations for other multicultural services practitioners. Among their suggestions, they called for greater awareness of the distinct needs of various cultural groups and how they interact with the campus culture, spreading the responsibility for diversity education across campus, and greater commitment of financial resources to support the work of multicultural student services.

Focus on Institutional Culture, Not Type

Although most liberal arts institutions share a general Carnegie classification, each liberal arts college's culture is different. Differences in campus histories regarding diversity and multiculturalism, the size and nature of its faculty, staff, and student population, and the local and regional community greatly influence the structure and mission of MSS and how it is perceived on campus. This diversity, like the broader student diversity with which these offices engage, must be examined campus by campus and not with broad brushstrokes. Some of the professionals we interviewed stated that although their title specifies a *multicultural* focus, that word had varying meanings across campus, and sometimes the scope of their responsibilities required greater attention to the majority campus population instead of the multicultural students they were charged to serve.

Diversity Education as Everyone's Job

A pervasive theme throughout the interviews was the feeling on the part of these administrators that they felt "the weight" and that they were "the one." The burden was not shared with others on campus, and other campus offices simply directed anything having to do with underrepresented students to their offices. These administrators sought to contradict this attitude and asserted the adage that "it takes a village" to do diversity education and to support and advance underrepresented students. It must be everyone's job in the institution to work for the success of all students, including those who are underrepresented.

Dedication, Time, and Money

Another common complaint from these administrators had to do with the limited budgets they had to do their work. The irony for many was that, unlike their public or community college counterparts, the higher tuitions at their private colleges and university would seemingly result in significantly large programming budgets. However, this was clearly not the case. Many administrators stated they were underbudgeted compared to their colleagues in other areas of student affairs, such as student activities or residence life, and colleagues in MSS at other institutions. The wide range of operating budget figures reported by Stewart and Bridges (Chapter 3) bears this out. These MSS officers felt that budgets were not only tools of fiscal management, but also were reflections of institutional priorities and values. In their opinion, if multicultural student services is purported to be essential to the educational experiences of faculty, staff, and students, then its budget should reflect that.

CONCLUSION

Liberal arts institutions provide an ideal setting for encouraging intellectual discourse, collaborative learning, and progressive social change (Chickering & Gamson, 1987). The individuals who serve in MSS evidence a strong commitment to supporting the institutional mission as related to diversity and inclusion. In such tightly coupled environments, as Birnbaum (1988) described liberal arts colleges, the mission and task of promoting diversity and multiculturalism ought to expand beyond the boundaries of any one office or program. Thus, a clear vision, definition, and commitment to structural diversity and improved climate for multicultural engagement, along with clear expectations for the role of MSS, are essential to helping to understand what underrepresented students do and learn while in college and whether or not they will persist to graduation. More importantly, a clear articulation of diversity and a commitment of personnel and resources to support multicultural student services and diversity education are essential to ensuring that all college students gain valuable experiences with diversity.

REFERENCES

Altbach, P. G., Lomotey, K., & Kyle, S. R. (1999). Race in higher education: The continuous crisis. In P. G. Altbach, R. O. Berdahl, & P. J. Gumport (Eds.), *American higher education in the 21st century: Social, political, and economic challenges* (pp. 109–148). Baltimore, MD: Johns Hopkins University Press.

Birnbaum, R. (1988). *How colleges work: The cybernetics of academic organization and leadership*. San Francisco, CA: Jossey-Bass.

Black co-eds across U.S. voice dissatisfaction with their treatment at college. (May 15, 1989). *Jet*. Retrieved from http://books.google.com

Brubacher, J. S., & Rudy, W. (2007). *Higher education in transition* (4th ed.). New Brunswick, NJ: Transaction Publishers.

Carnegie Foundation for the Advancement of Teaching. (n.d.). *Classification descriptions*. Retrieved January 20, 2010, from http://classifications.carnegie foundation.org/descriptions/basic.php

Chickering, A. W., & Gamson, Z. F. (1987, June). *Principles for good practice in undergraduate education* [Special insert to *The Wingspread Journal*]. Racine, WI: Johnson Foundation.

Chickering, A. W., & Reisser, L. (1993). *Education and identity* (2nd ed.). San Francisco, CA: Jossey-Bass.

Chronicle of Higher Education (2009). *The 2009 almanac of higher education* [supplemental issue]. Available at http://chronicle.com/almanac/

Council of Independent Colleges. (2009). *Making the case*. Available at http://www .cic.edu/makingthecase/data/index.asp#top

Guthrie, D. S. (1992). Mapping the terrain of church-related colleges and universities. In D. S. Guthrie & R. L. Noftzger Jr. (Eds.), *Agendas for church-related colleges and universities* (pp. 3–18). New Directions for Higher Education, no. 79. San Francisco, CA: Jossey-Bass. doi: 10.1002/he.36919927903

Harcleroad, F. F., & Eaton, J. S. (2005). The hidden hand: External constituencies and their impact. In P. G. Altbach, R. O. Berdahl, & P. J. Gumport (Eds.), *American higher education in the twenty-first century: Social, political, and economic challenges* (2nd ed., pp. 253–283). Baltimore, MD: Johns Hopkins University Press.

Kuh, G. D., & Umbach, P. D. (2005). Experiencing diversity. *Liberal Education, 91*(1), 14–21. Retrieved from http://www.aacu.org/liberaleducation/

Myers, M. T. (2001). Preparing students for an uncertain future. *Liberal Education, 87*(3), 22–26. Retreived from http://www.aacu.org/liberaleducation/

National Association of Independent Colleges and Universities. (2004). *Independent colleges and universities: A national profile.* Retrieved from http://www.naicu.edu/docLib/20080214_2004Profile1.pdf

Strange, C. C., & Banning, J. H. (2001). *Educating by design: Creating campus learning environments that work.* San Francisco, CA: Jossey-Bass.

Thelin, J. R. (2004). *A history of American higher education.* Baltimore, MD: Johns Hopkins University Press.

Wolf-Wendel, L. E., Twombly, S. B., Tuttle, K. N., Ward, K., & Gaston-Gayles, J. L. (2004). *Reflecting back, looking forward: Civil rights and student affairs.* Washington, DC: National Association of Student Personnel Administrators.

9

Multicultural Student Services at Public Institutions

Dorian L. McCoy

Sari, a new assistant director within the university's multicultural student services office, is overwhelmed by the complexity of getting something "simple" accomplished. She complains to her mentor, "Everyone's roles are so specialized, and no one seems to know what anyone else is doing. Furthermore, every time I try to start something new on behalf of diverse students on this campus, I trip over a half dozen political landmines along the way! What am I supposed to do?"

THE UNIQUE CHARACTER OF PUBLIC UNIVERSITIES

As discussed by Shuford (Chapter 2), multicultural student services (MSS) began during the turbulence of the 1960s and 1970s. State-supported (i.e., public) institutions in the United States dominated the spotlight during this time in history, with many of the most publicized events of the era involving students and administrators at these universities (e.g., Kent State and Jackson State riots, the *Dixon v. Alabama* case).

By receiving financial support through state revenues, public universities are in a very real sense owned by the people. Therefore, how these institutions attend to the education of students while responding to increasing demands for accountability from the public sets them apart from private institutions. Usually lacking the privilege of making decisions by consensus and collegiality within the simple, tightly coupled organizational systems that are often the norm in private colleges, public institutions are marked by greater levels of political maneuvering in highly complex, loosely coupled systems (Birnbaum, 1988). In the opening vignette, Sari is experiencing the confusion and frustration that can result from this.

In such an organizational climate, the demands of the many might silence the needs of the few, requiring negotiation and coalition-building with allies as necessary skills. For multicultural educators, the public university can present a formidable challenge to accomplishing their goals of supporting students who are usually the numerical minority on the campus. However, public universities often have greater access to financial resources than do private, not-for-profit campuses and are sometimes located in population centers that are more racially, ethnically, religiously, and sexually diverse than the locales that often surround private institutions (see Ferguson & Thomas-Rashid, Chapter 8). Public universities, therefore, are a unique environment and pose distinctive barriers and opportunities for educators in MSS.

BARRIERS TO MULTICULTURAL STUDENT SERVICES AT PUBLIC UNIVERSITIES

Despite the progress achieved by, and for, historically underrepresented and marginalized student groups during the last half of the 20th century, numerous barriers remain at public institutions. These barriers affect the organizational units charged with supporting and enhancing the experiences of students from these groups. This chapter provides an overview of several prominent barriers that affect administrators, practitioners/educators, and students in MSS, and it provides recommendations and strategies for addressing these barriers and opportunities for enhancing the educational experiences of students from historically underrepresented and marginalized groups. Sari's desperate plea to her mentor for help highlights several of these challenges.

Multicultural educators at public institutions continue to encounter barriers that prohibit them from effectively creating environments that are conducive to the success of students from historically underrepresented and marginalized populations. Barriers include but are not limited to issues of campus climate and organizational structure and limited human, fiscal, and spatial resources. Further scrutiny of these barriers is warranted to assess how they negatively impact MSS and the experiences of students from underrepresented populations.

Campus Climate

Prominent among the barriers at public institutions is the campus or institutional climate. Public institutions, particularly those in the South, often possess legacies and traditions of exclusionary practices that might have been enforced by civil laws and statutes (Griffin, Nichols, Perez, & Tuttle, 2008). Most public, predominantly White institutions (PWIs) were not established for students from historically underrepresented populations (Hurtado, Milem, Clayton-Pedersen, & Allen, 1998; Pewewardy & Frey, 2002). Most, if not all, PWIs have climates and cultural norms that privilege those who are White, male, and heterosexual; thus, their environments are perceived to be unwelcoming, hostile (Harper & Nichols, 2008), or chilly for students from historically underrepresented populations. As a result, these students might experience alienation, marginalization, and isolation on college campuses (Griffin et al., 2008; Longerbeam, Inkelas, Johnson, & Lee, 2007; Museus, Nichols, & Lambert, 2008; Sandeen & Barr, 2006).

Strange and Banning (2001) acknowledged the difficulties associated with creating inclusive campus environments for students of color, women, and lesbian, gay, bisexual, and transgender students. The students most often having trouble are rarely a numerical majority. Because these students do not make up a majority of the campus population, their needs and how the campus climate affects them are often overlooked or dismissed. In other words, the dominant campus culture continues to prevail, therefore preventing positive transformation of the campus climate for historically underrepresented and marginalized student groups.

According to Chesler, Lewis, and Crowfoot (2005), resistance to multiculturalism and multicultural change is normal and should be expected in "monocultural higher educational organizations" (p. 71). Those opposed to multiculturalism typically are concerned with a loss of personal power and privileges. These concerns provide educators in MSS an opportunity to inform those with apprehensions about the benefits of having a diverse and multicultural campus community. However, they also can create obstacles to developing programs and services to assist underrepresented students to survive and thrive in the campus environment in ways that honor and value the students.

Organizational Structure

The organization of multicultural student services at public universities might also serve as a barrier to providing quality programs and initiatives to students. No universal or ideal model exists for the organization of student affairs (Manning, Kinzie, & Schuh, 2006); the same can be argued for MSS. Typically, MSS units report to the vice president for student and campus life or someone within the student affairs hierarchy. However, some institutions have fragmented organizational models with various MSS functional units reporting to a student affairs unit and others reporting to an academic or administrative unit (see Stewart & Bridges, Chapter 3). The lack of consistent organizational lines can lead to disjointed administrative and programmatic efforts and create communication barriers. Therefore, the organization of MSS should occur in a manner that promotes student engagement and success (Manning et al., 2006).

One potential organizational model for MSS at public institutions is the "Affinity Model" (Ambler, 2000, p. 131). This particular model aligns or clusters all the functional units within MSS under the auspices of an executive level student affairs administrator/educator for diversity and multicultural initiatives. Units in an affinity model are clustered based on the services provided to students and the university community. Benefits of this model include each director or supervisor being an "expert" in that functional area and all multicultural subunits reporting to one administrator, who can advocate to other executive level administrators on behalf of multicultural educators and historically underrepresented and marginalized students. Disadvantages include communication among units and territorial concerns. In addition, students might have trouble navigating the bureaucracy associated with this model. Despite the concerns with affinity models, they are growing increasingly common at large public institutions (Ambler, 2000). See Figure 9.1 for an affinity organizational model for multicultural student services.

For small- and medium-size public institutions, the affinity model might be inappropriate. These institutions typically have fewer functional units,

Figure 9.1 Affinity organizational model for multicultural student services.

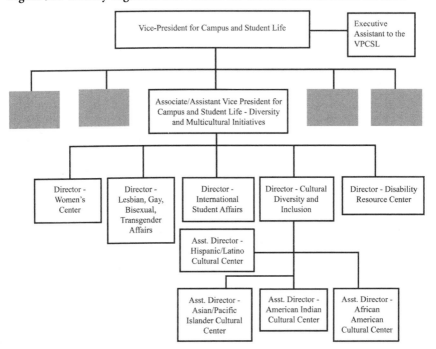

and multicultural educators might have responsibility for multiple functional areas. The organization of MSS at these institutions varies based on institutional resources and how student services are organized as an administrative unit.

Resources

In an era of declining legislative funding and university budget cuts, limited resources constrain the staffing of offices and the programs and services offered by MSS at public institutions. Budget cuts and competition for funds prevent the development of innovative recruitment programs for students from historically underrepresented populations, limit the scope of programs offered, and restrict hiring and salary increases for units that are often understaffed (see Stewart & Bridges, Chapter 3). Staffing is a grave concern because of the various roles, demands, and commitments of multicultural educators. Multicultural educators are often hyper-visible on their campuses, working varied and demanding hours, while serving as role models and mentors for students in less than welcoming environments. Limited resources are also a serious concern for multicultural educators working in private institutions as Ferguson and Thomas-Rashid (Chapter 8) also point out.

Location

environmental messages

Another barrier for multicultural student services is its physical or geographical location on campus. Unfortunately, most MSS offices and programs were established as the result of campus crises (such as the student sit-in at the University of Washington in 1968) and were allocated space on the periphery of campus or in smaller, less-prominent campus locations. Public institutions with strong commitments and values related to diversity and multiculturalism must continue efforts to have MSS units be highly visible and geographically centered on their campuses, which promotes inclusivity. The placement of offices and buildings on campus sends silent messages about the campus environment (Strange & Banning, 2001) and suggests how campus community members and visitors should perceive the campus in terms of its structural diversity and legacy of inclusion (Hurtado et al., 1998). However, budget cuts, reduced state appropriations, and finite space are challenges public institutions must confront in order to meet the needs of students.

Although this list of barriers is not exhaustive, these factors adversely affect the ability of MSS to effectively meet the needs of students from historically underrepresented and marginalized populations. It is the responsibility of public institutions to address and remove barriers that prevent student success.

OPPORTUNITIES FOR ENHANCING MULTICULTURAL STUDENT SERVICES AT PUBLIC INSTITUTIONS

It has been almost a half-century since MSS first emerged at public institutions and nearly two decades since Stage and Manning (1992) offered a model of the multicultural campus that would be inclusive and responsive to all members of the campus community. Yet this goal has not been

the roles of student affairs educators in general, and multicul-
; in particular, continue to expand as campuses place increased
diversity (Dixon, 2001; Talbot, 2003). "Cultural brokers"
(Stage & Manning, 1992, p. 15) must work to transform campus environments from a monocultural perspective to a multicultural one, with emphasis on organizational change and responsiveness for all members of the
campus community.

Educators in MSS at public institutions face some distinct opportunities
given the current social and political climate of the United States and the
emergent global society. The remainder of this chapter is devoted to exploring those opportunities and offering recommendations for enhancing multicultural student services at public institutions.

Developing Global Citizens

One of the foremost goals of diversity education and multiculturalism is to
produce graduates who will become effective citizens in a global society
(Dixon, 2001; Harper & antonio, 2008). Educating students for a global
society requires diverse student populations. Furthermore, there are numerous cognitive and social benefits for students when interacting with others
outside their own identity group (Harper & Nichols, 2008; Whitla, Howard, Tuitt, Reddick, & Flanagan, 2005). Societal success for future graduates
is most likely dependent on their ability to live, work, and function effectively with individuals who possess diverse backgrounds, lifestyles, and ways
of learning and knowing (Sandeen & Barr, 2006). As our communities
become more global, multicultural educators have pivotal roles in the development and education of all students. The greater structural diversity typically found at public universities provides rich opportunities for MSS
educators to promote this learning outcome among students.

Assessing the Campus Climate

An obligation exists for public institutions to assess the campus climate for
students of color, women, and other marginalized groups (Smith & Wolf-
Wendel, 2005). It is well documented that the campus climate affects the
persistence of students from historically underrepresented populations
(Locks, Hurtado, Bowman, & Oseguera, 2008; Museus et al., 2008; Whitla

et al., 2005). Unfortunately, cultural norms for students from underrepresented populations and institutional norms are often in conflict. Members of the dominant culture assume the campus climate, values, and norms are inviting and welcoming because they reflect their culture (Smith & Wolf-Wendel, 2005). This incongruence of cultures can lead to the marginalization and isolation of students from historically underrepresented populations.

Collaborative efforts among executive-level administrators, governing boards, and multicultural educators are essential for improving the campus climate and removing institutional barriers. Given their roles, it is the responsibility of governing boards and presidents to initiate constructive change in their campus climates (Chesler et al., 2005). This includes reviewing and revising strategic plans, institutional policies, and practices for inclusivity. Multicultural audits or campus assessments are potential methods for assessing the campus climate for diversity and multiculturalism (Chesler et al., 2005; Torres, Howard-Hamilton, & Cooper, 2003). Multicultural educators can advocate for the proactive implementation of policies that are reflective of various campus constituencies. Petitt and McIntosh (Chapter 13) further discuss climate assessments and their importance for MSS. In light of the more or less directive role of the state government in the affairs of public universities, it might also be important to secure the cooperation and collaboration of state coordinating or governing boards and legislative bodies in support of strategic planning, institutional policy reviews, and campus cultural audits.

Improving Retention Efforts

The retention of students from underrepresented populations is one of the most daunting challenges facing higher education. Students from these groups continue to post degree completion rates lower than the overall student population (Museus et al., 2008). A longstanding effort of PWIs has been to increase the number of students from underrepresented populations (Locks et al., 2008); however, enhanced retention initiatives are needed. Despite improved recruitment practices, public institutions have failed to provide students from underrepresented populations necessary support for their success after arriving on campus. Multicultural educators are essential to the development of retention initiatives that target underrepresented and marginalized students. Retention efforts include both academic support and providing opportunities for involvement in campus organizations, programs, and activities (Kuh, Kinzie, Schuh, & Whitt, 2005). Improved retention efforts result in enhanced structural diversity at public institutions.

The structure of state appropriations for higher education institutions sometimes exacerbates the retention issue. When state funding is tied to student enrollment numbers alone, institutions are rewarded for achieving high recruitment goals each semester. State funding formulas that emphasize graduation and degree completion might elicit more attention to student retention and persistence.

Collaborating With Academic Affairs

Collaborating efforts with academic affairs presents another opportunity for MSS to enhance the educational experiences of students from historically underrepresented populations. Improved retention and student persistence is often the responsibility of student affairs educators. Manning et al. (2006) argued this practice is problematic if it absolves academic affairs and other institutional units of responsibility for student success. Examples of collaborative initiatives between MSS and academic affairs divisions include providing academic support and skill development, offering mentoring and tutoring programs, and establishing study groups. Collaborative efforts not only enrich student learning but also enhance the services provided (Manning et al., 2006). Furthermore, multicultural educators can provide diversity training for academic affairs divisions and faculty. Public universities typically have more expansive course offerings and faculty departments focused on issues of diversity and multicultural populations. This presents an opportunity for programmatic collaboration with MSS. Kodama and Takesue (Chapter 15) further discuss ways for MSS to collaborate with academic affairs.

Hiring Multiculturally Competent Educators

Hiring multiculturally competent educators is essential for meeting student needs at public institutions. Pope, Reynolds, and Mueller (2004) defined multicultural competence as "a distinctive category of awareness, knowledge, and skills essential for efficacious student affairs work" (p. 9). The expectation that all student affairs educators become multicultural experts is not realistic; however, all student affairs educators should possess a level of multicultural knowledge that allows them to engage with students of diverse backgrounds and identities (Pope et al., 2004). The potential outcomes of hiring a multiculturally competent staff include but are not limited to enhanced programming (both educational and social) and the creation of more comfortable learning environments for students (Loo & Rolison, 1986).

Providing Safe Spaces

Multicultural educators must work to ensure that there are physical spaces on campus that are culturally sensitive to the needs of students from underrepresented and marginalized populations. Recognizing the hostility often directed toward students of color, women, and students who identify as lesbian, gay, bisexual, or transgendered, women's centers, ethnic and cultural centers, and various campus offices (e.g., Disability Services) provide students safe spaces or places of solace. Institutions must recognize the value of these safe spaces. The aforementioned centers, offices, and residence halls are often the hub of campus life for these students and present an opportunity for involvement in the campus community. These campus safe spaces are essential for providing students from historically underrepresented and marginalized groups locations to form meaningful relationships with other students and allies.

There is an apparent movement on some campuses to merge ethnic and cultural centers into one multicultural center. Patton (2006), however, offered words of caution for institutions considering such actions: "[M]erging individual culture centers to bring underrepresented groups under one roof has the potential to undermine the rich history that each of these groups brings to the campus" (p. 642). Elimination or the merging of specific cultural centers diminishes students' sense of inclusion on campus. Strange and Banning (2001) concluded that various campus communities thrive when space is dedicated to students who have shared characteristics and interests.

Inclusive Programming

The "coordination of diversity-related efforts and a focus on inclusion" (Harper & antonio, 2008, p. 9) presents an additional opportunity for multicultural student services. Multicultural educators are responsible for creating opportunities for students with diverse identities to engage, interact, and support each other. The benefits of engagement with peers from diverse backgrounds include increased cultural/identity awareness and appreciation, racial understanding, and satisfaction with college (Harper & Nichols, 2008; Locks et al., 2008).

Integration into campus organizations and activities tends to offer students from historically underrepresented and marginalized populations greater social options and enhances their integration into campus life (Griffin et al., 2008). Programs that celebrate diversity, promote inclusion, and enhance the educational experience for all students are essential for changing the campus climate (Talbot, 2003). "Students from diverse backgrounds and with diverse perspectives must be given opportunities to interact outside of the classroom through cocurricular workshops and programs, clubs and campus activities" (Griffin et al., 2008, p. 131). Taking into consideration that many members of the campus community were raised in homogeneous communities (Locks et al., 2008; Sandeen & Barr, 2006), such programs provide educational opportunities; promote positive cross-cultural, cross-racial, and cross-gender interactions; and promote involvement in campus programs and activities. Furthermore, these programs have the potential to educate the campus community about various forms of privilege (Chesler et al., 2005; Whitla et al., 2005).

Promoting Religious Tolerance

The role of multicultural student services has taken on added significance since the events of September 11, 2001, when religious tolerance in the United States most likely reached an all-time low (Sandeen & Barr, 2006; Smith & Wolf-Wendel, 2005). Despite the passage of time, the need to educate the campus community about religious pluralism remains. The development of programs emphasizing religious pluralism assists in fostering a campus climate of tolerance and inclusiveness for students who do not identify as Christian. Although private institutions, especially those that are religiously affiliated, typically employ full-time staff to plan and develop programs related to spirituality and religion, public institutions often seek support from off-campus entities (Dungy, 2003). MSS at public institutions are encouraged to develop partnerships with local religious organizations to further promote tolerance and understanding on campus. Jenny Small (Chapter 6) further discusses the inclusion of religious diversity within MSS programs and services.

THE FUTURE OF MULTICULTURAL STUDENT SERVICES AT PUBLIC INSTITUTIONS

debate

Despite the existence of historical and institutional barriers, the attacks of the past decade on affirmative action (*Grutter v. Bollinger* and *Gratz v. Bollinger*), and diversity programs, the necessity and vitality of multicultural student services at public institutions remains unquestioned. The United States Supreme Court upheld the notion that diversity in higher education is a constitutionally compelling interest (Ancheta, 2005; Evans & Chun, 2007). Multicultural educators continue their efforts to assist in creating campus climates that are conducive for students from historically underrepresented and marginalized groups to succeed in the dynamic and ever-changing environments of higher education. As evidenced by the examples provided in this chapter, the various roles and functions of MSS and multicultural educators will continue to evolve as higher education becomes more reflective of the global community in which we live.

REFERENCES

Ambler, D. A. (2000). Organizational and administrative models. In M. J. Barr, K. M. Desler, & Associates (Eds.), *The handbook of student affairs administration* (pp. 121–134). San Francisco, CA: Jossey-Bass.

Ancheta, A. N. (2005). After *Grutter* and *Gratz*: Higher education, race, and the law. In G. Orfield, P. Marin, & C. L. Horn (Eds.), *Higher education and the color line: College access, racial equity, and social change* (pp. 175–196). Cambridge, MA: Harvard Education Press.

Birnbaum, R. (1988). *How colleges work: The cybernetics of academic organization and leadership.* San Francisco, CA: Jossey-Bass.

Chesler, M., Lewis, A., & Crowfoot, J. (2005). *Challenging racism in higher education: Promoting justice.* Lanham, MD: Rowman & Littlefield.

Dixon, B. (2001). Student affairs in an increasingly multicultural world. In R. G. Winston Jr., D. G. Creamer, T. K. Miller, & Associates (Eds.), *The professional student affairs administrator: Educator, leader, and manager* (pp. 65–80). New York, NY: Brunner-Routledge.

Dungy, G. J. (2003). Organization and functions of student affairs. In S. R. Komives, D. B. Woodard Jr., & Associates (Eds.), *Student services: A handbook for the profession* (4th ed., pp. 339–357). San Francisco, CA: Jossey-Bass.

Evans, A., & Chun, E. B. (2007). *Are the walls really down?: Behavioral and organizational barriers to faculty and staff diversity.* ASHE Higher Education Report *33*(1). San Francisco, CA: Jossey-Bass.

Griffin, K. A., Nichols, A. H., Perez, D., II, & Tuttle, K. D. (2008). Making campus activities and student organizations inclusive for racial/ethnic minority students. In S. R. Harper (Ed.), *Creating inclusive campus environments* (pp. 121–138). Washington, DC: National Association of Student Personnel Administrators.

Harper, S. R., & antonio, a. l. (2008). Not by accident: Intentionality in diversity, learning, and engagement. In S. R. Harper (Ed.), *Creating inclusive campus environments* (pp. 1–18). Washington, DC: National Association of Student Personnel Administrators.

Harper, S. R., & Nichols, A. H. (2008). Are they not all the same? Racial heterogeneity among Black male undergraduates. *Journal of College Student Development, 49,* 199–214.

Hurtado, S., Milem, J. F., Clayton-Pedersen, A. R., & Allen, W. R. (1998). Enhancing campus climates for racial/ethnic diversity: Educational policy and practice. *The Review of Higher Education, 21,* 279–302.

Kuh, G. D., Kinzie, J., Schuh, J. H., Whitt, E. J., & Associates (2005). *Student success in college: Creating conditions that matter.* San Francisco, CA: Jossey-Bass.

Locks, A. M., Hurtado, S., Bowman, N. A., & Oseguera, L. (2008). Extending notions of campus climate and diversity to students' transition to college. *The Review of Higher Education 31,* 257–285.

Longerbeam, S. D., Inkelas, K. K., Johnson, D. R., & Lee, Z. S. (2007). Lesbian, gay, and bisexual student experiences: An exploratory study. *Journal of College Student Development, 48,* 215–230.

Loo, C. M., & Rolison, G. (1986). Alienation of ethnic minority students at a predominantly White university. *The Journal of Higher Education, 57,* 58–77.

Manning, K., Kinzie, J., & Schuh, J. (2006). *One size does not fit all: Traditional and innovative models of student affairs practice.* New York, NY: Routledge.

Museus, S. D., Nichols, A. H., & Lambert, A. D. (2008). Racial differences in the effects of campus climate on degree completion: A structural equation model. *The Review of Higher Education, 32,* 107–134.

Patton, L. D. (2006). The voice of reason: A qualitative examination of Black student perceptions of Black culture centers. *Journal of College Student Development 47,* 628–646.

Pewewardy, C., & Frey, B. (2002). Surveying the landscape: Perceptions of multi-cultural support services and racial climate at a predominantly White university. *The Journal of Negro Education, 71*(1–2), 77–95.

Pope, R. L., Reynolds, A. L., & Mueller, J. A. (2004). *Multicultural competence in student affairs.* San Francisco, CA: Jossey-Bass.

Sandeen, A., & Barr, M. J. (2006). *Critical issues for student affairs: Challenges and opportunities.* San Francisco, CA: Jossey-Bass.

Smith, D. G., & Wolf-Wendel, L. E. (2005). *The challenge of diversity: Involvement or alienation in the academy?* ASHE Higher Education Report, *31*(1). San Francisco, CA: Jossey-Bass.

Stage, F. K., & Manning, K. (1992). *Enhancing the multicultural campus environment: A cultural brokering approach.* New Directions for Student Services, no. 60. San Francisco, CA: Jossey-Bass.

Strange, C. C., & Banning, J. H. (2001). *Educating by design: Creating campus learning environments that work.* San Francisco, CA: Jossey-Bass.

Talbot, D. M. (2003). Multiculturalism. In S. R. Komives, D. B. Woodard Jr., & Associates (Eds.), *Student services: A handbook for the profession* (4th ed., pp. 423–446). San Francisco, CA: Jossey-Bass.

Torres, V., Howard-Hamilton, M. F., & Cooper, D. L. (2003). *Identity development of diverse populations: Implications for teaching and administration in higher education.* ASHE Higher Education Report, *29*(6). San Francisco, CA: Jossey-Bass.

Whitla, D. K., Howard, C., Tuitt, F., Reddick, R. J., & Flanagan, E. (2005). Diversity on campus: Exemplary programs for retaining and supporting students of color. In G. Orfield, P. Marin, & C. L. Horn (Eds.), *Higher education and the color line: College access, racial equity, and social change* (pp. 131–151). Cambridge, MA: Harvard Education Press.

10

Multicultural Student Services at Community Colleges

Eboni M. Zamani-Gallaher
Stanley Bazile

At a national conference of other directors of multicultural student services units, James represents his community college for the first time. As he listens to the discussions in the workshops, he realizes that his role and responsibilities look very different from those of his colleagues, who mostly work at four-year institutions. Cynthia, the senior student affairs officer at her community college, is attending the conference in hopes of finding out how other two-year institutions address issues of diversity and organize services to multicultural students.

THE LANDSCAPE OF HIGHER EDUCATION is rich with an assortment of institutions that provide postsecondary training, credentialing, and development for a wide array of collegians. Although there are 4,314 postsecondary institutions in the United States, well over 1,600 are public and private two-year institutions (Provasnik & Planty, 2008). Historically two-year institutions, often referred to as community colleges, are commonly at the margins of the larger discourse on postsecondary education in terms of policy development, state/federal financial support, and research focus among academicians (Cohen & Brawer, 2008; Zamani, 2006). Given the common neglect of community colleges, they are often viewed from a deficit model (for example, Brint & Karabel, 2006) and frequently stigmatized by misinformed public perceptions that do not illuminate the true value of this tier of higher education.

The great paradox of community colleges is the promise they hold of greater educational, occupational, and social mobility juxtaposed with the reality that these institutions were not conceived to expand access to the masses. They were created to stratify higher educational opportunities, suppress collegiate ambitions, and dissuade students from seeking career trajectories that would exceed low/middle-level workers to perpetuate the interests of elites (Brint & Karabel, 2006; Dougherty, 2006). However, the era when low-skill labor dominated the labor market has ended with the onset of rapid growth in high-skill/high-demand technical professions. Consequently, some analysts predicted robust job expansion in occupations requiring an associate's degree, positioning community colleges to respond to the nation's workforce development needs for competing in a global knowledge economy (Purnell, Blank, Scrivener, & Seupersad, 2004). *debate*

The current globally driven labor market illustrates the necessity for highly skilled laborers from diverse backgrounds. Community colleges, more so than their university counterparts, have mirrored the shifting demographics of society at large with divergent learners from all walks of life (e.g., racial/ethnic minorities, reentry students, older adult learners, students with disabilities). With the increase of nontraditional, low-income students from various cultural groups attending two- and four-year colleges, the organizational structure for the delivery of effective student services is paramount to collegiate satisfaction, retention, matriculation, and educational goal attainment.

Although all institutions of higher learning seek to educate and serve every student, this chapter highlights the unique ways in which community colleges meet the needs of a diverse student body. Specifically, the varying compositions and structures of community colleges are discussed, along with current data on characteristics of students, faculty, and administrators, to examine the context of multicultural student services (MSS) at community colleges.

THE COMMUNITY COLLEGE CONTEXT

In 1901 Joliet Junior College was established in Illinois, marking the birth of a sector in higher education that would become a crucial gateway for individuals seeking postsecondary education. By 1946 students were returning to college by the hundreds of thousands. This increase in student enrollment placed significant strain on the nation's higher education system. As a result, President Harry S. Truman established the Commission on Higher Education for American Democracy. The committee included twenty-eight members, with occupations that varied from educators to nonprofessionals; it was assigned the broad task of exploring possible original initiatives the nation's colleges and universities could engage in to respond to the growing need for education. In response, the 1947 Truman Commission Report called for creating a public community college system that would deliver a multitude of programs with low costs of attendance to meet the needs of local constituencies (Cohen & Brawer, 2008). Hence, the community college movement began to take shape. By the 1960s the growth in the community college sector exploded, resulting in the massification of higher education. Access to postsecondary education was extended across social groups, no longer reserved for the elite.

Community colleges have provided opportunities for higher learning to everyday people from all walks of life. These institutions have enrolled students that might not otherwise have any other postsecondary education options. To illustrate the growing importance of this sector to the higher education enterprise, in the 1970s roughly two million students attended community colleges. By the 1980s enrollment at community colleges had doubled to four million and by fall 2006 community colleges served more than 6.2 million individuals, accounting for 35% of all postsecondary students (Provasnik & Planty, 2008). More recent data suggest that community college students constitute 46% of all U.S. undergraduates, and community colleges register 41% of all first-time, first-year students and enroll nearly half of all students of color participating in postsecondary education (American Association of Community Colleges [AACC], 2008).

There has been a 741% increase in community college enrollments over the last 45 years (Provasnik & Planty, 2008). Despite the considerable number of undergraduate students who attend four-year institutions, projected trends are that community college enrollments will continue to grow

(Cohen & Brawer, 2008). A number of factors have contributed to the enlarged enrollment at community colleges: increasingly competitive admissions requirements at four-year institutions amid significant remediation needs among graduating high school students, the skyrocketing costs of college, and decreasing availability of grant-based financial aid concurrent with rising loan-based assistance (Cohen & Brawer, 2008).

Student Demographics

Among the growing number of students at community colleges are racially/ethnically diverse students. Student enrollments at community colleges, as reported by AACC in 2008, included 13% African American/Black, 15% Hispanic/Latino, 6% Asian/Pacific Islander, and 1% Native American. These students of color made up 35% of the student body of two-year institutional enrollments (AACC, 2008). Similar to four-year institutions, women constituted the majority of community college students, accounting for 60% of enrolled students. Dissimilar to four-year institutions is the proportion of traditional-age students enrolled. Full-time students aged 20 to 24 constituted 52.7% of enrollment at four-year institutions nationally; at community colleges, they made up only 33.8% of total enrollment (Almanac, 2008). The average age of a community college student was 29 years (AACC, 2008). Moreover, the majority of students who attended a two-year institution (59%) attended part-time. Additionally, 17% of community college students were single parents (AACC, 2008).

Community College Faculty and Staff Demographics

Access to higher education via community colleges has benefited several populations. Cain (1999) stated, "The public two-year colleges do not simply educate or credentialize. They change lives for the better. They change them radically and they change them permanently and they change them inexpensively" (p. 1). Based on the changing dynamics of higher education, the roles of postsecondary educators and administrators are both critical and complex in striving to provide optimal learning conditions that enable students to self-actualize. Therefore, it is vital that community college faculty and staff strive to aid students in navigating the sometimes rocky terrain of college environments. For nontraditional, culturally diverse students, barriers (both perceived and real) could hamper their collegiate satisfaction and academic progression.

Although the profile of students at community colleges has continued to change, the cultural pluralism of the faculty and staff at two-year institutions has not kept pace proportionately (Zamani, 2006). In fact, 81.2% of the 354,497 faculty members at public two-year institutions identified as White, non-Hispanic (Almanac, 2008). There appears to be parity by gender among two-year faculties with women totaling 48.7%; however, White men made up the majority of community college faculty members when examining faculty members by race/ethnicity and gender.

As is the case with faculty, administrative staff was also disproportionately represented relative to community college students of color. The 2008–2009 Almanac issue of *The Chronicle of Higher Education* reported that as of fall 2005 there were a total of 26,770 professional public, two-year college employees, and Whites represented 80% of executive, administrative, and managerial staff members. One percent of administrative staff at public two-year institutions were American Indian, 2.3% were Asian, 10.2% were African American/Black, Hispanics amounted to 5.6%, and the race was unknown for 1.1%.

Student Affairs and the Community College

Although there is a small cadre of administrators of color in higher education, many are stratified by institutional type. For instance, greater numbers of faculty and staff from racially/ethnically diverse backgrounds can be found at two- and four-year minority-serving colleges, such as historically Black colleges, predominantly Hispanic-serving institutions, and tribal colleges (Aragon & Zamani, 2002; Townsend et al., 1999). However, the vast majority of students of color attending college are not enrolled at minority-serving community colleges or four-year universities but at predominantly White institutions (Allen, 1992). These trends have created specific distinctions within and between postsecondary institutions in terms of who occupies administrative student affairs positions and what programs, policies, and services are advanced that are targeted to culturally diverse student populations.

Regarding student services, there are many parallels and differences when contrasting two- and four-year institutions of higher learning. The functions of student personnel work in four-year organizations overlap with those in community colleges; each sector is determined to provide the most favorable conditions for engaging student learning in and outside the classroom. Similar to their university counterparts, a central mission of community college student services is to apply a holistic approach in developing students through offering a vast array of services. These services include academic advising, admissions, campus activities, career services, college counseling, community service, disability services, financial aid, multicultural programming, orientation, student organizations, transfer/articulation, and service learning (Culp, 2005; Komives, Woodard, & Associates, 2003). To a lesser extent, student affairs in the community college includes residence life, health services, child care assistance, or Greek affairs. The aforementioned services are distinctly organized from one community college to the next (Robinson-Wright & Smith, n.d.).

According to Lett and Wright (2003), an institution's student affairs mission must include the following goals: healthy student development, successful progression toward graduation, and multicultural initiatives. What little literature is available indicates that numerous student affairs offices at community colleges are lacking diversity, because the overwhelming majority of community college student affairs officers (CCSAOs) are White males (Wilson-Strauss, 2005; Zamani, 2006). Research by Opp (2001) and Pope (2002) contended that the key to recruiting and retaining students of color is to address barriers to success, provide mentoring, and most especially have chief CCSAOs who can serve as mentors and role models, because these dynamics positively impact equitable outcomes for two-year students of color.

COMMUNITY COLLEGES, STUDENT AFFAIRS, AND MULTICULTURAL SERVICES

Multicultural student services at two-year institutions are generally housed under student affairs and generally referred to as the student life or multicultural affairs office. The overall function of these units is to offer programs that recruit, increase access, and promote academic assistance for students of color. Some institutions strive to retain and foster matriculation via transfer to four-year colleges, certificate and associate's degree conferral, and aid in transitioning students from school to work (Prairie State College, 2008). Beyond providing student support, programs, and leadership opportunities at community colleges, MSS professionals also serve as advisors for culturally diverse student organizations (e.g., The Black Student Association, Hispanic Student Club, GLBT Union, and Society of Students with Disabilities). For example, it is the charge of the Prairie State College Student Life and Multicultural Affairs Department and the aim of MSS units at other community colleges to ensure a culturally congruent climate, aid student development, and broaden opportunities to learn by fostering civic engagement and student leadership (Prairie State College, 2008).

As James and Cynthia are coming to realize in the opening vignette, research examining community college multicultural student services is virtually absent in the extant literature. What presently serves as a foundation for framing MSS work on two-year campuses is the literature on multicultural competence in student affairs (Castellanos, Gloria, Mayorga, & Salas, 2008; King & Howard-Hamilton, 2003). Pope, Reynolds, and Mueller (2004) stated, "Despite the significant role that the student affairs profession has played in responding to multicultural issues on campus, there is limited student affairs literature that specifically addresses multicultural concerns" (p. 5). Community college research is marginalized relative to higher education administration and student affairs literature. Hence, there is a dearth of literature squarely focused on the linkages between MSS and student affairs at two-year institutions.

Piland, Hess, and Piland (2000) discussed how little research illustrates culturally pluralistic educational experiences provided for community colleges students. Their research examining student learning encounters of 434 community college students with multicultural and diversity education found that student experiences were enriched when multicultural/diversity content was included. Overall, the results indicated that community college students desired to have more courses with this content. However, White male students expressed the least interest in multicultural coursework in comparison to women and minority students. One example of how community colleges could attend to MSS, as well as build the relationship between academic and student affairs units, is through courses that address diversity and pluralism. Sedlacek and Roper (1988) argued that teaching courses such as "Education and Racism" illustrates an academic role that MSS personnel can fill. Therefore, MSS administrators need to aspire to having exemplary multicultural awareness, knowledge, and skills because these professionals can contribute to the cultural competencies and intercultural maturity of collegians at two-year institutions (King & Baxter Magolda, 2005; Pope et al., 2004).

Innovation in Community College Multicultural Student Services

Our review of the literature found no empirical studies on the effectiveness of MSS at community colleges or the career satisfaction of student affairs professionals, but there are a few MSS programs at select two-year institutions that we considered to represent best practices. One such initiative is the Multicultural Student Leadership Training Program sponsored by the Sylvania Multicultural Center at Portland Community College. This leadership training initiative is a yearlong, paid internship for 10 students of color. The student leaders selected work as peer tutors and student coordinators. Each student leader participates in extensive training and a leadership retreat, is expected to work 10–12 hours each week, must maintain a minimum cumulative GPA of at least 2.5, and must register for six or more credit hours each semester (Oliveros, 2008). The aim of the Multicultural Student Leadership Training Program is to assist students in self-actualizing as campus leaders as well as embed opportunities for students to put the tenets of social justice, student advocacy, and multiculturalism into practice (Oliveros, 2008).

Another example of best practices in MSS at community colleges is in the Office for Student Life and Multicultural Affairs at Prairie State College (PSC) in Chicago Heights, Illinois. This office prides itself on providing preenrollment and transfer advice, helping students complete financial aid applications, sponsoring tours to four-year universities, and offering bilingual assistance in college exploration (Prairie State College, 2008). Akin to the bilingual assistance offered by PSC, Santa Barbara Community College District is responding to the diverse, growing population of English as a second language (ESL) learners. Under the Student Life Program, the Multicultural Student Services Officer is also in charge of activities for international students such as social events, field trips, and campus tours for local language schools (Santa Barbara Community College District, 2008). Given that roughly two-fifths of international students attending U.S. colleges and universities are enrolled at community colleges, representing 8% of public community college enrollments, MSS at two-year institutions have also become involved with study abroad and global studies (AACC, 2008).

Pierce College, located 45 minutes outside of Seattle, understands that the community college student is not always from the local community. Pierce College provides institutional fact sheets in eight languages other than English, including Chinese, Indonesian, Japanese, Korean, Portuguese, Spanish, Thai, and Turkish. In addition, Pierce's Multicultural Leadership Institute (MLI) offers community cultural events such as foreign language social chat sessions. Participation in the chats requires no language fluency to join and is free of cost to students and to the public. The foreign language social chat sessions are offered in Chinese, Korean, Japanese, Russian, Spanish, English for ESL learners, and American Sign Language. Additionally, MLI prides itself on the following motto: EMBRACE, "Educating Myself for Better Racial Awareness and Cultural Enrichment" (Pierce College, 2006). Pierce has a range of services, including diversity training workshops, overseas service-learning projects, the diversity book club, "munch-n-learn" events, and visual/cinema cultural art events.

Although the functions of multicultural student services should embrace a variety of international and domestic diversity issues, many community college MSS efforts are often supported through the federal TRIO Student Support Services (SSS) grants. The purpose of the TRIO program is to provide a multitude of academic and personal support services for first-generation college students with limited income or disabilities. Effective SSS units on community college campuses can aid in improving retention, persistence, and graduation rates of the targeted students (Bellevue Community College, 2004).

Gauging the academic progression of culturally diverse students is vital to enhancing services and programs that are beneficial for divergent student populations. The Multicultural Affairs Program, in collaboration with the High Technology Center, at Glendale Community College in Arizona developed a student tracking/monitoring system in an effort to be proactive in offsetting potential problems (e.g., student attrition/withdrawal, academic probation, financial aid probation, to improve lag-time with stop-out patterns, etc.). The "StudentPal" program was created to improve the performance and outcomes of racially/ethnically diverse students (Mendoza & Corzo, 1996). With StudentPal, multicultural affairs at Glendale Community College has the ability to analyze student level data in terms of their course load trends, GPA by age, and zip code. This new tracking program has expanded the college's capacity to serve students and made the unit better equipped to respond to faculty referrals, provide early warnings to students, as well as develop targeted retention initiatives for students of color (Mendoza & Corzo, 1996).

CONCLUSIONS AND IMPLICATIONS
FOR PRACTICE

Debat

With demographic trends projecting that U.S. society will be increasingly diverse, with large numbers of students from underrepresented, marginalized groups seeking higher learning, multicultural student services' mission and range will be of great importance. This chapter sought to highlight how MSS units are critical at community colleges in meeting the academic and personal needs of culturally diverse students. Yet, student affairs units housing MSS at two-year institutions are questioned by some, rendering them vulnerable at community colleges. For example, rarely is the existence of units such as academic affairs, business affairs, or administrative affairs questioned; rather, there is a general consensus that these units are a necessity (Helfgot, 2005). In some respects, student services are often seen as an afterthought.

> There are times when the functions provided by student affairs are embraced by the institution, and student affairs professionals are welcomed as full partners in the educational enterprise. At other times, however, student affairs is viewed as a drain on institutional resources or fluff that adds little or no value to the enterprise. (Helfgot, 2005, p. 6)

In spite of being devalued by some, student affairs practitioners at community colleges work tirelessly to serve a range of students. This task is becoming harder to do as the enrollment population has become more diverse. Although a diverse student body provides a plethora of benefits to students, staff, and the institution, it also brings a number of complicated dynamics, especially because this growing population is not specific to one demographic. Thus, the work of MSS professionals at two-year institutions of higher education is notable. Arguably, MSS work is challenging and rewarding for practitioners at community colleges because they are the architects that design programs and an atmosphere where all members of the community feel welcome and affirmed.

Having a culturally pluralistic staff is essential to fostering greater student success. The pipeline of student services personnel with the critical skill sets to lead diverse initiatives under the auspices of multicultural student services is limited. Although community colleges enroll multiple marginalized populations, including race/ethnicity alongside social class, gender, disability, sexual orientation, and religious diversity, based on the limited literature on multicultural affairs in community college settings, it is unclear to what extent such offices have expanded services to persons across the spectrum of these differences. The exemplars featured in this chapter clearly illustrate services to racially/ethnically diverse populations or diversity education on those subjects. Given that community college populations are growing and becoming increasingly diverse, it is paramount that future research explores the ways in which two-year institutions respond to the divergent student populations entering, with greater sensitivity and awareness of the multiplicity of identities students have as shaped by all of their ascribed characteristics.

REFERENCES

Allen, W. R. (1992). The color of success: African American college student outcomes at predominantly white and historically black public colleges and universities. *Harvard Educational Review, 64,* 26–44.

Almanac issue 2008–09. (2008, August 29). *The Chronicle of Higher Education, 45*(1). Retrieved from http://chronicle.texterity.com/chronicle/almanac200809/

American Association of Community Colleges (2008, January). *Community college fast facts.* Retrieved August 23, 2008, from http://www2.aacc.nche.edu/research/index.htm

Aragon, S. R., & Zamani, E. M. (2002). Promoting access and equity through minority serving institutions. In M. C. Brown (Ed.), *Equity and access in higher education: Changing the definition of educational opportunity* (Readings on Equal Education, *18,* 23–50). New York, NY: AMS Press.

Bellevue Community College (2004, May 19). *TRIO Student Support Services.* Retrieved June 19, 2008, from http://bellevuecollege.edu/trio/

Brint, S., & Karabel, J. (2006). Community colleges and the American social order (reprint). In B. K. Townsend, D. D. Bragg, K. Dougherty, F. S. Laanan, & B. V. Laden (Eds.), *ASHE Reader on Community Colleges* (4th ed., pp. 63–74). Boston, MA: Pearson Publications.

Cain, M. S. (1999). *The community college in the twenty-first century: A system approach*. Lanham, MD: University Press of America.

Castellanos, J., Gloria, A. M., Mayorga, M. M., & Salas, C. (2008). Student affairs professionals self-report of multicultural competence: Understanding awareness, knowledge, and skills. *NASPA Journal, 44,* 643–663.

Cohen, A. M., & Brawer, F. B. (2008). *The American community college* (5th ed.). San Francisco, CA: Jossey-Bass.

Culp, M. C. (2005). Increasing the value of traditional support services. In S. R. Helfgot & M. C. Culp (Eds.), *Special issue: Community college student affairs: What really matters* (pp. 33–49). New Directions for Community Colleges, no. 131. San Francisco, CA: Jossey-Bass.

Dougherty, K. J. (2006). The community college: The impact, origin, and future of a contradictory institution. In B. K. Townsend, D. D. Bragg, K. Dougherty, F. S. Laanan, & B. V. Laden (Eds.), *ASHE reader on community colleges* (3rd ed.; pp. 753–782). Boston, MA: Pearson Publications.

Helfgot, S. (2005). Core values and major issues in student affairs practice: What really matters? In S. R. Helfgot & M. C. Culp (Eds.), *Special issue: Community college student affairs: What really matters* (pp. 5–18). New Directions for Community Colleges, no. 131. San Francisco, CA: Jossey-Bass.

King, P. M., & Baxter Magolda, M. B. (2005). A developmental model of intercultural maturity. *Journal of College Student Development, 46,* 571–592.

King, P. M., & Howard-Hamilton, M. (2003). An assessment of multicultural competence. *NASPA Journal, 40,* 119–132.

Komives, S. R., Woodard, D. B., Jr., & Associates. (2003). *Student services: A handbook for the profession* (4th ed.). San Francisco, CA: Jossey-Bass.

Lett, D., & Wright, J. (2003). Psychological barriers associated with matriculation of African American students at predominantly White institutions. *Journal of Instructional Psychology, 30,* 189–196.

Mendoza, J., & Corzo, M. (1996). *Tracking/monitoring program to enhance multicultural student retention.* Retrieved from ERIC database. (ED399999)

Oliveros, C. (2008, March 31). *Multicultural student leadership training program.* Retrieved June 19, 2008, from http://www.pcc.edu/resources/culture/documents/student-leadership-application-2008.pdf

Opp, R. D. (2001). Enhancing recruitment success for two-year college students of color. *Community College Journal of Research and Practice, 25,* 71–86.

Pierce College (2006, March 14). *The MCSS center—multicultural student services.* Retrieved July 22, 2008, from http://www.pierce.ctc.edu/edsupport/mcss

Piland, W. E., Hess, S., & Piland, A. (2000). Student experiences with multicultural and diversity education. *Community College Journal of Research and Practice, 24,* 531–546.

Pope, M. L. (2002). Community college mentoring: Minority student perception. *Community College Review, 30*(3), 31–45.

Pope, R. L., Reynolds, A. L., & Mueller, J. A. (2004). *Multicultural competence in student affairs.* San Francisco, CA: Jossey-Bass.

Prairie State College (2008). *Student services: Student life and multicultural affairs office—The goals of SL/MA.* Retrieved August 16, 2008, from http://prairiestate.edu/ss-msa.html

Provasnik, S., & Planty, M. (2008, August). *Community colleges: Special supplement to the Condition of Education 2008.* Washington, DC: National Center for Education Statistics, U.S. Department of Education.

Purnell, R., Blank, S., Scrivener, S., & Seupersad, R. (2004). *Opening doors, support success: Services that may help low-income students succeed in community college.* New York, NY: Manpower Demonstration Research Corporation.

Robinson-Wright, U. M., & Smith, S. G. (n.d.). Community colleges. *Education encyclopedia: StateUniversity.com.* Retrieved from http://education.stateuniversity.com/pages/2464/Student-Services.html

Santa Barbara Community College District (2008, September). *Multicultural student services officer.* Retrieved from http://www.sbcc.edu/hr/classificationinformation/multicultural%20student%20services%20officer%20Dec-05.doc

Sedlacek, W. E., & Roper, L. D. (1988). *Student personnel professionals in academic roles: A multicultural example.* Retrieved from ERIC database. (ED296271)

Townsend, B. K., Guyden, J. A., Hutcheson, P. A, Laden, B. V., Pavel, D. M., & Wolf-Wendel, L. (1999). Beyond a distinctive student body: Possibilities for practice. In B. K. Townsend (Ed.), *Two-year colleges for women and minorities: Enabling access to the baccalaureate* (pp. 225–244). New York, NY: Falmer Press.

Wilson-Strauss, W. E. (2005). *Graduate preparation for community college student affairs officers.* Unpublished doctoral dissertation, University of Florida.

Zamani, E. M. (2006). African American student affairs professionals in community college settings: A commentary for future research [reprint]. In B. K. Townsend, D. D. Bragg, K. Dougherty, F. S. Laanan, & B. V. Laden (Eds.), *ASHE reader on community colleges* (3rd ed., pp. 173–180). Boston, MA: Pearson Publications.

11

Multicultural Student Services at Minority-Serving Institutions

Historically Black Institutions

Kevin D. Rome Sr.

Leslie is in hir[1] sophomore year at a historically Black college in the South. Ze knows that what sets hir apart from the rest of the Black students on campus is hir gender identity; ze has come to acknowledge hir identity as genderqueer. However, there is nowhere on campus for hir to talk about hir issues with a trusted adult. Na'im is in his junior year at the same college. As a Muslim student, he often feels ostracized and has been mocked on campus by other students. Although the required weekly chapel programs are supposed to be interfaith, the presider always begins and ends by praying "in Jesus's name." His requests for a truly religiously pluralistic chapel program seem to be going unheard.

A S EXPLORED BY KUPO (Chapter 1), higher education was largely restricted to young, wealthy, White men prior to the mid-20th century. Very few institutions had race-blind admissions policies, and even those that did admit Black and other non-White students segregated

---

[1] Please see the Introduction for discussion of the use of gender-neutral pronouns in the opening vignette for this chapter.

167

them on campus (Anderson, 1988; Thelin, 2004). The emergence of preparatory schools, colleges, and universities committed to the education of African Americans was principally responsible for making higher education and
upward mobility accessible to these citizens (Anderson, 1988). Historically
Black colleges and universities (HBCUs) are institutions founded prior to
1964 for the purpose of educating African Americans at the college level;
103 institutions are recognized as HBCUs by the federal government
(Brown & Davis, 2001).

Founded by various religious denominations and private philanthropists,
HBCUs provided an education in either a classical liberal arts curriculum or
an industrial (vocational) curriculum (Anderson, 1988). Over time, this simple distinction has evolved such that these institutions represent a range of
institutional types, including two-year and four-year institutions, private and
public schools, liberal arts colleges and research universities, as well as single-
gender and coeducational academic environments (Brown & Davis, 2001).
HBCUs are distinguished from predominantly White institutions (PWIs)
by unique characteristics. Among these are that HBCUs have a tradition of
providing access for African Americans to higher education (regardless of
academic preparation), social networks for African American students and
alumni, and programming geared toward the African American experience
(Palmer & Gasman, 2008). Further, Brown and Davis (2001) argued that
HBCUs have a "unique social contract" and act as "social agencies" for
educational access, as well as "social equalizers" (p. 33) by providing social
capital to students who otherwise would not have access to full participation
in American society.

HBCUs have a "tradition of inclusion" (Jewell, 2002, p. 9) in that they
never practiced exclusionary admissions, residency, or student activities policies (Anderson, 1988), and their students were at the forefront of civil rights
protests during the 1960s and 1970s (McAdam, 1982). Nevertheless, student enrollments developed to be racially homogeneous, owing mainly to the
interacting effects of racism and inadequate funding to support competitive
program development and institutional advancement (Anderson, 1988; Jewell, 2002). Despite the racial homogeneity of the student body, other forms
of diversity do characterize HBCUs in terms of social class, sexual orientation and gender identity, religion and faith, as well as age, ability, and first-
generation status (Jewell, 2002). HBCUs also have student groups who are
racial minorities on the campus that identify as White, Latino, or Native

American, as well as international students (often from the African Diaspora) who enroll at these institutions (Jewell, 2002). Therefore, the question of how these institutions build multicultural competence within the student body, as well as preparation for engaging diversity and supporting pluralism, is relevant.

However, the distinctive character of HBCUs, including their historical legacy of inclusion, predominantly Black student enrollment, and presumed cultural consistency, suggests that multicultural student services (MSS) at these institutions would take a different shape. This topic has not been addressed in the literature previously, so there is no information upon which to base a general discussion of MSS at HBCUs. When researching the nature of multicultural student services at these institutions through reviewing institutional websites and discussions with other colleagues at HBCUs, there was very little information available on the existence of such offices. Although there were student organizations that addressed issues of diversity, the institutions did not have specific offices focused on multicultural issues.

I worked for several years as the chief student affairs officer at Morehouse College, a historically Black, private, liberal arts college for men, and I am intimately familiar with its institutional history and student services. At Morehouse, multicultural student services are diffused throughout the campus without institutional coordination by any single unit or administrator. This could be a characteristic endemic to historically Black colleges because of the lack of specific administrative offices devoted to multiculturalism. This arrangement has its benefits, because it spreads responsibility and ownership throughout the campus. However, as illustrated by the opening scenario involving Leslie and Na'im, the drawback is that there is no central unit accountable for ensuring that the needs and issues of a broad range of diverse students are addressed and supported. This chapter looks at a single campus that is representative of the attitude and approach toward MSS provided at HBCUs. Morehouse is not illustrative because it is a "typical" HBCU. In fact, in many ways, it is not typical, given its all-male student enrollment and stronger financial position and elite status among HBCUs (Butler, 1977). Rather, Morehouse's approach to MSS is illustrative because the structural diversity of its student body and historical development and approach to diversity is consistent with other historically Black institutions (Brown & Davis, 2001; Jewell, 2002). Therefore, the nature and character of issues of difference, privilege, and inclusion at Morehouse are similar to most other HBCUs.

MOREHOUSE COLLEGE

The following briefly summarizes the historical development and faculty and student demographics of Morehouse College. This discussion helps contextualize the approach to multicultural student services at Morehouse and might be helpful for understanding how MSS is approached at other HBCUs as well.

Historical Development

In 1867, two years after the Civil War ended, Augusta Institute was established in the basement of Springfield Baptist Church in Augusta, Georgia. Founded in 1787, Springfield Baptist is the oldest independent African American church in the United States. The school's primary purpose was to prepare Black men for the ministry and teaching. Augusta Institute was founded by the Reverend William Jefferson White, an Augusta Baptist minister and cabinetmaker, with the encouragement of the Reverend Richard C. Coulter, a former slave from Augusta, Georgia, and the Reverend Edmund Turney, organizer of the National Theological Institute for educating freedmen in Washington, DC. In 1879, Augusta Institute was invited by the Reverend Frank Quarles to move to the basement of Friendship Baptist Church in Atlanta and changed its name to Atlanta Baptist Seminary. Later, the seminary moved to a four-acre lot near the site on which the Richard B. Russell Federal Building now stands in downtown Atlanta. In 1885, the institution relocated to its current site in Atlanta's West End community. The campus encompasses a Civil War historic site, a gift from John D. Rockefeller, where Confederate soldiers staged a determined resistance to Union forces during William Tecumseh Sherman's famous siege of Atlanta in 1864. In 1897, Atlanta Baptist Seminary became Atlanta Baptist College (Jones, 1967).

Atlanta Baptist College was named Morehouse College in honor of Henry L. Morehouse, the corresponding secretary of the Northern Baptist Home Mission Society. Morehouse received full accreditation by the Southern

Association of Colleges and Schools in 1957 (Jones, 1967). Today, Morehouse College is located on a 66-acre campus in Atlanta and enjoys an international reputation for producing leaders who have influenced national and world history (Jones, 1967).

College Demographics

Morehouse College enrolls approximately 2,800 men from 40 states and 18 countries outside the United States (Morehouse College, 2006). The largest population of international students derives from the Caribbean and the continent of Africa. The college also takes pride in the diversity of its staff and professors. Morehouse's most recent fact book indicated that approximately one-third of its faculty were women or from an ethnic background other than African American (Morehouse College, 2006).

Affiliation

Morehouse College is located in the Atlanta University Center, a consortium of six institutions where undergraduates may cross-enroll in each of the undergraduate institutions. The member institutions of the Atlanta University Center are Clark Atlanta University; the Interdenominational Theological Center, a federation of seven theological seminaries; Morehouse College; the Morehouse School of Medicine; Morris Brown College, a coeducational liberal arts college related to the African Methodist Episcopal Church; and Spelman College, an independent liberal arts college for women (Morehouse College, 2006).

Institutional Philosophy of Diversity

The institutional diversity philosophy at Morehouse College is that the entire college addresses and is committed to multiculturalism. Every academic department, center, and student services unit has special programs that are directed at particular issues of multiculturalism. Robert Franklin (2007), the current president of Morehouse College and the moral leader of the institution, addresses various topics related to how one should treat his brother (sister) in his book, *Crisis in the Village*. It is leadership from the top that creates an environment for addressing multiculturalism at the college.

This model, as well as similar models at other historically Black colleges, needs empirical evidence to support this approach to addressing multiculturalism (Dwyer, 2006).

In his book, Franklin (2007) spoke to such issues as healthy men's relationships. He also addressed ethical and moral leadership as necessary traits in this society. Such strong messages from the top leadership at Morehouse provided direction for accepting differences on the campus. When a college or university has a president or chancellor who exemplifies such principles, it promotes an environment that welcomes multiculturalism. However, contradictory messages, such as noninclusive messages about gender expression sent by the college's dress code policy (discussed further in what follows), can undermine that dominant philosophy.

Diversity and Difference at Morehouse College

At first glance, it might appear that Morehouse College is a homogeneous environment, composed predominantly of African American men from throughout the United States. It is also reasonable to conclude that a monolithic culture exists in such an environment. The reality of multiculturalism at a place such as Morehouse College is impacted by many factors, including but not limited to religion, gender, sexual orientation, nationality, class, and geographic background, or a combination of these traits.

International Diversity

One might assume that multiculturalism in an all-male, predominantly African American environment would refer only to those students who are non-African American. Although it is true that those students who are not African American contribute to the diversity of the college, efforts to address multiculturalism at Morehouse College are focused predominantly on the diversity that exists among African American men and others of African descent. Given this, the college recognizes the importance of exposing its students to global diversity. The college selected "Enhancing the Global Competence of Morehouse Students" as the topic of its Quality Enhancement Plan (QEP). The QEP is a requirement for reaccreditation by the Southern Association of Colleges and Schools.

Global competence may be addressed through the curriculum, programming, traveling abroad, international students, faculty, staff, and other means. Additionally, studying abroad can result in greater cross-cultural skills and global understanding for students (Kitsantas, 2004). As a result of developing its Quality Enhancement Plan, Morehouse created two new positions. A study abroad director was created to increase emphasis on students studying abroad, and a new international student recruiter was developed to focus on increasing the number of international students attending the college. This is particularly important at a time of budget cuts and reductions in resources. The creation of the new positions at the college emphasizes a commitment to global diversity and multiculturalism.

International students make up approximately 3% of the 2,800 students enrolled at Morehouse. International students are serviced through the Andrew Young Center for International Affairs (AYC), which is charged to provide leadership to the college's international education objectives and promotes an institutional culture of internationalism. The center's mission is the globalization of the college's academic programs, curricula, and activities and the preparation of students for service in the global community. Its vision is directed at developing the global leadership skills of both international and domestic students (Morehouse College, 2006).

Religion

Religion has played an integral role at Morehouse College from its inception and genesis in the basement of Springfield Baptist Church. Many of the founders and early students of the institution were Christian clerics. The school was an outlet for producing more educated African American ministers and teachers (Jones, 1967). Spirituality plays a significant role in the lives of most African American college students (Riggins, McNeal, & Herndon, 2008). The role of religion and the Martin Luther King Jr. International Chapel, under the leadership of Dr. Lawrence Carter, has a significant impact on Morehouse College. Yet Morehouse students today represent a variety of religious and faith backgrounds and belief systems. The college has adapted to serve and support students who do not identify as Christians as well as educate students about other faiths.

Interdenominational religious services are offered each Sunday on the campus. Speakers from various faiths are invited to lecture in the chapel. At special services and events in the chapel, one can expect to hear a prayer or message from a Jewish or Buddhist person or someone from another faith not typically represented in a predominantly African American community. Students from various faith traditions serve as chapel assistants, who provide support for programs and services by serving as ushers and speakers.

Gender Identity and Expression

Gender is inextricably tied to identity at a unisex institution. This can be particularly complex when gender and race are the catalyst for the formation of the college. Studies have suggested that a relationship exists between racial identity and gender for African American men (Brooks & Good, 2001; Caldwell, 2000; Lazur & Majors, 1995; Wester, Vogel, Wei, & McLain, 2006). Morehouse College takes pride in addressing such delicate issues and producing highly educated and talented African American male graduates.

From the students' introduction to the campus during new student orientation through the final upper-division senior courses, there is an emphasis on the development of manhood. Currently, the Morehouse College Male Initiative has been launched to study factors that lead to the academic success of African American men. The effort also looks at the identity development of African American men. One goal of the program is to provide a model for academic success for African American and other minority men in higher education.

Identity development and manhood development are not constructed in isolation at Morehouse. Morehouse has a sister institution, Bennett College, a women's college located in Greensboro, North Carolina. The proximity of Spelman College and Clark Atlanta University provide ample opportunity for students at Morehouse to interact and develop relationships with female college students. Morehouse and Spelman collaborate on programming and share a joint homecoming. The two schools have rituals of assigning brother–sister partnerships during the students' first year. There also exist brother–sister partnerships between residence halls on the campuses. It is no surprise that marriages between Morehouse and Spelman students are common occurrences.

However, there is diversity in gender expression among the students at Morehouse College. Within all-male environments, the pressure to conform to socially accepted masculine gender roles and expression can be intense

(Harper, 1996; Johnson, 1997). The institutional response to transgender and gender nonconforming students remains unresolved, not only at Morehouse but across all HBCUs (Jewell, 2002). Recently, Morehouse announced dress codes that reinforce traditional, masculine modes of gender expression (Gasman, 2009; Jaschik, 2009), and the conservatism of this policy resembles those at many other HBCUs (Harper & Gasman, 2008). As Gasman (2009) also expressed, such noninclusive policies signal a troubling, and possibly hostile, climate for transgender men at Morehouse College.

Sexual Orientation

Sexual orientation has been and continues to be a difficult issue to address at historically Black colleges and universities, particularly those with past or current religious ties (Jewell, 2002). Dealing with race, faith, and sexual orientation is a complicated task (Poynter & Washington, 2005). The subject of gay and bisexual students is also unresolved at Morehouse College, as it is at many historically Black institutions (Harper & Gasman, 2008). As the population of college students who have nonheterosexual or transgender identities grows (Sanlo, Rankin, & Schoenberg, 2002), it is imperative that the college be more responsive to the needs of such students. Morehouse College, like all other colleges and universities, should address this issue and develop a framework to deal with the students. Support groups exist on the campus and in the community, but the college does not provide resources for these organizations (McCready, 2004).

Social Class

Morehouse College predominantly espouses the values of the African American middle class, and it is difficult to argue against the increasing influence of the African American middle class (Malveaux, 2002). It is also important to point out the diversity of socioeconomic levels of the students who matriculate at the college and at historically Black institutions generally (Jewell, 2002). Morehouse College has to balance providing an environment that is acceptable to a demanding middle- and upper-class African American population, while making those who derive from lesser means feel comfortable in the environment.

Perusal of the alumni list or current student enrollment of Morehouse reveals the names of the sons of many noted celebrities, dignitaries, and politicians. However, the majority of the students attending the institution do not have recognizable surnames. It takes a concerted effort on the part of the institution to provide an environment that makes such a mix of students feel comfortable in the same environment. This is done by intentionally encouraging the normalization of each student's experience and treating each student as if his success is important to the college.

Geographic Background

As stated earlier, Morehouse College enrolls students from throughout the world but particularly throughout the United States. Students from various geographic locations share a bond and kinship. There are observable distinctions among students from the West Coast, Southwest, Midwest, North, East, and, most notably, the South, given that the college is located in the heart of the South. Adjustments must be made for students who have never visited or spent much time in the Deep South to acclimate them to a very different way of life.

This mixing of heterogeneous regional cultures is not always peaceful. There have been incidents throughout the years that have created conflict between students from various regions of the country. However, the regional cultural diversity has positive manifestations as well. There are strong affinity clubs that represent states or cities and operate as student organizations. One's geographic background typically serves as a source of pride and motivation.

Identity Salience and Intersectionality

Identity salience might be the most difficult issue to address at an all-male, predominantly African American college. Regardless of the aforementioned characteristics of students, how one chooses to identify varies as much as the hues that may be found in the environment. Cross's Black racial identity development model (1971, 1991) is helpful in addressing racial identity, but not all students identify primarily by their racial identity. In an environment such as Morehouse College, a student may choose to identify according to his religion, gender, sexual orientation, nationality, class, geographic background, or racial identity singularly, or in any combination of those mentioned. Therein lies the challenge and rewards of addressing multiculturalism at Morehouse College and other HBCUs.

Addressing Multiculturalism

Multiculturalism at Morehouse College is formally addressed through academic programs and centers, student services and student organizations, and the Martin Luther King Jr. International Chapel. Because of the size limitations of this chapter, it is not possible to list all of the multicultural programming that takes place at the college. However, many of the ongoing programs that address multiculturalism are highlighted.

Academic Programs and Centers

As mentioned earlier, the faculty is responsible for much of the multicultural education on campus. Multiculturalism is infused throughout the curriculum in all of the academic programs at Morehouse College. The Division of Humanities and Social Sciences provides foreign language classes that all Morehouse College students are required to take. There is an emphasis on language and culture. The Morehouse Research Institute also provides research on the diversity and challenges of African American men.

The Division of Science and Mathematics, through its environmental studies program, focuses on the cultural aspects of the human–environment interaction. Students in the psychology department participate in psychology research projects at sites throughout the world that provide exposure to various cultures. Also, engineering students complete two years at Morehouse College and then complete their final years of study on campuses throughout the United States, providing them with diverse educational and interpersonal experiences.

The Division of Business and Economics provides students an opportunity to focus on international business. Outstanding students in the division are provided an all-expense-paid international trip through the Spring Tour program. The trips are intended to expose students to various cultures throughout the world. Trip destinations have included India, Dubai, New

Zealand, Australia, England, Scandinavia, Portugal, Spain, Italy, China, and other international locations.

Academic centers play an important role in addressing multicultural issues for Morehouse students. The Leadership Center hosts the Oprah South African Leadership Project and the African President-in-Residence program. The Bonner Office of Community Service provides opportunities for students to participate in service-related activities throughout the world. These offices are critical to the experience of students at Morehouse.

As noted earlier, Morehouse selected globalization as the topic of its Quality Enhancement Plan for its SACS accreditation. The effort of this plan is housed in the Andrew Young Center for International Affairs (AYC). Most notably, the AYC provides the following: Center Faculty and Student Fellows Program; International Affairs Fellowship Program; Medal for Social Justice; Diplomat-in-Residence Program; Intensive Modern Foreign Language Program; International Exchange/Study Abroad Programs; International Student Services; International Studies Program; Institutional Capacity-Building Initiatives; and Morehouse College International Affairs Society. Global understanding and international competence are strengths among Morehouse's multicultural education initiatives.

Student Services and Student Organizations

The Division of Student Services provides cultural programming, along with assisting students to provide cultural programming for the campus and Atlanta University Center. The division provides various cultural weeks, programs, panels, and speakers. The critical aspect of most programming at the college is that it is coordinated by students. Student organizations are responsible for almost weekly cultural programming across a broad range of diverse topics.

Students take responsibility for educating their peers, the campus, and the community on multicultural issues. Students also provide forums to share their international and cultural experiences abroad. Some examples of programming includes: Safe Space Week, International Student Fair, African Diaspora Week, DuBois International Hall, Dual Conscientiousness of Being Black and Latino on Campus, Study Abroad Fair, and Male and Female Relationships.

Martin Luther King Jr. International Chapel

The Martin Luther King Jr. International Chapel is the crown jewel of the Morehouse College campus. The chapel promotes the philosophies of Mohandas K. Gandhi (Indian spiritual leader and nonviolent civil resistance activist), Dr. Martin Luther King Jr. (religious leader and nonviolent civil rights activists), and Daisaku Ikeda (Buddhist philosopher and peace builder) primarily through the Science and Spiritual Awareness week. The theme for the week in 2008 was "A Spiritually Engaged Global and Ethical Education." The week focuses on the diversity of religious beliefs that exists and invites speakers and ministers from various faiths and cultures to talk about nonviolence.

The chapel is also the forum for speakers to address students on various cultural topics. The Crown Forum is a campus-wide forum that all students must attend each Thursday during their tenure at the college. All first-year students are required to attend chapel on Tuesday, and this is where they receive information on various topics related to diversity, multiculturalism, self-awareness, and any other issues that the students might face.

Relevant Issues to Consider

There are several relevant issues to consider when assessing the multicultural efforts at Morehouse College. Race, gender, resources, history, and geographic location greatly influence the college's issues associated with addressing multiculturalism. Morehouse College recognizes that African Americans are not a monolithic group and that there is a vast diversity within the African American community. Unlike many PWIs, Morehouse College cannot make the assumption that "one size fits all" for its African American students. It would be a fallacy to assume that there is one category that can capture the identity of the Morehouse student beyond the traditional saying that a new student enters as a "Man of Morehouse" striving to be a "Morehouse Man." Students may identify across a range of races, ethnicities, nationalities, sexual orientations, social classes, and religions, among other identities.

Depending on the developmental identity level or self-actualization of students at Morehouse College, a student might not consider race as a relevant factor in identifying himself. There are students who identify predominantly by their religious affiliations, their sexual orientations, or even their parents' home countries. During my time at Morehouse, I have met trans-gender students who identified more as women. There were also students who considered themselves Christians and argued that race was less impor-tant than religion. These can be challenging aspects of an institution with strong religious affiliations and a rich history of educating African American men.

Likewise, exploring the diversity of Black students at HBCUs would uncover students hailing from the United States, Africa, the Caribbean, South America, and throughout the world. Each ethnic group brings various aspects of its culture whether the student is studying abroad, is a first genera-tion American, or has been in the United States for generations. The student might be the first in the family to attend college, or maybe family members have attended college for several generations. The student might come from a very wealthy family, a middle-class family, or a very poor family. The student might have grown up in a two-parent household or that of a single parent. These variables, along with the uniqueness of each student, create diversity within the student culture.

Challenges

African American men are challenged with succeeding in higher education at epidemic levels. The miracle of Morehouse College has been that it is able to take African American men from high-performing and low-performing high schools and meet their academic challenges, while addressing the diver-sity that exists among the student population. It is also important to acknowledge how the multiculturalism of the college creates relationships among students who would never have connected if they were on a much larger campus.

Finances. Morehouse College is challenged financially like many historically Black, private, liberal arts institutions. The staffing patterns are much lower than many large or more well-financed institutions. Many efforts to address multicultural issues are combined with the teaching or administrative roles of faculty and staff. There is not a special office to address issues of diversity or multiculturalism. As illustrated previously, these issues are addressed aca-demically through core courses and specialized major courses. Most faculty and staff recognize the importance of a well-rounded education that exposes students to multiculturalism.

Location. The history and geographic location of Morehouse College collectively contribute to many of the attitudes on the campus regarding diversity. Morehouse, as an institution with strong religious roots and ties, may be characterized as socially conservative. This is relevant when considering issues of sexual orientation, nonconforming gender roles, and the presence of White students. Atlanta, Georgia, is considered one of the more liberal cities in the South; however, there still exist campus and community attitudes that are not understanding or accepting of certain issues of difference.

Alumni. Atlanta is a southern city with a considerable amount of ethnic and cultural diversity. It is a city known for its involvement in the Civil Rights Movement and was the home of Morehouse's most illustrious alumnus, the Reverend Dr. Martin Luther King Jr., and many other noted civil rights leaders. Morehouse College has a rich history and impressive tradition of developing strong African American male leaders. Despite the increased diversity of the city, there are alumni who are steeped in the history and past of Morehouse and do not understand or agree with the diverse identity assertions of current students.

As the college evolves and more diversity is expressed, the campus will experience some "growing pains" and confrontations among outspoken alumni, faculty, staff, and students. The many calls and letters received from alumni that address concerns about the identities and personas of current students reflect this. Alumni and current students express concerns about the multicultural programming provided on campus that addresses nontraditional topics for the campus, such as sexual orientation, hip-hop identity, or other contemporary issues facing all historically Black colleges, as well as colleges and universities in general.

Challenges with providing multicultural programming at an all-male, predominantly African American institution have been identified. An overwhelming majority of the programming is directed toward African American issues. It is a challenge to have faculty and staff consider the diversity that exists on the campus and not program exclusively for African American men. The institution is not immune to similar issues faced at PWIs, where programs are heavily directed toward the majority population. It is important to note that the close proximity of Spelman College assists in providing at least a more gender-balanced approach to programming.

IMPLICATIONS

The question of who is responsible for addressing issues of multiculturalism at HBCUs is one to which each institution should give account. If the responsibility remains largely in the hands of students, then what is the role of the institution? Although the practice of allowing students to drive initiatives that impact multicultural issues might be a model practice for other colleges and universities, there should also be a parallel track for the college or university to take direct institutional responsibility for providing consistent multicultural programming, education, and services. It is critical that institutions explore options that work on their particular campuses and that work with faculty, staff, and administrators to create a welcoming environment for all students. Students have a shared responsibility to advocate for their needs and to make sure that their institution acknowledges cultural differences. Working collectively with students to address the campuses' needs is ideal; however, if the onus remains primarily on students, then the services will probably fall short.

One limitation of such an approach is that the needs of the most organized and outspoken populations will receive the most attention. This can be seen in the concerns expressed by students who identify as gay, bisexual, transgender, and gender nonconforming, concerning the lack of support provided for such students. While preparing this chapter, I reviewed the websites of several HBCUs in search of offices exclusively providing services to lesbian, gay, bisexual, and transgender (LGBT) and gender-queer student populations. I was not able to locate such an office, nor were any freestanding multicultural offices located on HBCU campuses. This stands out as a significant area of difference and inclusion that HBCUs must address.

CONCLUSION

A commitment to multiculturalism in various forms permeates the Morehouse College campus. Like other historically Black institutions, the college does not have a specific office that is responsible for addressing the topic. However, it is the expectation that every member of the college community is committed to embracing and supporting multiculturalism. There is still a great deal of work that needs to focus on multicultural issues at Morehouse and other HBCUs. The fact that I was unable to locate an office dedicated to multiculturalism at any of the schools whose websites I viewed might send a message that there is not a recognized need, commitment, or priority for such issues. Resources could be the driving factor at some of the institutions, but that cannot be the excuse for all.

Diffusing multicultural education and support throughout the campus might work well or appear to work well for historically Black colleges, but more empirical data are needed to support such approaches. The strategy at Morehouse College is not out of line with other historically Black colleges (Jewell, 2002). The approach is not perfect, but the college manages to create a welcoming environment for many of the students who attend. I can imagine that most HBCUs and their students would defend such an approach, but the students associated with the groups that appear to be underrepresented and the most silenced might have a different opinion. Embracing the diversity within the African American community, as well as across the global community, is critical for historically Black institutions, like Morehouse College, to continue to lead in providing an education that reflects the most noble democratic ideals of U.S. society.

REFERENCES

Anderson, J. D. (1988). *The education of Blacks in the south, 1860–1935*. Chapel Hill: University of North Carolina Press.

Brooks, G. R., & Good, G. E. (Eds.). (2001). *The new handbook of psychotherapy and counseling with men: A comprehensive guide to settings, problems, and treatment approaches* (vol. 2). San Francisco, CA: Jossey-Bass.

Brown, M. C., II, & Davis, J. E. (2001). The historically Black college as social contract, social capital, and social equalizer. *Peabody Journal of Education, 76,* 31–49.

Butler, A. L. J. (1977). *The distinctive Black college: Talladega, Tuskegee, and Morehouse*. Metuchen, NJ: Scarecrow.

Caldwell, L. D. (2000). The psychology of Black men. In L. Jones (Ed.), *Brothers of the academy* (pp. 131–139). Sterling, VA: Stylus.

Cross, W. E., Jr. (1971). Toward a psychology of Black liberation: The Negro-to-Black conversion experience. *Black World, 20*(9), 13–27.

Cross, W. E., Jr. (1991). *Shades of black: Diversity in African American identity*. Philadelphia, PA: Temple University Press.

Dwyer, B. (2006). Framing the effect of multiculturalism on diversity outcomes among students at historically Black colleges and universities. *Educational Foundations, 20*(1/2), 37–59.

Franklin, R. M. (2007). *Crisis in the village.* Minneapolis, MN: Fortress Press.

Gasman, M. (2009, October 22). More than appearances. *Inside Higher Ed.* Retrieved from http://www.insidehighered.com/views/2009/10/22/gasman

Harper, P. B. (1996). *Are we not men? Masculine anxiety and the problem of African-American identity.* New York, NY: Oxford.

Harper, S. R., & Gasman, M. (2008). Consequences of conservatism: Black male undergraduates and the politics of historically Black colleges and universities. *Journal of Negro Education, 77,* 336–351.

Jaschik, S. (2009, October 19). What the Morehouse man wears. *Inside Higher Ed.* Retrieved from http://www.insidehighered.com/news/2009/10/19/morehouse

Jewell, J. O. (2002). To set an example: The tradition of diversity at historically black colleges and universities. *Urban Education, 37,* 7–21. doi: 10.1177/0042085902371002

Johnson, A. G. (1997). *The gender knot: Unraveling our patriarchal legacy.* Philadelphia, PA: Temple University Press.

Jones, E. A. (1967). *A candle in the dark: A history of Morehouse College.* Valley Forge, PA: Judson Press.

Kitsantas, A. (2004). Study abroad: The role of college students' goals on the development of cross-cultural skills and global understanding. *College Student Journal, 38,* 441–452.

Lazur, R. F., & Majors, R. (1995). Men of color: Ethnocultural variations of male gender role strain. In R. F. Levant & W. S. Pollack (Eds.), *A new psychology of men* (pp. 337–358). New York, NY: Basic Books.

Malveaux, J. (2002, July 4). Class matters for economic prosperity. *Black Issues in Higher Education, 19*(10), 32.

McAdam, D. (1982). *Political process and the development of Black insurgency, 1930–1970.* Chicago, IL: University of Chicago Press.

McCready, L. T. (2004). Understanding the marginalization of gay and gender nonconforming black male students. *Theory Into Practice, 43,* 136–143.

Morehouse College. (2006). *Introduction to Morehouse College.* Retrieved October 29, 2008, from http://www.morehouse.edu/admissions/coursecatalog/pdf/009-30.pdf

Palmer, R., & Gasman, M. (2008). It takes a village to raise a child: The role of social capital in promoting academic success for African American men at a Black college. *Journal of College Student Development, 49*(1), 57–70.

Poynter, K. J., & Washington, J. (2005). Multiple identities: Creating community on campus for LBGT students. In R. Sanlo (Ed.), *Gender identity and sexual orientation: Research, policy, and personal perspectives* (pp. 41–47). New Directions for Student Services, no. 111. San Francisco, CA: Jossey-Bass.

Riggins, R. K., McNeal, C., & Herndon, M. K. (2008). The role of spirituality among African-American college males attending a historically Black university. *College Student Journal, 42,* 70–81.

Sanlo, R., Rankin, S., & Schoenberg, R. (Eds.). (2002). *Our place on campus: Lesbian, gay, bisexual, transgender services and programs in higher education.* Westport, CT: Greenwood.

Thelin, J. R. (2004). *A history of American higher education.* Baltimore, MD: Johns Hopkins University Press.

Wester, S. R., Vogel, D. L., Wei, M., & McLain, R. (2006). African American men, gender role conflict, and psychological distress: The role of racial identity. *Journal of Counseling & Development, 84,* 419–429.

12

Multicultural Student Services at Minority-Serving Institutions

Tribal Colleges

Les D. Riding In
Robert Longwell-Grice

"The tourist said, 'Sir, are you brown from the sun?'

The old Indian said, 'No ma'am, I'm Jim from the earth.'"
(White Hat, 2003)

Cora, called Kai (meaning "willow tree") by her grandmother and other older relatives, read the above quote in her Introduction to Navajo History class offered at her college and laughed out loud in an expression of understanding, as did many of her classmates. Although Cora did not grow up on the nearby reservation, she wanted to attend this tribal college for the opportunity to connect with her Navajo community and learn the value of indigenous knowledge and philosophy.

A S ILLUSTRATED IN THIS EXCHANGE ABOVE and innately understood by Cora, majority culture has always had trouble understanding American Indians. Mainstream media commonly depicts American Indians as prolific artisans, attending powwows and being deeply religious. This generalization has led many non-Indians to incorrectly believe that American Indians are one generic group of people, when, in fact, there are more than 500 tribes in the United States, each with its own history, language, and customs (Horse, 2005). This representation is often manifested at mainstream institutions, where administrators, advisors, and professors make nominal efforts to recognize the history and culture of Native American students (Austin, 2005) without fully incorporating them into the academic community. Today, athletic teams use mascots that promote American Indian stereotypes, and attempts to eradicate these mascots have been met with extreme hostility (Longwell-Grice & Longwell-Grice, 2003). In this environment, academic achievements by Native American students at mainstream institutions are far from commendable. The latest data from 2002 showed that Native Americans make up less than 1% of all college students nationally and earned less than 1% of all degrees conferred (U.S. Department of Education, as cited by Guillory & Wolverton, 2008).

As reflected in Cora's example in the opening vignette, tribal colleges and universities (TCUs) were created to counter the marginalization of Native American students at mainstream universities while, at the same time, preventing further disengagement by young Native American students from tribal languages and customs. Classes on tribal history and language are offered as part of the core curriculum, not as peripheral study (Gagnon, 2001). Some tribal colleges offer innovative curricula that include degree programs that specialize in tribal leadership or native soil conservation. As a result, tribal college graduates are able to have an immediate positive impact in their communities and tribe.

In this chapter, our intent is to help readers better understand how student development and co-curricular activities contribute to the promising healing properties of tribal colleges, particularly in multiculturalism efforts. The chapter begins by providing a brief history of the tribal college movement and reporting the current demographics of tribal colleges. Next, the discussion moves to framing multiculturalism at tribal colleges, highlighting particular practices at some of the colleges. Finally, implications and final thoughts about how tribal colleges address issues of multiculturalism are presented.

HISTORY OF TRIBAL COLLEGES

It is not our intent to provide a history of the very complex relationship American Indian tribes have had with all levels of mainstream education. At the least, it has been a troubling history, marred with stories of native language loss, forced removal of children from their parents, and other sobering details that have been loosely documented in the literature. Some of this history is covered by Kupo (Chapter 1). As westward expansion threatened land occupied by indigenous peoples, colleges would be used as acculturation agents for assimilating American Indians into the dominant culture. Natives were not, understandably, eager to accept these offers of education, as they had resisted earlier attempts by educators to "Christianize" them, a consistent goal of educational efforts toward Native Americans. The Seneca Chief Red Jacket, commenting upon these efforts, said,

> Instead of producing that happy effect which you so long promised us, its introduction so far has rendered us uncomforted and miserable. You have taken a number of our young men to your schools. You have educated them and taught them your religion. They have returned to their kindred and color neither white men nor Indians. The arts they have learned are incompatible with the chase and ill adapted to our customs. They have been taught that which is useless to us. (Velie, 1979, pp. 141–142)

To reclaim education as a process of cultural valuing instead of cultural assimilation, Native Americans would have to be at the center of its design and administration. The idea of an Indian college had been contemplated for decades, but Crum (2007) argued that three major developments of the 1960s were primarily responsible for the development of the tribal college consortium: the rise of Indian activism in the 1960s, the socioeconomic reforms of the Great Society, and the notion of Indian self-determination that surfaced in the 1960s and became policy in the 1970s.

According to Crum (2007), tribal people of the 1960s were fully aware that the dominant society had never encouraged higher education for the vast majority of American Indians. Today, tribal colleges are symbolic of the contemporary American Indian: one who values modern educational methodology while recovering indigenous knowledge. Perhaps Native scholar Angela Cavender Wilson (2004) stated it most appropriately: "Native academics with intellectual strength would be wise to . . . work toward the recovery of indigenous traditions as part of our scholarly agenda and commitment to our tribal communities" (p. 72).

A commitment to improving tribal communities, particularly in creating economic opportunities and entrepreneurship, was paramount (Fogarty, 2007). After all, these communities were familiar with the perils of social and economic isolation: extreme poverty, unemployment, high school drop-out rates, addiction rates among the nation's highest, suicide rates double the national average, and alcohol-related deaths being far too common (Martin, 2005). Although TCUs were designed to be safe havens for Native American knowledge, they also must provide immediate job training in high-need reservation economies, legitimize culture as fundamental to education, and prepare their students to participate in a larger economy (Fogarty, 2007).

TRIBAL COLLEGE DEMOGRAPHICS

Today, there are more than 32 tribal colleges located across the United States. According to the American Indian Higher Education Consortium (AIHEC, 2006), there are more than 16,000 students enrolled in tribal colleges. Of these students, approximately 80% are American Indian, with 7% non-Indian men, 19% non-Indian women, 52% American Indian women, and 28% American Indian men. In 2003–2004, first-year student retention rates were reported at 46%. The report also included data on factors negatively affecting retention rates. The participating TCUs reported what they believed were the most important factors impeding college completion for their students. Twenty-three TCUs listed family obligations; twelve listed maintaining off-campus employment, financial problems, and lack of preparation; and eleven listed transportation. Other factors included lack of daycare services and family problems.

The AIHEC report (2006) stated that among first-time tribal college enrollees, 69% had earned a high school diploma, 21% earned a GED, and 10% did not graduate from high school at all. Along with issues associated with underpreparedness, AIHEC argued that socioeconomic factors might also impede the academic success of tribal college students. Most notable was the $13,998 average family income of students, far below the national poverty level of $19,157. Because of these socioeconomic factors, 83% of tribal college students received financial aid. Another significant socioeconomic factor affecting the recruitment and retention of tribal college students was the fact that a full 25% of the TCU student population were single parents with children.

Despite the numerous challenges confronting tribal college students, tribal colleges continue to make a difference in many individual students' lives. According to AIHEC (2006), 2,372 students graduated from TCUs in

2004–2005. These students graduated from a variety of disciplines and technical certification programs, ensuring that their impact would be far-ranging. The report also stated that many of these same graduates would transfer into baccalaureate programs at other institutions to complete baccalaureate and graduate degrees.

Upon stepping into a Native American community, one would immediately recognize the diversity of the people. This diversity existed in Native American communities long before European colonization, because life depended on the "interconnections among family, kin (extended family), clan, tribe, intertribal bonds and external allies" (Benham & Mann, 2003, p. 172). Accordingly, Guardia and Evans (2008) identified eleven core values that were commonly held by Native Americans: sharing, cooperation, noninterference, present-time orientation, being versus doing, extended family orientation, respect, harmony and balance, spiritual causes for illness and problems, group dynamics, and importance of the tribe over the individual. Guardia and Evans cautioned readers not to overgeneralize Native American populations, because tribal worldviews vary. However, collectively, these core values create a group identity for American Indians and demonstrate a care for the greater community. Today, this interconnectedness resonates throughout Indian communities and is reflected in the great diversity that exists at all TCUs.

FRAMING MULTICULTURALISM

Although most tribal colleges do not have an office dedicated to understanding and promoting multiculturalism, the tribal colleges do generally have student development activities designed to help Native American populations understand their role in context with the larger world economy. Many of these efforts are infused into the curriculum, where indigenous knowledge and research are often used to analyze modern problems. One example is in the area of sustenance and environmental protection. In 2006, the American Indian and Alaska Native Climate Change Working Group was formed at Haskell Indian Nations University to bring together leading geoscientists with indigenous environmental researchers and American Indian students studying climate change (Wildcat, 2008). The group, which has partnered Haskell with four other major universities, reinforces the important role of indigenous knowledge to a national audience (Wildcat, 2008).

This group is one example of how tribal colleges are often regarded as a bridge that links two cultures: a Native American culture that values group identity and cooperation and a mainstream culture that values competition and individual accomplishment. This duality is expressed in tribal college mission statements and other visionary documents. This dual mission is not too dissimilar from what multicultural student services (MSS) attempt to do on predominantly White campuses for racial and ethnic minority student populations. Linking these two cultures is a difficult task, considering many tribal college students have lived on the reservation or Indian land most of their lives. These students must be prepared to participate in a global society, but not at the expense of forfeiting traditional knowledge and customs. As a result, the most innovative strategies toward meeting the diverse needs of a mostly Native American student population are directed toward this dual mission and, over time, prevent attrition of tribal college students.

ILLUSTRATIVE PRACTICES SUPPORTING PLURALISM AND DIVERSITY AT TRIBAL COLLEGES

Rooted in the Native American worldview previously described, some additional strategies documented in school websites or Native American publications that address Native American students' concerns and contribute to the local communities surrounding the college follow. Common among these approaches is the use of service-learning, global awareness, and an emphasis on reconnecting tribal college students to Native American elders, traditions, and language.

Salish Kootenai College

Located on the Flathead Indian Reservation in Montana, the college prepares native students for participation in mainstream culture through a required service-learning course appropriate with the student's chosen major. Students must serve 30 hours of community service in addition to class time. Additionally, the college offers multiple academic outreach programs with the surrounding community and state institutions. One such example focuses on science education. The Big Sky Partnership partners Salish Kootenai College, Montana reservation's K–8 instructors, and tribal leaders with Montana's state university faculty. The goal of the Big Sky Partnership is to create a community-based science curriculum appropriate for K–20 science education at all of Montana's learning institutions.

In 2007–2008, Native American students at Salish Kootenai College were roughly 75% of the total student population. Like other tribal colleges, the Native American student population is a critical mass. However, student development activities are designed to meet the general student population. To meet the needs of a diverse population, Salish Kootenai College has incorporated a social integration strategy based on the Family Education Model (Guillory & Wolverton, 2008). The strategy incorporates a student's family and extended family in campus events, creating a community-based campus environment. Additionally, the college has a retention officer who has the primary responsibility for contacting students who are not attending class and making a personal connection with them. Through personal contact and involving the student's family, the college is in a position to better understand and address each student's unique predicament.

Stone Child College

Stone Child College recently moved to a new campus centrally located on the Rocky Boy Reservation in Montana. This larger campus enables Stone Child to provide additional meeting and classroom space. Among the new services is a day care facility, designed to care for young children while their parents attend class. The new campus also attempts to incorporate aspects of universal design by accommodating students in wheelchairs.

Like Salish Kootenai, Stone Child recently hired a full-time retention officer who maintains personal contact with any students who are at risk of dropping out. The campus actively involves the community by regularly incorporating tribal elders into its programs. One particularly successful program uses tribal elders as mentors for current students. Another program, the Elder on Campus program, provides spiritual guidance to students through one-on-one contact.

Leech Lake College

Leech Lake awards the Honorary Degree for Elders (HDE), a degree that is designed to incorporate the knowledge and wisdom of elders in the community. Those who are interested in pursuing the HDE must complete 64 credit hours in any subject. Elders in the program are exempt from Western evaluation models (to which other degree programs at Leech Lake must adhere). Further, elders do not have a financial obligation to the college.

Although this program is similar to other elder programs at tribal colleges, Leech Lake makes a unique effort to ensure that elders feel engaged and valued in contemporary society.

Fond Du Lac Tribal and Community College

Located in Cloquet, Minnesota, Fond Du Lac Tribal and Community College has more than 2,700 enrolled students. Although the college promotes the Anishinaabeg culture and history, there is a secondary emphasis "to celebrate the cultural diversity of our community and promote global understanding" (Fond Du Lac, 2005–2007, p. 3). This commitment to diversity is seen in the architecture of the campus buildings; the materials used to build the structures are reflective of the various communities the campus serves. The architects of Fond Du Lac Tribal and Community College also use circular themes to stress common purpose, and many buildings are designed to remind students and staff that they share the same earth and sky.

Fond Du Lac is home to the Institute for Objective Human Understanding, a grant-funded program that promotes global understanding through various learning opportunities. The college also engages international students in Anishinaabeg culture. One way this is done is through the Cultural Immersion Program, a two-week program during which tribal elders teach the students about Anishinaabeg customs and traditions.

Northwest Indian College

Located in Bellingham, Washington, Northwest Indian College has hosted the Annual Summit on Indigenous Service Learning since 2007. This summit demonstrates the importance that Northwest Indian College gives to service learning activities. The college believes that service learning leads to lifelong learning, which allows its students to continually learn about greater society. Additionally, Northwest Indian College believes that a student who commits to service learning contributes to the colleges' strategic initiative of "bringing traditional ways into living contact with contemporary society" (Northwest Indian College, 2007, p. 4).

Oglala Lakota College

Located on the Rosebud Reservation in south-central South Dakota, Oglala Lakota College has dedicated itself to service-learning. However, they quickly learned that merging service-learning academic credit required faculty support. With that in mind, Oglala Lakota College provides funding to faculty who are willing to incorporate service-learning projects into their class syllabi. One example of the school's dedication to service-learning is seen through one class that requires students to assist in community literacy outreach programs. Students can take four class periods to complete the project. The goal of this service-learning project is to improve literacy rates of children on the Rosebud Reservation.

Lac Courte Oreilles Ojibwe Community College

The Lac Courte Oreilles Ojibwe Community College (LCO) serves the Ojibwe Reservation and surrounding area in Wisconsin. Concerns about the decline in Indian male college attendance led to the formation of the Men's Talking Circle group at LCO. This group discusses challenges that impede graduation for male students. Among the topics are academic preparation, substance abuse, transportation, and the social stigma associated with attending college. LCO is one of the few (if not only) tribal colleges that engage male students to come forward and speak about these sensitive issues.

LCO also received a National Science Foundation grant to fund an Elder-in-Residence program. Similar to the program at Stone Child, the program has elders visit the campus for up to one week to visit with students and faculty about Ojibwe knowledge. This program ensures that Native American knowledge is fused with modern teaching models, so students will incorporate vital Native American insight into their formal learning.

Tohono O'odham Community College

Tohono O'odham Community College (TOCC), located in Sells, Arizona, began offering classes in January 2000. In keeping with TOCC's vision to "enhance greater participation of the Tohono O'odham Nation in the local, national, and global community" (TOCC, n.d.), the college has incorporated a brown bag series of relevant, global topics. Recent programs, sponsored by TOCC faculty, include presentations on topics such as understanding Hinduism and the emergence of China in the 21st century.

TOCC also has established an Apprenticeship Program, which won the 2006 State of Arizona Rural Outstanding Apprenticeship Program of the

Year Award. Past apprenticeships include refurbishing homes of elders, including wiring appliances and general repair. TOCC social work students also participate in other service-learning projects, such as cemetery cleaning and cookouts for foster children. The service-learning projects hope to have students positively engage in social problems, such as child neglect and family violence.

LOOKING IN TO LOOK OUT

Because of the near eradication of Native American culture and history by Western colonial imperialism and American racial prejudice, Native American students are in critical need of authentic education regarding their own identities and cultural history. As Pope and Reynolds (1997) described in the characteristics of multicultural competence, "a belief in the value and significance of [one's] own cultural heritage and worldview [is] a starting place for understanding others who are culturally different" (p. 271). It is from this place of cultural and personal authenticity and wholeness that genuine cross-cultural engagement becomes possible. Through this broad range of programs and initiatives, tribal colleges support and facilitate the deep connection of Native American students to their culture, thereby laying the foundation for students to attain broad multicultural understanding regarding social issues that also affect non-Native American populations and from which to reach out to global contexts.

IMPLICATIONS

Tribal colleges have implemented strategies to create a welcoming atmosphere for all students. These strategies have successfully increased transfer of Native American students to mainstream, four-year institutions. However, unless Native American students transferring from tribal colleges have strong support at their new institutions, their transition remains difficult to navigate. Although these students might never reach critical mass at major universities, college student professionals at mainstream universities have an obligation to learn about the issues confronting Native American students, such as tribal sovereignty. Additionally, Martin (2005) recommended that student affairs professionals become more welcoming not only to Native American students, but to the students' families as well. Martin further recommended that student support programs become more integrated with the academic campus. Student affairs staff working together with academic affairs will create a more comfortable campus, Martin argued. This is important for all universities with Native American students; however, it is a priority for universities that are located near tribal colleges or Indian country.

FINAL THOUGHTS

The literature on Native American education and indigenous models of learning is still very limited, and student development theory as it applies toward Native Americans is fragmented at best. Those who perform traditional student development functions at tribal colleges must accomplish their tasks without an existing, well-documented theory or framework. Particularly in the area of multiculturalism, tribal colleges tend to define multiculturalism as meeting the broader needs that their student population encounter on a daily basis.

We have presented only a few examples of how tribal colleges address broader issues of their student population. It is important to understand that even though some issues, such as sexual orientation, gender identity, and social class, are not directly documented, it does not mean that the colleges are failing to address these issues. Additionally, tribal colleges have only been a part of the higher education community since 1968, with the founding of Navajo Community College, now Diné College, in Tsaile, Arizona. At the start of the tribal college movement, much time was spent proving that Indians could legitimately run a college (Boyer, 2005). Boyer (2005) argued tribal colleges must provide "new accountability" that focuses heavily on assessment data. In other words, now that tribal colleges exist, they must demonstrate they are indeed making a difference and improving outcomes for Native American students. Providing these data to assessors and other interested parties is a priority before other matters, such as formally addressing a broader range of multicultural issues. Moreover, tribal colleges must keep in mind their role as stewards of indigenous history and culture. Therefore, the colleges give greater concentration toward ensuring academic credibility, while maintaining the engagement of elders in the college community.

Perhaps more than any other institutional type, tribal colleges must have the support of their tribal council and the local community (Stein, 2003). As the most respected persons in the community, the elders are often the vocal representation of that support. Therefore, bringing other diversity issues into the curriculum might require consultation with and perhaps persuasion of these elders. Such collaboration and partnership would ensure that multicultural education is offered in a framework that still reflects indigenous values of mutual respect, honoring the earth, and the worth of every individual toward the betterment of the community. Given these foundational values, we have little doubt that over time tribal colleges will incorporate education about and support of issues related to sexual orientation, gender identity, and interracial education and cooperation with other marginalized racial/ethnic groups in the United States. As stated earlier, informal education and support on these issues might very well take place on tribal college campuses. However, more research on this aspect of tribal college education and student life needs to be done.

REFERENCES

American Indian Higher Education Consortium. (2006). *American Indian measures for success factbook 2005: Tribal colleges and universities report.* Washington, DC: Author.

Austin, R. D. (2005). Perspectives of American Indian nation parents and leaders. In M. J. Tippeconnic Fox, S. C. Lowe, & G. S. McClellan (Eds.), *Serving Native American students* (pp. 41–48). New Directions for Student Services, no. 109. San Francisco, CA: Jossey-Bass.

Benham, M., & Mann, H. (2003). Culture and language matters: Defining, implementing, and evaluating. In M. Benham & W. Stein (Eds.), *The renaissance of American Indian higher education: Capturing the dream* (pp. 165–192). Mahwah, NJ: Erlbaum.

Boyer, P. (2005). To be or not to be?: TCUs probe identity questions as they "indigenize" their institutions. *Tribal College Journal of Higher Education, 16*(3), 10–14.

Crum, S. (2007). Indian activism, the great society, Indian self-determination, and the drive for an Indian college, 1964–71. *American Indian Culture and Research Journal, 31*(1), 1–20.

Fogarty, M. (2007). Commitment to building prosperous nations [electronic version]. *Tribal College Journal, 18*(3), 12–17.

Fond Du Lac Tribal and Community College. (2005–2007). *Student handbook.* Cloquet, MN: Author.

Gagnon, G. O. (2001). Keeping the tribal colleges tribal [electronic version]. *Tribal College Journal, 12*(3), 37–40.

Guardia, J. R., & Evans, N. J. (2008). Student development in tribal colleges and universities. *NASPA Journal, 45,* 237–264.

Guillory, R. M., & Wolverton, M. (2008). It's about family: Native American persistence in higher education. *The Journal of Higher Education, 79,* 58–87.

Horse, P. G. (2005). Native American identity. In M. J. Tippeconnic Fox, S. C. Lowe, & G. S. McClennan (Eds.), *Serving Native American students* (pp. 61–68). New Directions for Student Services, no. 109. San Francisco, CA: Jossey-Bass.

Longwell-Grice, R., & Longwell-Grice, H. (2003). Chiefs, braves and tomahawks: The use of American Indians as university mascots. *NASPA Journal, 40*(3), 1–12.

Martin, R. G. (2005). Serving American Indian students in tribal colleges: Lessons for mainstream colleges. In M. J. Tippeconnic Fox, S. C. Lowe, & G. S. McClennan (Eds.), *Serving Native American students* (pp. 79–86). New Directions for Student Services, no. 109. San Francisco, CA: Jossey-Bass.

Northwest Indian College. (2007). *Northwest Indian College strategic plan, 2004–09.* Retrieved from http://www.nwic.edu/sites/default/files/docs/geninfo/strategic plan.pdf

Pope, R. L., & Reynolds, A. L. (1997). Student affairs core competencies: Integrating multicultural awareness, knowledge, and skills. *Journal of College Student Development, 38,* 266–277.

Stein, W. J. (2003). Developmental action for implementing an indigenous college: Philosophical foundations and pragmatic steps. In M. Benham & W. Stein (Eds.), *The renaissance of American Indian higher education: Capturing the dream* (pp. 25–59). Mahwah, NJ: Erlbaum.

Tohono O'odham Community College. (n.d.). *College vision and goals.* Retrieved from http://www.tocc.cc.az.us/goals.htm#vision

Velie, A. R. (1979). *American Indian literature: An anthology.* Norman: University of Oklahoma Press.

White Hat, C. R. (2003). *American Indians and chemical dependency.* Unpublished doctoral dissertation, Iowa State University, Ames.

Wildcat, D. (2008). We are all related—Indigenous people combine traditional knowledge, geosciences to save planet. *Tribal Journal of American Indian Higher Education, 20*(2), 24–27.

Wilson, A. C. (2004). Reclaiming our humanity: Decolonization and the recovery of indigenous knowledge. In D. Mihesuah & A. C. Wilson (Eds.), *Indigenizing the academy: Transforming scholarship and empowering communities* (pp. 69–87). Lincoln: University of Nebraska Press.

Part Four

Building Bridges

THESE CHAPTERS DISCUSS the myriad ways that MSS must work to build bridges that connect itself to other units and divisions within colleges and universities, as well as developing critical coalitions with advocates and allies in previously unconsidered places.

13

Negotiating Purpose and Context

Becky Petitt
David McIntosh

A recent cultural audit revealed that many multicultural students did not know there were multiple offices to support multicultural students or what support they could expect to receive. Also, the findings showed that the offices' mission statements did not clearly align with the university's language about issues of diversity and pluralism that reflected historical issues but not present realities. Dorothy, the chief diversity officer on campus and the one who commissioned the review, is puzzled and concerned. However, it is clear that steps need to be taken to rectify this situation. She calls for a retreat with the directors of the multiple multicultural centers on campus to review the report and strategically plan for the future.

BROADER INSTITUTIONAL CONTEXT

MULTICULTURAL STUDENT SERVICES (MSS) units have histori-cally led college and university efforts to prepare students for our global, diverse, and interconnected world. Because these units were among the first to "interrupt the usual" by challenging institutional culture, norms, and processes that disadvantaged underrepresented students, they played a key leadership role in establishing the institutional context for diversity. The task of transforming traditional institutional culture was no trivial undertaking; preexisting institutional interests were (and still are) powerful forces. When considering the work of MSS units, as Dorothy must now do in the opening scenario, it is important to understand the unique history and culture of the particular institutions within which they are situated. This contextual understanding is of particular importance with regard to units located on predominantly White college and university campuses. Institutions that were not designed with underrepresented students in mind prove more difficult to navigate (Aguirre, 2000; Stanley, 2006; Stanley & Lincoln, 2005). It is important for observers of these units to acknowledge the historical backdrop of a particular institution and to bear in mind that these units operate within historically constructed and hierarchically arranged frameworks. Many institutions have long memories and traditions that negatively impact the work of diversity change agents.

Although most MSS units are located in student affairs divisions, their reach has been broad, extending well beyond traditional institutional boundaries. Professionals in these units have served as leading campus authorities on diversity in higher education, served as spokespeople on the university's behalf regarding diversity issues, led campus-wide training efforts for students, faculty, and staff, and taught credited courses, to name a few of the many important roles they have played. The recent emergence of chief diversity officers (CDOs) on college and university campuses has necessitated renegotiation of the role of MSS within this new context.

The presence of the CDO signifies an increased institutional commitment to diversity. Typically occupied by a tenured member of the faculty and situated within the university president's cabinet (Williams & Wade-Golden, 2007), the CDO is responsible for facilitating the comprehensive institutional diversity agenda and increasing the university's capacity to engage diversity. Thus, having increased the diversity infrastructure, raised the profile and importance of diversity efforts, and hired a senior scholar to fulfill this important role, several institutions have realigned reporting lines to have MSS report to the CDO.

Although Williams and Wade-Golden (2007) noted that this portfolio model creates the opportunity for greater synergy, most universities have allowed MSS units to remain within the student affairs division, which has created unintended, but significant, consequences for these units and the diversity agenda as a whole. The absence of direct lines of reporting and communication presents the opportunity for confusion, and MSS units risk being undifferentiated from the CDO and vice versa. Therefore, it is imperative that MSS units and CDOs view their relationship as interdependent and mutually reinforcing. As strategic partners, they should work together, and with other diversity-related committees and taskforces, to align, leverage, and maximize their shared goals.

It is also vitally important that MSS anchor and align their mission and work within the broader university mission. Their mission statements should clearly articulate how their work advances the core university mission of teaching, research, and service. Further, to the extent their work is grounded in the unique history, culture, and traditions of their institutions, the more effective their efforts will be. Though MSS challenge and strive to change exclusionary systems, they must find means to advocate change in ways that are congruent with the unique culture of the university. For example, Texas A&M University, a very tradition-rich and family-oriented university, responded to campus acts of incivility by coining the phrase "*Respect Is an Aggie Value.*" This community expectation was woven into many high-profile speeches, such as the president's "State of the University" address, new student orientation sessions, first-year and university convocation addresses, and residence hall training. This message was reinforced with language such as: "We Are the Aggie Family," "Those who would intentionally disrespect or offend any member of our community are not real Aggies," and "Aggies take care of each other." Defining and redefining an Aggie as one who respects and cares for the entire Aggie Family has proven a successful strategy in advancing their diversity agenda through subtle, yet meaningful cultural shifts.

Cultural shifts of this nature require strong, committed presidential leadership. Presidents play a pivotal role in the success of diversity initiatives, because people pay attention to where presidents invest their time, resources, and attention. When the president is unequivocal about the diversity imperative and takes responsibility for setting the vision and holding people accountable for outcomes in a consistent way, it adds power and greater potential for broad engagement. Although the voice and commitment of the president is essential, the president's job is to communicate priorities, define the problems and opportunities, and engage content experts to implement institutional transformation. Further, a visionary president should establish systems and processes that are not person-dependent—systems and processes that will outlast her or his tenure and lead to sustained progress.

MULTICULTURAL ORGANIZATIONAL DEVELOPMENT

Building capacities that transform and maintain organizational change is essential. Multicultural organizational development (MOD) theory is a useful framework to guide this process. Jackson and Holvino (1988) viewed MOD as several threads that, when woven together, produce welcoming and inclusive organizations. These threads are that a multicultural organization (a) is diverse in cultural representation, (b) has an equitable distribution of power and influence, (c) supports the elimination of oppression, and (d) supports multicultural perspectives in the larger society. Grieger (1996) and Pope and Reynolds (1997) added that MOD is a systemic, systematic, planned, proactive, comprehensive, and long-range process. We further add that MOD is an enduring pursuit. The objective is ever-evolving and dynamic, as the context shifts and changes over time.

Many MSS units teach and provide professional support to other campus units as they work to develop multiculturally competent organizations. Because of this important leadership role, multicultural services units, themselves, are encouraged to continue their growth and learning with regard to cultural competence. Because advocating for socially just organizations is one of their core tenets, these organizations are expected to model such environments through their inclusive knowledge, skills, abilities, and practices. Many individuals hired to work in MSS are passionate practitioners who have not been formally prepared for their roles and do not possess content-specific credentials that inform their work (Johnstone & Kanitsaki, 2008). We do not suggest that these professionals are any less competent and capable of carrying out their work. Rather, in academia, understanding, drawing from, and building upon scholarship are critical. To establish and maintain credibility, members of these units should continue to deepen their skills through ongoing professional development.

Multicultural competence should be required of all members of the higher education community (Pope, Reynolds, & Mueller, 2004), because of the nature of social life as discussed by several scholars (Kumagai & Lypson, 2009; Ober, Granello, & Henfield, 2009; Rogers-Sirin & Sirin, 2009). According to these authors, individuals' daily thoughts and decisions are impacted by personal values and mental models, and there is often reluctance to acknowledge personal biases. Being reflective and candid about our lack of important cultural knowledge about many groups is essential. In a society demarcated by power and privilege, underexposure to culturally rich information about nondominant cultural groups is common. However, this lack of exposure might unintentionally cause harm when one acts from a position of ignorance. It is imperative that all educators develop new awareness, knowledge, and skills, as the world and our campuses become more globally interconnected. Moreover, multicultural competence, like multicultural organizational development, is a process and a journey. It is not a destination that can be reached or an assignment one can complete (Kumagai & Lypson, 2009; Ober et al., 2009; Rogers-Sirin & Sirin, 2009).

Organizations must be explicit about diversity-related competencies they want their organizational and institutional staff, students, and faculty to obtain. There is a need to define what a multiculturally competent professional is, what experiences lead to multicultural competence, and how such competence is measured. Drawing on the collective wisdom of many who have written about multicultural competence (Gayles & Kelly, 2007; Grieger, 1996; Jackson & Holvino, 1988; Pope, 1993; Pope & Reynolds, 1997; Shapiro, Sewell, & DuCette, 1995; Woods, 2004), a multiculturally competent professional possesses the following knowledge and abilities:

Knowledge

- ◆ Knowledge of one's own cultural and personal biases
- ◆ Knowledge of diverse cultures and oppressed groups
- ◆ A complex understanding of culture and the way it influences worldviews
- ◆ An understanding of the social, cultural, and historical systems that shape our experiences
- ◆ An understanding of the roles of power and conflict in relationships
- ◆ A deep understanding of organizational development and change

Abilities

- ◆ Ability to communicate effectively across differences
- ◆ Ability to interrogate one's own assumptions
- ◆ Ability to notice and interrupt oppression
- ◆ Ability to resolve conflict

♦ Ability to be cognitively agile
♦ Ability to manage developmental tension

Additionally, these competencies should be woven into institutional structures, policies, and practices. They should be included in position descriptions, serve as criteria for hiring decisions, be included in ongoing educational opportunities, and be part of performance appraisals, linked to merit, compensation, and promotion systems. Every possible linkage should be explored so the expectation of multicultural competence is clear, connected, continuous, and well grounded.

ASSESSMENT

Although often cited as important practice for all units, assessment often takes a backseat to other more pressing issues, such as programming, dialoging with students, and planning future initiatives (Bresciani, Zelna, & Anderson, 2002). The reality is that assessment is a tool that can enhance each of these pressing needs, but for the purposes of this chapter, we discuss how assessment enables practitioners to build capacity for enduring progress.

The benefits of diversity, multicultural competence, and the value added by MSS must be documented. "Without a body of evidence that demonstrates an impact, diversity investments can be challenged, leadership decisions can be questioned, and effective planning may be hampered" (Anderson, 2008, p. 15). It is imperative that practitioners in MSS forcefully articulate their efficacy, thus assessment should be an essential element of their work.

Assessment can serve many useful functions: It provides feedback regarding the efficacy of the work, it illuminates the needs of end users (students, staff, faculty, or even the community at large), and it focuses efforts on the areas of greatest need for the campus (Bresciani et al., 2002; Maki, 2004). Further, assessment results represent a powerful mechanism for communicating with constituents regarding the nature of work being conducted and the demonstrable effect of that work. In this era of increased accountability and shrinking budgets, having data to support decisions and tell the stories of success is essential. However, assessment is not a magic bullet that can solve all problems; rather, the assessment process is a tool that can powerfully advance the unit's mission.

The process of creating a specific assessment plan for an MSS unit is beyond the scope of this chapter; however, there are several important points to highlight so practitioners can leverage assessment to build capacity for an MSS unit. First, an essential step is to identify the intended outcomes, mission, and purpose. If done collaboratively, this process will not only identify what is important and bring all members of the unit into alignment, but will also ensure that everyone within the unit is invested in the outcomes (Angelo, 1999). This serves as a tangible reminder of individuals' contributions to the whole and allows people to see themselves as important contributors in the unit's work.

The second way to leverage assessment to build capacity is to recognize its iterative nature (Bresciani et al., 2002; Maki, 2004). Because the nature of the work done by MSS units is dynamic and changing to meet the needs of a diverse world, the nature of the assessment must match this dynamic and fluid character. For many units, this requires a shift in the way practitioners see their day-to-day work. Building assessment in as a daily component for most educational practitioners might require that the culture of the organization be refocused to value assessment. The old adage, "what is valued gets done," seems particularly germane here. Building a culture that values and expects inquiry serves to institutionalize assessment and rely on assessment to inform practice (Bresciani et al., 2002; Maki, 2004).

Third, an audit of the MSS unit's work might be necessary to ensure that each of the outcomes that the unit seeks to accomplish has a method of delivery as well as criteria that serve as indicators of success. For example, if a unit decides an outcome will be "students will have the opportunity to discuss how globalization affects their education," there must be some activity or program with the purpose of meeting this outcome (Bresciani et al., 2002; Maki, 2004). To gather information regarding an intervention's success, criteria must be established that will denote what the participants have learned, developed, or understood as a result of this activity or program. Bloom's taxonomy (see Krathwohl, 2002) might be particularly helpful in choosing words to describe learning outcomes and criteria of effectiveness. Once the criteria for success have been established, a method to measure those criteria (such as a survey, a focus group, taking note of a desired behavior, etc.) is necessary. A useful activity as described by Marilee Bresciani (2003) is to complete an Outcome Delivery Mapping Worksheet (Figure

13.1), which helps link outcomes with activities or initiatives. This helps to ensure that there is at least one delivery mechanism for each outcome.

Fourth, gathering assessment data requires considering the question: "What type of information will be most compelling?" There are many types of data (e.g., quantitative survey data, focus group data, qualitative interview data), but, for the purposes of assessment, it is not necessary to focus on the methodology until it is clear what type of data is required: direct evidence, indirect evidence, or dashboard indicator (Bresciani et al., 2002; Ewell & Jones, 1993). Direct evidence is feedback whereby the end user (typically the student) provides a demonstration of their understanding, skills, or abilities (Bresciani et al., 2002; Klein, Kuh, Chun, Hamilton, & Shavelson, 2005; Palomba & Banta, 1999). Indirect evidence allows the end user to reflect and report or describe their learning, growth, or skill development (Bresciani

Figure 13.1. Program delivery map.

Results	
Desired Outcomes	Intervention to Achieve Outcome
1.	1.
2.	2.
3.	3.
Evaluation	
Criteria for Evaluation	Method for Evaluation
1.	1.
2.	2.
3.	3

Note: Adapted by David McIntosh from Bresciani (2003)

et al., 2002; Klein et al., 2005; Palomba & Banta, 1999). Dashboard indicators are perhaps the easiest to gather and include data such as the number of people to attend a program or the number of staff members who inquire about services (Bresciani et al., 2002). Each of these types of data has advantages and disadvantages. For example, dashboard indicators are typically easier to gather but are rarely sufficient to make decisions or evaluate the achievement of an outcome. Direct measures are quite effective in demonstrating outcome achievement but are often difficult to gather. Indirect measures can be easier to gather but can be more challenging to interpret. Because each of these types of data provides different information, it is important to consider how data will be used and what means are available for data-gathering—only then can decisions be made regarding the type of data that is compelling, assists in making decisions for the unit, and answers the questions that are most important (Bresciani et al., 2002).

Climate Assessment

Aside from outcomes-based assessment as described previously, climate assessments are a powerful tool for understanding how different people understand, interpret, and are made to feel within the campus community (Anderson, 2008; Hurtado, Milem, Clayton-Pedersen, & Allen, 1998; Milem, Chang, & antonio, 2005; Worthington, 2008). This powerful assessment can assist in describing not only what the campus environment is, but also where focused attention is needed to improve the campus climate. In turn, this can advise MSS units in designing initiatives that are most needed by the campus (Hurtado et al., 1998; Milem et al., 2005).

A campus-wide climate assessment is typically a large-scale project that can be expensive and time consuming. Before embarking on such an assessment, it is important to gather easily accessible data. First, many campuses participate in some sort of national assessment instrument, such as the NSSE (National Survey of Student Engagement) or CIRP (Cooperative Institute Research Program). Within many of these instruments are questions regarding students' attitudes toward diversity, engagement with people who are different from themselves, and comfort level in discussing issues related to diversity. Analyzing the responses to these questions provides a baseline for understanding how students perceive the campus environment, but it is important to note that these instruments often do not delve into the depth that might be necessary for a campus climate assessment (Hurtado, Griffin, Arellano, & Cuellar, 2008).

Next, there are dashboard indicators and indirect evidence measures that campuses likely compile. For example, there is almost certainly presence data, which simply documents the numbers of people by category, typically race and gender. A five-year spread of these data can powerfully illustrate the campus trend for recruitment and retention of underrepresented students, faculty, and staff. Further analysis can provide richer data: to disaggregate these numbers by position type; disaggregate the number of full, associate, assistant, and clinical professors by race and gender; or disaggregate the number of executives, administrators, managers, secretarial, and service employees by race and gender will begin to shape a narrative about the campus environment. The presence data provide a baseline for understanding if the campus is making progress in recruiting and retaining traditionally underrepresented people and whether traditionally underrepresented people are excluded in promotion opportunities. To take this analysis another step farther, many institutions participate in a data-sharing consortium (such as IPEDS), which compiles data on peer institutions. Comparing data will provide compelling information that can assist in creating a campus-wide conversation as well as create a mandate for further action.

A type of indirect evidence that might also be easily accessible is an exit survey. Exit surveys are typically completed when a student or employee leaves the institution. This type of data complements the trend data described previously with information about why people leave an institution. Other sources of data to consider include surveys of students who transfer out of the institution or surveys asking graduating students about their experiences. These sources of indirect evidence probably already exist and might already be analyzed, so they can easily be used in a preliminary analysis of potential campus issues.

Another opportunity to gather data prior to launching a climate assessment is to conduct an audit of the diversity initiatives currently taking place on the campus. It is quite likely that the MSS unit is not the only unit conducting diversity work on campus (particularly on larger campuses). Presumably, programs and initiatives exist to meet a diversity need, and by auditing the current diversity initiatives, their outcomes, and their assessment techniques, a great deal can be learned about the needs of the campus community, including which groups might be underserved and if there is a duplication of effort (which could indicate opportunities for collaboration). Hurtado (2003, 2005) examined campus diversity initiatives (as an avenue for teaching students about interacting in a pluralistic society) and created a typology for classifying campus diversity initiatives, which will certainly assist practitioners in conducting such an audit.

A diversity initiative audit serves as a strong start for understanding the campus climate. The data collected will assuredly raise more questions than they have answered, and a campus climate assessment will be an appropriate vehicle for seeking answers to these questions. However, investing time in examining existing information to know what specific information is necessary will produce a much sharper and more focused campus climate assessment, giving results greater clarity and utility.

The next step is to decide whether a local or outside instrument will be employed to answer the emergent questions. The primary advantage to launching a local instrument (one that is designed in-house, perhaps in conjunction with the campus assessment office or other invested constituents) is that the instrument, methodology, sample, and the like, are locally controlled. As such, investigators can pursue answers to the most pressing questions. The cost of having complete control is complete responsibility for formulating questions, which is more tedious than it might initially seem. The next step is choosing a method, whether survey, focus groups, or interviews, followed by gathering the data. Depending on the means available for survey administration, a software package that allows electronic distribution of the instrument will be necessary. Qualitative data will require having trained facilitators to conduct interviews or focus groups. Consideration must also be given to issues of sample (requisite number of respondents and sufficient response rate) and, finally, a method to analyze the data is necessary, so that meaning can be made of the results.

Given all of the responsibilities for a local instrument, it might be more efficient to employ an external consultant to assess the campus climate. An outside climate survey has the major advantage of a company or research institute taking responsibility for formulating the questions, deciding on the method, gathering data, and offering preliminary analysis. Many outside climate surveys also offer the option of comparing results with mission- or size-equivalent or regional peer institutions. The potential downside of using an external survey is losing control of many aspects of the process. For example, many questions will be mandated so that results can be compared across institutions. Although it is likely that many institutions have some of the same questions regarding the climate, it is equally likely that the preliminary analysis of dashboard indicators and indirect data will lead to questions that are not addressed in a generalized climate survey. Many outside instruments allow users to add questions that are tailored to individual institutions, but there could be more questions in need of answers than question space available.

Regardless of the type of campus climate assessment chosen, one aspect remains constant: It will be necessary to make meaning of the data and implement the results in a compelling way to tell the story that informs practice. For example, what does it mean about a campus when 20% of students engage in meaningful conversations with someone of a different background? How will this data point be used to inform practice? With whom should this information be shared? Only once this critical step is complete will it be possible to make decisions that are grounded in data, create a narrative that communicates the areas of greatest need for the communities the MSS unit supports, and design initiatives, programs, or interventions to best meet these needs (Hurtado et al., 2008).

This discussion would not be complete without acknowledging that assessment, more broadly speaking, is deeply political. When questions are asked about return on human and financial investments, whose needs are or are not being met through certain initiatives, and whether those initiatives are effective and worthwhile, it can introduce a good deal of anxiety. In some instances, units or individuals unable to convey their effectiveness risk termination. Therefore, it behooves an organization to create its own internal accountability mechanisms to measure its effectiveness, use the results to recalibrate, if necessary, and document success. Although many dislike the time-consuming nature of assessment and resist it until it is foisted upon them by another organizational unit, accountability is ever upon us (particularly because of the nature of our work), ever-expanding, and here to stay.

ENCOUNTERING RESISTANCE

Multicultural organizational development and assessment are profoundly political pursuits. That these accountability-driven commitments would stimulate resistance is no surprise. Indeed, resistance should be anticipated and engaged. Good practitioners set diversity-related standards and expectations and then use assessment to hold community members accountable. Institutional transformation seeks to alter prevailing systems of power and the behaviors of the people who coordinate to keep webs of exclusion in place. Thus, it arouses insecurities and anxieties. Change agents should explore the roots of resistance, be aware of its many manifestations, and develop skills to negotiate and engage it.

Among the many reasons people resist multicultural transformation are (a) challenges to fundamental societal beliefs (Chan & Treacy, 1996); (b) fear that the benefits of an inequitable system will cease to accrue; (c) threat to the power and decision-making privileges of those in control; (d) fear of the (real or imagined) advancement of gender and ethnic minorities; (e) competition for scarce resources; and (f) nonminorities feeling overlooked because they do not see themselves represented in diversity initiatives (Applebaum, 2008; Stevens, Plaut, & Sanchez-Burks, 2008). Additionally, resistance could come because the mandate for change is, "tacitly or explicitly, a kind of criticism undertaken by outsiders and imposed upon an in-group" (Burack & Franks, 2004, p. 87). It threatens the intact group in ways that often cause them to close ranks and continue to exclude marginal group members, and there is a "tendency to idealize the group *as it is*, not as it might be at some point in the future" (Burack & Franks, 2004, p. 87, emphasis added).

Resistance has many other faces, all of which require distinct responses. Resistance can be as subtle as silence, nonattendance, acts of omission, isolation, and lack of recognition. Although these are often invisible acts of intransigence, their accumulation and persistence serve to institutionalize the marginalization of change agents and their work. Resistance can also be overt. Some might deny outright the existence of inequality, refuse to accept data-supported justifications, fail to cooperate with the MSS office or provide critical information needed to advance its agenda, openly criticize and undermine its work, or provide partial or short-term funding for multicultural initiatives. Regrettably, resistance occasionally comes from administrators who were responsible for creating MSS units. Evelyn Hu-DeHart (2000) posited that their behavior is rooted in fear of strengthening a force of free-thinking, independent-minded, critically evaluating professionals with an intellectual base of their own.

Engaging, not avoiding or ignoring, resistance is an important survival skill. We encourage MSS professionals to view resistance as a source of energy that has the potential to enrich their efforts and help shift deeply embedded mental models and ways of behaving. If not assertively addressed, sites of resistance can persist and draw critical attention away from laudable efforts.

Interventions used by MSS professionals might include a number of tactics. First, they should acknowledge the discomfort multiculturalism introduces. Second, we recommend they notice and name the resistance, then engage in deep, searching dialogue to explore common ground. Third, MSS professionals can develop interventions to draw in those who are disengaged or who feel disenfranchised by their efforts. Fourth, we urge MSS professionals to carefully attend to their discursive framing of their priorities so they do not inadvertently create an insider/outsider binary (Iverson, 2007). Fifth, staff in MSS should explicitly include nonminorities in their efforts as allies (Stevens et al., 2008). Sixth, MSS staff can produce evidence of how the institution as a whole benefits from a more diverse and welcoming environment. Finally, we encourage MSS professionals to engage in difficult dialogues.

Equally important for MSS staff is the sometimes challenging but highly rewarding work of coalition-building. It is imperative that these staff develop relationships within, across, and among identity groups to build a strong infrastructure. Programs and people should be networked, multidimensional, integrated, comprehensive, and characterized by trust and strategic planning. Texas A&M University provides another useful illustration. They established an informal Diversity Network that meets twice each semester. Individuals who are formally charged with diversity initiatives are convened and encouraged to share ideas, strategies, programs, challenges, and resources. Many important outcomes and synergistic activities have resulted from this informal, yet meaningful, effort.

IMPLICATIONS

Although each campus is unique, with its own set of challenges and opportunities, MSS units have several factors in common. They are all partners in the educational enterprise. They all seek to transform the academy into a more inclusive, welcoming environment. They all have some level of understanding about organizational behavior and the workings of power and privilege. Finally, they all devote attention to multicultural organizational development both at the micro (individual unit) and macro (institutional) levels. However, leadership strategies for advancing campus diversity will vary across institutions, because they must be tailored to different campus frameworks and address different institutional needs (Anderson, 2008).

To remain relevant, MSS units must continue to speak to the higher mission of the university and work collaboratively with the many other units charged with multicultural organizational transformation. They should also engage in ongoing professional development to continue growing in their knowledge and skills and to evolve their practice. Furthermore, they should focus considerable attention on systemic change that alters the culture, structure, mental models (Kezar, 2003), and webs of exclusion that privilege some and disenfranchise others. Finally, they should anticipate and respond nimbly to resistance and develop a culture of evidence to support diversity. When MSS units can adroitly engage these strategies, the possibility of institutional renewal and sustainable outcomes is much more promising.

REFERENCES

Aguirre, A. (2000). *Women and minority faculty in the academic workplace: Recruitment, retention, and academic culture.* ASHE-ERIC Higher Education Report, *27*(6). San Francisco, CA: Jossey-Bass.

Anderson, J. A. (2008). *Driving through change: Transformative leadership in the academy.* Sterling, VA: Stylus.

Angelo, T. (1999). Doing assessment as if learning matters most. *AAHE Bulletin, 59*(9), 3–6.

Applebaum, B. (2008). "Doesn't my experience count?" White students, the authority of experience and social justice pedagogy. *Race, Ethnicity, and Education, 11,* 405–414.

Bresciani, M. J. (2003, December). Identifying projects that deliver outcomes and provide a means of assessment: A concept mapping checklist. *NetResults: E-Zine.* Retrieved from http://www.naspa.org/membership/mem/pubs/nr/PrinterFriendly.cfm?id=1291

Bresciani, M. J., Zelna, C. L., & Anderson, J. A. (2002). *Assessing student learning and development: A handbook for practitioners.* Washington, DC: National Association of Student Personnel Administrators.

Burack, C., & Franks, S. (2004). Telling stories about engineering: Group dynamics and resistance to diversity. *NWSA Journal, 16*(1), 79–95.

Chan, C., & Treacy, M. (1996). Resistance in multicultural courses: Student, faculty, and classroom dynamics. *American Behavioral Scientist, 40,* 212–221.

Ewell, P. T., & Jones, D. P. (1993). Actions matter: The case for indirect measures in assessing higher education's progress on the National Education Goals. *Journal of General Education, 42,* 123–148.

Gayles, J., & Kelly, B. (2007). Experiences with diversity in the curriculum: Implications for graduate programs and student affairs practice. *NASPA Journal, 44,* 193–208.

Grieger, I. (1996). A multicultural organizational development checklist for student affairs. *Journal of College Student Development, 37,* 561–573.

Hu-DeHart, E. (2000). The diversity project, institutionalizing multiculturalism or managing differences?: Institutions embrace diversity—in theory. But they don't do much to implement it. *Academe Online.* Retrieved from http://www.aaup.org/AAUP/pubsres/academe/2000/SO/Feat/hu.htm?PF = 1

Hurtado, S. (2003). *Preparing college students for a diverse democracy: Final report to the U.S. Department of Education.* Ann Arbor, MI: Center for the Study of Higher and Postsecondary Education.

Hurtado, S. (2005). The next generation of diversity and intergroup relations research. *Journal of Social Issues, 61,* 595–610.

Hurtado, S., Griffin, K. A., Arellano, L., & Cuellar, M. (2008). Assessing the value of climate assessments: Progress and future directions. *Journal of Diversity in Higher Education, 1,* 204–221.

Hurtado, S., Milem, J. F., Clayton-Pedersen, A., & Allen, W. (1998). Enhancing campus climates for racial/ethnic diversity: Educational policy and practice. *Review of Higher Education, 21,* 279–302.

Iverson, S. (2007). Camouflaging power and privilege: A critical race analysis of university diversity policies. *Educational Administration Quarterly, 43,* 586–611.

Jackson, B., & Holvino, E. (1988). *Multicultural organization development.* (Program on Conflict Management Alternatives at the University of Michigan, Working Paper, No. 11). Ann Arbor: University of Michigan.

Johnstone, M., & Kanitsaki, O. (2008). The politics of resistance to workplace cultural diversity education for health service providers: An Australian study. *Race, Ethnicity, and Education, 11,* 133–154.

Kezar, A. (2003). Enhancing innovative partnerships: Creating a change model for academic and student affairs collaboration. *Innovative Higher Education, 28*(2), 137–156.

Klein, S. P., Kuh, G. D., Chun, M., Hamilton, L., & Shavelson, R. J. (2005). An approach to measuring cognitive outcomes across higher-education institutions. *Journal of Higher Education, 46,* 251–276.

Krathwohl, D. R. (2002). A revision of Bloom's taxonomy: An overview. *Theory into Practice, 41,* 212–218.

Kumagai, A., & Lypson, M. (2009). Beyond cultural competence: Critical consciousness, social justice, and multicultural education. *Academic Medicine, 84,* 782–787.

Maki, P. L. (2004). *Assessing for learning.* Sterling, VA: Stylus.

Milem, J., Chang, M., & antonio, a. (2005). *Making diversity work on campus: A research based perspective.* Washington, DC: Association of American Colleges and Universities.

Ober, A., Granello, D., & Henfield, M. (2009). A synergistic model to enhance multicultural competence in supervision. *Counselor Education & Supervision, 48,* 204–221.

Palomba, C. A., & Banta, T. W. (1999). *Assessment essentials: Planning, implementing and improving assessment in higher education.* San Francisco, CA: Jossey-Bass.

Pope, R. (1993). Multicultural-organization development in student affairs: An introduction. *Journal of College Student Development, 34*(3), 201–205.

Pope, R. L., & Reynolds, A. L. (1997). Student affairs core competencies: Integrating multicultural awareness, knowledge, and skills. *Journal of College Student Development, 38,* 266–277.

Pope, R. L., Reynolds, A. L., & Mueller, J. A. (2004). *Multicultural competence in student affairs.* San Francisco, CA: Jossey-Bass.

Rogers-Sirin, L., & Sirin, S. (2009). Cultural competence as an ethical requirement: Introducing a new educational model. *Journal of Diversity in Higher Education, 2,* 19–29.

Shapiro, J., Sewell, T., & DuCette, J. (1995). *Reframing diversity in education.* Lancaster, PA: Technomic.

Stanley, C. (Ed.). (2006). *Faculty of color: Teaching in predominantly White colleges and universities.* Bolton, MA: Anker.

Stanley, C., & Lincoln, Y. (2005, April). Cross-race faculty mentoring. *Change, 37*(2), 44–52.

Stevens, F., Plaut, V., & Sanchez-Burks, J. (2008). Unlocking the benefits of diversity: All-inclusive multiculturalism and positive organizational change. *The Journal of Applied Behavioral Science, 44,* 116–133.

Williams, D., & Wade-Golden, C. (2007). *The chief diversity officer: A primer for college and university presidents.* Washington, DC: American Council on Education.

Woods, M. (2004). Cultivating cultural competence in agricultural education through community-based service-learning. *Journal of Agricultural Education, 45*(1), 10–20.

Worthington, R. L. (2008). Measurement and assessment in campus climate research: A scientific imperative. *Journal of Diversity in Higher Education, 1,* 201–203.

14

Developing Collaborations Within Student Affairs

Walter M. Kimbrough
Carretta A. Cooke

Kwon is the director of multicultural affairs and has been trying for months to establish a collaborative partnership with residence life to do more than just a one-hour sensitivity training workshop for resident assistants. Gayle, the coordinator for student activities, serves as the advisor for the student programming board and has been frustrated this year by group members' collective unwillingness to consider events and artists that would have a more diverse appeal. She knows she needs help but is unsure whether it is appropriate for her to consult with Kwon and unclear about his responsibilities as the director of multicultural affairs.

As DISCUSSED BY SHUFORD (Chapter 2), multicultural student services (MSS) were begun in earnest over the last quarter of the 20th century. They were developed from coast to coast: for example, the University of Virginia in 1976, Ohio State University in 1970, and Washington State University in 1986 (Hale, 2004). In most cases, campus unrest played an integral part in the development of these offices. As offices created often in response to such tension, the mere appearance of MSS on campuses in some ways established a dynamic that began to isolate and segregate the

218

populations they served shortly after the major battles for integration had been won.

MSS offices, created in many cases not as the result of well thought-out strategic planning, but as the result of student agitation, ended up being placed haphazardly on campuses. In most cases, the offices were situated in student affairs divisions, but they continue to exist in academic affairs divisions and other areas. This chapter examines MSS when it is housed in student affairs, with special attention to the fit these offices might have in this unit and how they can become integral parts of the division and the campus.

FITTING WITHIN STUDENT AFFAIRS

In Hale's 2004 book, *What Makes Racial Diversity Work in Higher Education*, three contributing authors provided examples of the genesis of MSS offices and their placement on their campuses. The book's discussion begins with the University of Virginia (UVa). Turner (2004) defined the goals of the office as (a) to provide a supportive environment through contact with African American students, (b) to enhance the sensitivity of the larger community, (c) to provide support to parents and guardians, (d) to monitor and assess the university's climate, and (e) to enhance relationships in the local community. The UVa program provided a number of services, including peer advisors, faculty-student mentoring, a parents' association, and the Black cultural center (Turner, 2004).

In another example from Jones (2004) at Washington State University, the provost proposed the creation of a division of minority affairs within student affairs. The institution provided counselors for each protected racial underrepresented group, as well as two recruiters for students of color. The division's focus was "to increase the enrollment of students of color and to provide counseling (academic, personal, financial and social) and other support services to reduce the attrition of students of color" (Jones, 2004, p. 132). Six years after opening, the division was renamed Multicultural Student Services and moved to the area of the vice provost for Human Relations and Resources.

In the book's final example, according to Stewart (2004), Ohio State University's minority affairs office was created during a time of unrest on the campus in the late 1960s to 1970, epitomized by the Kent State incident that shook all of higher education, especially those schools in Ohio. During this tumultuous time, Ohio State added an Office of Minority Affairs, the Department of Black Studies, and the Center for Women's Studies. Although MSS at Ohio State initially focused on Black students, it later expanded to include other groups. The office's major programs included recruitment, retention, academic advancement, and recognition programs (Stewart, 2004).

These three examples have shared models for the operation of multicultural student services. All had been, at least at one time, part of the student affairs division. These offices, along with the vast majority of similar offices on campuses today, have as a major focus the integration of students of color into the institution's overall campus life. The heavy emphasis on the out-of-class experience makes the alignment of MSS within student affairs a natural fit.

THE FUNCTION OF STUDENT AFFAIRS IN THE MODERN COLLEGE AND UNIVERSITY

Historically, student affairs saw its largest expansion after World War II, when student enrollments grew mainly because of the matriculation of larger numbers of first-generation, racially/ethnically diverse students, and women (Ambler, 1993). This period served as an "end run," where those left out of the elitist educational system were granted access, and the nation saw attainment of higher education as a right and not a privilege. Through the early 20th century, the model for faculty was to be engaged with students both in and out of class. Faculty involvement gradually decreased in the era of the modern university with the emergence of the German research model as ushered in by Charles Eliot at Harvard (Rudolph, 1990).

When campuses first hired deans of men and women, those persons were selected for their "ability to develop or manage a variety of programs and services in behalf of students" (Appleton, Briggs, & Rhatigan, 1978, p. 20). By the 1960s, student affairs had grown into large, complex units headed by a chief student affairs officer. Ambler (1993) suggested "the civil rights movement of African Americans spilled onto the nation's campuses, creating tension and confrontation over long-ignored societal ills" (p. 109). With the disruptions by student protests, including antiwar groups, colleges and universities recognized a need for dedicated and professionally trained educators to facilitate a positive out-of-class learning environment for students.

Ambler (1993) surveyed over 100 institutions to determine the services, structure, and span of control of student affairs divisions. He found broad responsibilities, with some divisions housing functions that had been part of the academic affairs unit, including admissions, records, advising, and remedial services. In other instances, divisions had responsibility for campus safety, athletics, and even public relations. Many of the divisions were responsible for auxiliary services that are key areas for student out-of-class experiences, such as the residence halls, health services, and student unions.

With its breadth of oversight, the division of student affairs is an appropriate home for efforts to improve the quality of life for students of color. Much of the literature that addresses improving the overall performance of students of color is done from a student affairs framework, and often the recommendations for improvement are targeted toward student affairs, rather than academic units. Kuh, Schuh, Whitt, and Associates (1991) noted that two-thirds of college students' time when they are awake is devoted to activities other than attending class or studying. In light of this, Kuh et al. offered recommendations for colleges and universities to engage students purposefully. They offered special recommendations for improving the college experience and success of students of color, including:

1. Emphasize in word and action, at every opportunity, the importance of a multicultural learning community to the institution's educational purposes.
2. Develop orientation workshops for new students of color, hosted by currently enrolled students and faculty.
3. Create opportunities for students of color to meet regularly with one another and with university administrators to discuss concerns.
4. Establish cultural awareness weeks around themes of unity and diversity and observe special holidays and celebrations, such as Black Heritage Month, Cinco de Mayo, and Martin Luther King Jr.'s birthday.
5. Recognize students of color for their service and academic achievements. (Kuh et al., 1991, pp. 354–355)

MSS provides suitable leadership on these issues. Its placement in student affairs is strategic in that the unit's leader would be a peer with other key division leaders, who would serve as partners for accomplishing these goals. Special orientation sessions for students of color should be coordinated with the overall orientation schedule, and best practices in orientation can be shared for these focused events. Opportunities to meet with key administrators, especially those who supervise the cocurriculum where students spend most of their time, and key colleagues of the department's director are invaluable. The student activities office would serve as a great partner in planning events, leadership experiences, and the like for students of color and to ensure that they become engaged in general campus activities.

As presented in the three examples shared in Hale's (2004) text, MSS offices perform a wide variety of functions. The breadth of these functions has made it feasible for these areas to be housed in numerous areas. However, a key function is to provide social integration for students of color. These offices are responsible to provide the peer, faculty, or staff mentoring designed to ensure a connection between students and the institution. Numerous programmatic activities and events are planned in MSS offices, ranging from culturally specific educational events, to heritage theme month events. In addition, student groups whose primary purpose is support for students of color are often advised in these offices.

Another major function, however, is the academic component of MSS work. These offices generally take the lead in providing academic services, including tutoring and academic advising. In some instances, MSS offices are major components of the recruiting process, and they are tasked with increasing the diversity on the campus. These offices can help set the tone for the academic expectations of incoming students.

The impact of MSS offices is tremendous, with the bulk of the activities taking place within the realm of student affairs. However, these offices often are viewed from an institution-wide perspective as the natural leader to develop plans for creating an inclusive campus community. In fact, over the past decade, chief diversity officer positions have been established at places like the University of Virginia and the University of Wisconsin–Madison in an attempt to impact the overall diversity of the campus (see Petitt & McIntosh, Chapter 13, for further discussion). These positions pull MSS out of the student affairs division, thereby raising its visibility, because the chief diversity officer typically reports directly to the president or chancellor. Although this might pose some challenges, many of the persons who hold positions as chief diversity officers have a student affairs background and a thorough understanding of the importance of maintaining partnerships with student affairs.

Multicultural student services, however, might best be served within the context of a division of student affairs. Given the formative history of student affairs and the diversity issues on campuses today, cultivating and sustaining a strong relationship between MSS and the other units in the division of student affairs provides the best opportunity to maximize resources for the best interest of all students. Nevertheless, as the vignette involving Kwon and Gayle illustrates, how MSS can work effectively with other student affairs units is not always clear.

The following case study explores ways that MSS worked effectively within the division of student affairs at Old Dominion University (ODU). This institution is an urban commuter campus with a large student of color population. Student engagement was a challenge with fewer than a quarter of students residing on campus. Thus, a partnership between MSS and many offices on campus was critical in improving student persistence and graduation rates.

A CASE STUDY OF MULTICULTURAL STUDENT SERVICES IN STUDENT AFFAIRS

Cultural program planning and implementation for diverse audiences is an essential part of multicultural student services. Often, MSS offices are expected to plan programs and activities for the entire campus without substantial budgets, so survival strategies are paramount to achieving and succeeding. Collaborating with other student affairs offices and forging creative partnerships with colleagues on the academic side of the institution proved to be the key to successful programming. At times, they also played a pivotal advising role with cultural student organizations, leading to creating opportunities for innovative event planning among and between student groups and multicultural affairs offices.

Creativity and ingenuity are critical elements to successful program and event planning for multicultural student services. At Old Dominion University, this was accomplished through creating campus community partnerships that were embedded in the MSS mission. In collaboration with the student activities office, several initiatives were extremely successful for the department and ultimately, the student organizations as well.

For example, Black History Month planning required involvement from student organizations, student affairs offices, and academic departments. Planning began in the late summer and included working with student activities to make sure that funding for some programs would be granted to the student organizations involved in planning the month's events. The academic departments would also be contacted to see if there was interest in creating programs or providing financial support for a program. Often, MSS could work with academic colleagues who would serve as facilitators for lectures and panels. This increased their visibility with the students and often engaged them in ways they would not have been afforded if they were not willing and engaged participants with multicultural student services.

In addition, there were several initiatives grounded in academic affairs that required collaborations with MSS to ensure their success. The annual University Film Festival, for example, was planned to be focused on diversity through film as a core aspect of its mission, and MSS was a natural conduit for dialogue regarding film selection and themes for the events. This resulted in hosting such films as *Daughters of the Dust* and *Smoke Signals*, with their directors conducting discussions throughout the festival.

At Old Dominion, the camaraderie among the student affairs staff also afforded MSS the opportunity to think outside of the box when creating large-scale programs. MSS sponsored the first Kwanzaa program that involved the Hampton Roads community, and the funding for this program came not only from office support, but from most of the cultural student organizations, as well as from some community-based groups. The first year of the Kwanzaa program saw more than 500 persons in attendance and featured African dance, gospel performances, poetry readings, a fashion show, and an African marketplace. This undertaking could not have been accomplished without additional funding from student activities and the president's office.

To accomplish many of MSS's programmatic strategies, the staff found it easy to foster collegial relationships throughout the university; this might have been because the university was finding its niche as an academic institution in the Hampton Roads area. There was a willingness to be involved in diversity programs, and innovative programs were welcomed by the students and others within the university. The office also made ODU the first school in the Commonwealth of Virginia to have a position (as a graduate assistant-ship) that was focused on the gay, lesbian, bisexual, transgendered community and its issues, so the office was considered to be on the cutting edge of multicultural programming and diversity events.

The largest collaborative initiative took place when the office worked in partnership with the Filipino community of Hampton Roads and raised more than $100,000 to open the first Filipino American Student Cultural Center on the East Coast. The initiative also created a Filipino Studies minor and gave students the opportunity to view the cultural contributions of their community in broader academic and social frameworks. National and international media coverage accompanied the center's opening as well as a visit by the Philippines' ambassador to the United States for the opening gala.

STRATEGIES FOR SUCCESSFUL COLLABORATION

Many other mechanisms must be used by MSS offices to increase overall participation in its programs and endeavors. On many campuses, to increase the viability of MSS, it is essential to create bridges with other places and spaces on campuses to have universal buy-in for programming. It can be helpful for staff to reach out to student governments; in some instances, their programming budgets often exceed the department's budget allotment. Some campuses also have student programming boards, and it might be helpful to look to those boards for partnerships on shared programming initiatives. This can be especially useful to plan large-scale concerts that have broad appeal to students.

It is important to think about the advantages of these partnerships beyond their potential financial benefits, for example, as ways in which such collaborations can increase student participation and connect the mission of MSS to a broader university context. This ensures the office's viability and visibility throughout the campus community. MSS offices are urged to extend their outreach beyond partnerships based solely on racial and ethnic issues—to encompass a broad range of diversity issues and how those issues intersect with race and ethnicity. Strategic planning should include creating a strong framework for inclusive partnerships and collaborations that benefit the campus community.

To accomplish this, it is crucial to make sure that consistent contact is made through outreach with various college and university affinity groups through a variety of means. This could mean meeting with them on an individual basis or through an organized forum, such as a planning retreat for student leaders. During these kinds of events, it is helpful to approach the groups with ideas that support cooperation with the MSS unit's mission and with their goals for program planning. If multicultural events are planned well in advance, it might be useful to send an electronic calendar of events to a wide variety of organizations and offices and request cosponsorship of upcoming events as well as to make recommendations for cosponsorship of programs that serve their needs and meet the overarching goals of multicultural student services.

Nevertheless, collaborating with student groups requires that MSS professionals be aware of a few pitfalls to avoid. First, the learning opportunity for students should be emphasized. Clarity about expectations of the collaboration is essential. If their contribution is solely financial, then the group should understand the parameters of financial stewardship, particularly when collaborating with a university department. Also, if a group is interested in cosponsoring, but cannot give financial support for the endeavor, student groups are often the greatest source to ensure that the venue is filled for the event. Student groups are able to create amazing events with and without guidance from university officials, and many of those activities can meet the goals of MSS as well as increase cultural awareness on campus. Therefore, MSS should engage students and student organizations in the process frequently. This will benefit the office and increase its currency to a broader campus collective.

Another vehicle that MSS can use to build strong collaborations is to look to colleagues at other institutions in the local area. Often, speakers and performers block-book an event and offer reduced fees if they are able to come to an area and do multiple events. Institutional partnerships with other institutions can benefit from sharing facility space. These collaborations build a foundation for successful cultural programming.

As MSS begins to build new partnerships, professionals in these offices should keep in mind that other offices might reject their requests for collaboration, particularly if the rationale for collaboration is not clearly communicated. Therefore, MSS staff should be clear about why they are approaching another unit, organization, or department for involvement. There should be a logical impetus to motivate another group's involvement. A female Asian American author who writes about environmental issues could provide a partnership opportunity not only with Asian American and environmental student organizations, but also with academic units, such as Asian American or ethnic studies, women and gender studies, environmental studies, and other health- and science-related departments. See Kodama and Takesue (Chapter 15) for a more expansive discussion on building collaborative partnerships between MSS and academic affairs units.

MSS offices should also make sure that their departmental mission statements, goals, and objectives are clear and focused so that when outreach is being made to these external constituencies they can grasp what MSS is and how MSS fits into the overall strategic plan of the university. MSS units are sometimes viewed as silos within the university structure, and this often causes MSS units to be marginalized and not valued partners. When seeking new partnerships, the potential collaborator will need a cogent understanding of MSS's mission and goals as well as who its work impacts.

CONCLUSION

It is important for MSS units to build and create traditions with their students and the campus community, especially given the changing student demographic on U.S. campuses and the fact that many students have varied cultural expectations and experiences. To that end, partnerships and collaborations across institutions break down barriers of misunderstanding and diminish cultural stereotypes, especially when disparate entities partner on new programs. Creating opportunities for student engagement in areas that previously have not been viewed as viable is an exciting and exacting undertaking. There should also be a willingness on the part of professionals in MSS to let go of their own reluctance to reach out to new entities and seek collaborations that benefit all students, not just students of color. Although race is a major issue that higher education continues to address, MSS must also take the lead in broadening the conversation to include issues of gender, sexual orientation, disability, and religion, as discussed by the authors in section two of this volume.

REFERENCES

Ambler, D. A. (1993). Developing internal management struggles. In M. J. Barr & Associates (Eds.), *The handbook of student affairs administration* (pp. 107–120). San Francisco, CA: Jossey-Bass.

Appleton, J. R., Briggs, C. M., & Rhatigan, J. J. (1978). *Pieces of eight: The rites, roles, and styles of the dean by eight who have been there.* Portland, OR: National Association of Student Personnel Administrators Institute of Research and Development.

Hale, F. W., Jr. (Ed.). (2004). *What makes racial diversity work in higher education.* Sterling, VA: Stylus.

Jones, L. (2004). The development of a multicultural student services office and retention strategy for minority students. In F. W. Hale Jr. (Ed.), *What makes racial diversity work in higher education* (pp. 124–145). Sterling, VA: Stylus.

Kuh, G. D., Schuh, J. H., Whitt, E. J., & Associates. (1991). *Involving colleges: Successful approaches to fostering student learning and development outside the classroom.* San Francisco, CA: Jossey-Bass.

Rudolph, F. (1990). *The American college and university: A history.* Athens: University of Georgia Press.

Stewart, M. A. (2004). Effective minority programs at the Ohio State University. In F. W. Hale Jr. (Ed.), *What makes racial diversity work in higher education* (pp. 146–163). Sterling, VA: Stylus.

Turner, M. R. (2004). The office of African-American affairs. In F. W. Hale Jr. (Ed.), *What makes racial diversity work in higher education* (pp. 112–123). Sterling, VA: Stylus.

15

Developing Collaborations With Academic Affairs

Corinne Maekawa Kodama
Kisa J. Takesue

Simon, an academic advisor in the College of Arts and Sciences, has noticed that several of his students of color who are first-generation students have taken a course for academic credit focusing on study skills. It seems to help them with strengthening their grades, and these students seem happier than other first-generation students of color who are not in the class. He wonders how students get into the class, and he would like to spread the word, but he does not know who to contact. Across campus, Maurice is trying to think of ways to get more faculty involved in programs offered by multicultural student services. He is new to campus, unsure of how to identify allies and supporters, and has been warned of likely resistance.

FOR MORE THAN TWO DECADES, higher education researchers have been promoting the importance of collaboration between student affairs and academic affairs (Kellogg, 1999). The *Student Learning Imperative* (American College Personnel Association, 1994) emphasized the need for student affairs to forge partnerships with faculty, with the desired outcome of a "seamless learning" experience in which intellectual and social development occur both in and out of the classroom. *Powerful Partnerships,* a joint report by three major professional organizations of higher education, made the case that student learning can be improved only when both academic affairs and student affairs share the responsibility for educational enhancement (American Association of Higher Education, American College Personnel Association, & National Association of Student Personnel Administrators, 1998). More recently, *Learning Reconsidered* (Keeling, 2004) argued for the importance of integrated learning from all segments of campus to provide a holistic learning process and experience. Additionally, the DEEP (Documenting Effective Educational Practices) research team found multiple examples in which collaboration across divisional lines improved the quality of life for students (Kinzie & Kuh, 2004). Although multicultural student services (MSS) units might be located in student affairs, academic affairs, or another university division, much of the literature on student affairs–academic affairs collaborations is relevant to multicultural student service collaborations. This chapter focuses on collaborations between MSS and academic affairs.

In addition to promoting integrated learning, collaboration between MSS and academic affairs increases the likelihood that diversity efforts are integrated into all areas of the institution (Shuford & Palmer, 2004). The Association of American Colleges and Universities and the American Council on Education have produced research that explores and affirms the ways in which campus diversity enhances the educational experience, not just for individual students, but the greater campus community (Milem & Umbach, 2008). In addition to the educational benefits, practical considerations such as resource sharing are particularly relevant with shrinking higher education budgets. However, as Simon and Maurice illustrate in the opening vignette, collaboration might be intuitive but is not without effort.

In a climate of increased expectations and calls for collaboration, MSS professionals should first clarify the purpose, feasibility, and desired outcome of such alliances. Magolda (2005) argued that we should not collaborate merely for the sake of collaboration, but should always ask whether such partnerships truly improve students' quality of life and are good for involved partners. Martin and Samuels (2001) stated that partnership arrangements should not necessarily be centered on permanent or long-term arrangements, but instead should be appropriate to the moment and continually evaluated for measurable returns. Thus, an important part of collaboration is assessing what is possible and meaningful for a particular campus at a particular time.

BENEFITS OF COLLABORATION

One of the most important steps toward successful collaboration with academic affairs is for MSS staff to be able to clearly understand and articulate what they can offer academic affairs. Historically, MSS has played an integral role in the development of courses and academic studies, particularly in the field of ethnic studies (Shuford & Palmer, 2004). Staff members with a background in student affairs are uniquely positioned to impact change in students regarding diversity issues (Hurtado, Milem, Clayton-Pedersen, & Allen, 1999). Staff with student development backgrounds can be a resource for faculty in terms of theoretical understandings of identity, racial dynamics, and student development and growth as well as applied skills such as organizational dynamics, group facilitation, and individual counseling (Alvarez & Liu, 2002).

In turn, MSS can be informed by the knowledge and research backgrounds of faculty, particularly those with a background in ethnic or cultural studies, cultural psychology, or other related interests. Faculty in cultural and ethnic studies can provide MSS staff and students with the historical and sociopolitical contexts for multicultural programming or social justice issues (Alvarez & Liu, 2002).

Additionally, partnerships with academic affairs might more closely align MSS with institutional power. The political reality of most campuses is that organizational power resides in academic affairs. The closer one is to the decision-making center of campus, the greater one's visibility, sustainability, and, ultimately, effectiveness. This alignment might be particularly important in today's anti–affirmative action climate, which has challenged many diversity-based programs. In fact, collaborating with academic affairs might be part of a larger "survival strategy" to maintain multicultural initiatives and programs if student affairs units are being challenged in a way that academic affairs units are not.

CHALLENGES TO COLLABORATION

There are real cultural differences between student affairs and academic affairs that are important to understand before embarking on collaboration. Faculty focus on the generation and dissemination of knowledge, autonomy rooted in academic freedom, and collegiality, whereas student affairs professionals focus on addressing students' multiple needs, respecting differences, developing citizen-leaders, and increasing students' self-awareness and self-direction (Magolda, 2005). Views on diversity might vary by academic discipline (Milem & Umbach, 2008) and thus affect the selection of collaborative partners.

It is also important to recognize that faculty members have competing demands on their time, and some activities are more valued in the tenure and promotion review process than others. Research productivity and quality are generally the most important criteria, with service work (like collaborating with MSS) often considered second-tier. In the case of junior faculty, requests for participation in nonacademic work might be burdensome (or even a distraction) in the process of obtaining tenure. Thus, one should be aware of how an additional responsibility might impact a faculty member and make sure to include collaborators across all ranks of the faculty.

Another obstacle to collaboration is the differential in power and prestige on a particular campus that can make the ideal of egalitarian exchange unrealistic (Cook & Lewis, 2007; Magolda, 2005). Sometimes there is an assumption that academic affairs, and faculty in particular, will take the lead in partnerships and student affairs professionals will provide supplemental assistance. Magolda (2005) observed partnerships in which student affairs staff took sole responsibility for logistical details and seemed to willingly take a deferential role toward the faculty. In such instances, practitioners are not engaged as active educators but merely planners to do the busy work. The key is to find ways to structure collaboration to use all the abilities and strengths of different partners across the university (Magolda, 2005).

ASSESSING THE CLIMATE FOR COLLABORATION

Practitioners in MSS should define levels and means of collaboration that are feasible and meaningful to them, their work, and their campus rather than emulate models that are unrealistic for their circumstances. Campuses vary tremendously, and what works in one setting might not be appropriate for another. Therefore, understanding the campus climate is crucial to defining goals and understanding the ultimate success of diversity outcomes

(Milem, Chang, & antonio, 2005). Hurtado and others (1999) set forth a comprehensive framework identifying aspects of climate that are important to examine before embarking on campus-wide diversity initiatives. A few of these factors are particularly relevant in preparing for MSS–academic affairs collaborations (and a self-assessment checklist is provided at the end of this chapter).

Support for Diversity

Perhaps the most significant element to assess is the campus climate for diversity initiatives. This assessment should include consideration of the historical legacy of the institution, its mission statement, compositional diversity (students, staff, and faculty), and the existence of diversity initiatives (Milem et al., 2005). Taken together, these elements can serve as a measure of how committed and consistent the institution is on diversity issues and how future multicultural collaborations might proceed.

Institutional Type

The type of institution also has an impact on the campus culture related to collaboration: public or private; residential or commuter; research university, liberal arts college, or community college. For example, research universities have more rigid reporting lines and structures as well as "silos" that can make collaboration difficult. Liberal arts and residential campuses might have more opportunities for collaborative programs outside the classroom, whereas work at commuter institutions might be most effective if focused inside the classroom. The size of the institution also matters; it might be easier to develop collegial and collaborative relationships with faculty on a smaller campus, because there are fewer people wearing more "hats" (Degen & Sheldahl, 2007). This dynamic contrasts with working on a larger campus, where responsibilities might be divided among separate units that might not interact with each other much, if at all.

Organizational Structure

Much of the work in multicultural student services is closely aligned with the values of student affairs. However, MSS units might be housed in academic affairs or another area of the university, each reporting line having implications for campus impact and access to decision making. MSS units located in academic affairs might find it easier to collaborate with other academic units, given shared reporting structures and personal relationships. Some campuses might even have more than one department responsible for multicultural student services, perhaps one in student affairs and one in academic affairs. This type of arrangement might pose either advantages or obstacles to collaboration, depending on the clarity of mission, division of responsibilities, and relationships among the personnel across the units.

Related to the organizational structure is understanding the campus norm for collaboration. On some campuses collaboration between academic and student affairs is common, whereas on others, it is rare. The level of respect and appreciation between these different spheres is crucial in laying the groundwork for a realistic collaboration (Kinzie & Kuh, 2004). If university divisions operate completely separate from each other and rarely assemble for discussions, the likelihood of a successful collaboration will be slim.

Mission and Personnel

The mission of an MSS unit should guide the direction of any future collaboration. Does the mission focus on academic support, programming, or cultural awareness? How does this fit with the overall mission of the institution? Just as the mission specifies the direction of a unit's programs and services, it should also guide the types of collaborations that may develop with academic affairs.

The educational and professional training of MSS staff can have an impact on how staff might be perceived by faculty and academic administrators. An MSS director with a doctorate in a traditional academic field might have more credibility among faculty than someone with a student affairs degree or without a doctorate. An ethnic studies degree might be valued on a campus with cultural and ethnic studies departments but be less credible at an institution with more mainstream arts and sciences faculty. Previous teaching experience might give staff inroads into teaching a course or having input into curricular issues. Staff with research backgrounds can generate or interpret data, providing credibility for forging partnerships with academic faculty and administrators. It is important not only to consider the academic background of new hires if academic partnerships are desired, but also to use the strengths that existing staff might bring to these collaborations.

PRACTICAL IDEAS FOR COLLABORATION

Although there is existing literature on student and academic affairs collaborations focusing on systemic and organizational change, it can be challenging to find concrete examples for partnerships, particularly between MSS and academic affairs. Therefore, the following section includes practical suggestions for MSS/academic affairs collaborations.

Research

On many campuses, research is a priority, because it generates funding dollars, results in publications, and increases the institution's academic prestige. Moreover, hard data speak to academic administrators and faculty in a way that nothing else can, particularly at a research university. Data can be used to educate the campus about students and multicultural issues, gain legitimacy for multicultural initiatives, and lay the groundwork for establishing collaborations with academic affairs.

Many national grants or agencies require a section about diversity in grant proposals as a condition of funding, which is a prime opportunity for multicultural programs to partner with academic units. These partnerships could be as simple as providing student data to a principal investigator or could be more collaborative in terms of generating ideas for programs that would meet the conditions of the grant and increase the likelihood of funding.

Multicultural student services can also generate research that might require expertise from academic colleagues. For example, an MSS professional might benefit from input and assistance from faculty on a research project. Not only could this partnership raise awareness and visibility, but it also might give an MSS unit access to additional resources (e.g., research databases, statistical programs) and assistance in data analysis.

Inside the Classroom

The most obvious area for academic affairs collaborations is within the classroom. Research has demonstrated the positive impact of diversity courses or related content on students' openness to diverse ideas (Milem et al., 2005; Pascarella & Terenzini, 2005). Reaching students in the classroom is particularly important for campuses with a large number of commuter or nontraditional-age students who are not as engaged outside their classes

(Kuh, Gonyea, & Palmer, 2001). This is highlighted by National Survey of Student Engagement data, which showed that commuters were less likely to participate in enriching educational experiences (a category that included climate for diversity) and campus educational resources (Kuh et al., 2001). There are also students who never set foot in an MSS office, whether owing to personal prejudices, identity issues, or merely a lack of time, so an MSS presence in a classroom might be their first and perhaps only exposure to MSS and its programs and services.

Teaching is the most direct and obvious way to provide visibility and impact for an MSS office, although university policies differ on nonfaculty teaching appointments. Some institutions require that nonfaculty be affiliated with an academic department through an adjunct or temporary position. Other campuses might have first-year orientation, career exploration, or other developmental courses that allow nonfaculty to teach with some flexibility in the curriculum.

Teaching a course is not the only way to make an impact; a single lecture can be a useful collaboration. Depending on staff members' academic background and expertise, guest lecturing might be possible, in areas from ethnic studies to education, political science to sociology. In addition to direct instruction, visiting classes to promote an upcoming program can be an effective avenue for publicity, particularly if the curriculum is relevant to the program's goals. For example, writing courses might be an effective place to publicize a visit by an author, communications courses for a media presentation, honors courses to recruit peer mentors, and so forth. Such presentations can also be effective ways to provide general information about services to a captive audience. If faculty members are not willing to devote class time for a personal visit, often they will distribute an announcement, a more direct way of reaching students than other forms of publicity.

Service-Learning

Service-learning is another area perfect for collaboration between MSS and academic affairs, because service-learning activities combine out-of-class experiences with an intentional focus on academic learning outcomes (O'Grady, 2000). Service-learning can bolster some of the goals of an MSS unit and has increased in popularity and funding in recent years. MSS staff with community connections might help faculty find appropriate agencies or locations for projects as well as provide expertise in individual and group processing of service-learning experiences (Alvarez & Liu, 2002). Faculty can provide the historical context and academic analysis for the issues and communities that are being served. However, multicultural-oriented service-learning initiatives must be carefully considered on both sides, given the potential for perpetuating stereotypes and a colonialist mentality (O'Grady, 2000). Proper and thorough processing of service-learning experiences at community sites is the best way to prevent privileged students from leaving the service experience with previously held stereotypes more deeply embedded and using the service experience only as a missionary outlet without reflecting on what the agency and its clients have to teach them.

Academic Contests

Working collaboratively with an academic department on an academic competition can be implemented as a one-time activity or on an ongoing basis. Essay contests on a multicultural topic can encourage writers to think about new issues and provide thoughtful analysis for others to read. Art contests can produce designs for logos, posters, or other publications and give visibility to student work for an artistic portfolio. Encouragement, including extra credit, from faculty and academic departments can increase student submissions, and awards might be more meaningful if faculty members serve as judges. These types of collaborations can bring valued attention to students' talents, particularly if their work is published in a newsletter, website, or other public venue. This visibility might be particularly important for students with multicultural interests who have not otherwise found recognition or an appropriate outlet to express their talents.

Multicultural Speakers and Programs

Collaborating with academic affairs on multicultural speakers or performers can be an effective and fairly easy partnership. MSS staff can ask faculty colleagues for recommendations of a colleague with relevant multicultural research interests, an author of a book used in existing courses, or a notable figure in popular culture. Often academic departments have limited funds for this type of event, given the budgetary priority placed on direct instruction. Thus, cosponsorships with MSS might be of great benefit to an academic department by providing an enrichment opportunity for their students and faculty, while concurrently introducing a new audience to MSS.

Whether or not an academic unit is an official cosponsor, it might still be useful to include faculty in program planning to lay the groundwork for future, more meaningful collaborations. Faculty might be asked to give students extra credit for attending an activity. Inviting faculty and administrators to an invitation-only gathering to meet guest speakers and discuss their work provides an opportunity for them that also brings exposure to multicultural student services.

Mentoring Programs and Student Organizations

Establishing a mentoring program between students and faculty allows faculty to learn more about MSS and how it serves and impacts students. Mentoring programs provide an opportunity for faculty to connect with other student-centered faculty and staff and learn about student development issues from a student services perspective. Participation in a mentoring program might be also be an opportunity for junior faculty in underrepresented groups to connect with senior colleagues outside their departments, resulting in a positive impact on faculty retention.

MSS staff often serve as advisors to student organizations, and faculty might also be willing if there is a relevant connection. This can help share the advising load and bring in new advocates at the same time. It is also a great way to increase student–faculty contact outside the classroom, which has been shown to be particularly important for students of color (Pascarella & Terenzini, 2005). Advising an organization provides faculty with valuable insight into students' cocurricular lives as well as campus climate issues. A faculty member who has firsthand knowledge of a student organization's difficulty with funding or recruiting members might be more likely to serve as an advocate around these issues in other settings. Other ways to include faculty with multicultural organizations are to invite them to speak at an organization's meeting or have them as a special guest at an event.

Libraries

College and university libraries have found interesting ways to collaborate with student affairs (and specifically with MSS) through peer education, first-year programs, service-learning, mentoring programs, and academic skills workshops (Albin et al., 2005; Walter, 2005). MSS staff can also work with libraries to suggest books, films, or other multicultural resources and perhaps share the cost of these purchases. MSS offices that house their own small libraries can promote their holdings with faculty and academic departments as well as involve them in new acquisitions.

Committees

Having a faculty member serve on a search committee for a staff opening in MSS can increase awareness about a department, its mission and goals, and what qualifications are needed for a professional staff member. This experience gives the faculty member or academic administrator a stake in the future of the MSS office from a personal and professional standpoint; it also cultivates another advocate. Other related collaborations could include serving on a scholarship committee or an advisory board.

Additionally, including faculty or academic administrators in an advisory capacity can bring institutional credibility to an MSS office, particularly if it is located in student affairs. Faculty can offer a different perspective into the issues that face MSS and serve as a conduit for making connections with academic administrators. Conversely, it can be useful for MSS staff to serve on academic affairs committees such as summer programs, orientation, academic advising, and admissions and recruitment.

Consultations and In-Service Trainings

Staff in MSS can also serve as resources for faculty through consultation or workshops on topics such as basic information about students served by the office, cultural competency training, or differences in teaching/learning styles. MSS staff who have an understanding of racial identity and student development theories can offer faculty their expertise in facilitating the often emotional and confusing feelings that arise in classroom discussions around race and ethnicity (Alvarez & Liu, 2002). MSS staff can also help faculty design activities that are developmentally appropriate to the needs of students and perhaps bring practical or experiential applications to an academic course (Alvarez & Liu, 2002).

CONCLUSION

To make a campus-wide impact on diversity issues, it is crucial that MSS professionals find ways to collaborate with academic affairs. Although these collaborations might take a different form at each institution, effective diversity work needs to be integrated throughout the campus (Hurtado et al., 1999; Milem et al., 2005; Pope, Reynolds, & Mueller, 2004). From a practical perspective, collaborations with academic affairs often gives MSS more credibility within the academy, a different perspective on effecting change on campus, a wider net of advocates and allies, and access to students whom an MSS unit might not otherwise encounter.

Developing these collaborations need not be intimidating or complicated; the key is to conduct a careful assessment of external and internal factors that might affect the future success of collaborations. It is important to define what "meaningful" collaboration looks like and to acknowledge that each campus community has unique challenges and opportunities that will inform decision making. Diversity work across our institutions should continue to be explored with integrated and coordinated efforts to enhance learning (Hurtado et al., 1999). We cannot afford to compartmentalize multicultural work in discrete university divisions, when working together will bring many opportunities to improve the climate for diversity. The value of integrating multicultural student services with academic affairs cannot be underestimated when there is so much work to be done.

APPENDIX
Self-Assessment Checklist:
Issues to Examine Before Embarking
on Academic Affairs Partnerships

The following list of considerations is not exhaustive, but is meant to give practitioners a start in thinking about the many aspects that can impact collaborations.

Institutional Structure

- ◆ Does MSS report to academic affairs, student affairs, or another area?
- ◆ How stratified is your institution (and specifically your reporting line)?
- ◆ How much influence/input does MSS staff have with existing decision makers?
- ◆ Are there examples where academic and student affairs units work together already (committees, programs, course offerings)?
- ◆ Is there more than one MSS-type office, and if so, what is the relationship between these units?

Campus Climate for Diversity

- ◆ What is the racial/ethnic composition of your student body, staff, and faculty? What is the structural diversity of the institution for other social groups (gender, sexual orientation, gender identity, ability, age)?
- ◆ Does the curriculum include a "diversity" course requirement(s)?
- ◆ Is there a dean, vice president, or senior administrator charged with a diversity focus?
- ◆ Are there existing academic departments with a multicultural focus (e.g., ethnic studies, LGBT studies)?
- ◆ What kinds of issues, successes, and failures has your institution had with multicultural initiatives?

Mission

- ◆ What is the mission of the MSS office?
  - Retention, cultural awareness, recruitment, education, other?

- Student, staff, or faculty focused? All groups?
- Cross-cultural or targeted to specific groups (e.g., ethnicity-specific, LGBT)

◆ Does MSS serve the campus as a whole or mostly within a college/department?

◆ What is the history of MSS within the institution (grassroots establishment or top-down; grew out of proactive efforts or a reaction to a situation)?

◆ What is the overall mission of the institution? How does multiculturalism fit into that?

Composition of Multicultural Student Services Staff

◆ What are the educational backgrounds of MSS staff members?

◆ Do any MSS staff members have research or college teaching experience?

◆ What are the educational backgrounds (academic or professional) of key academic administrators and decision makers on campus?

◆ What experiences or personal relationships do the MSS staff members have with people in academic affairs (including committee work, departmental meetings, etc.)?

Classroom Collaborations

◆ Are there service-learning courses?

◆ Does your campus have a higher education/student affairs preparation program?

◆ Can nonfaculty teach courses (i.e., orientation courses, seminars)?

◆ Is there the opportunity for team-teaching between faculty and administrative staff?

REFERENCES

Albin, T., Currie, L., Hensley, R. B., Hinchliffe, L. J., Lindsay, B., Walter, S., & Watts, M. M. (2005, April). *Meeting the student learning imperative: Building powerful partnerships between academic libraries and student services.* Presented at the National Meeting of the Association of College and Research Libraries, Minneapolis, MN.

Alvarez, A. N., & Liu, W. M. (2002). Student affairs and Asian American studies: An integrative perspective. In M. K. McEwen, C. M. Kodama, A. N. Alvarez, S. Lee, & C. T. H. Liang (Eds.), *Working with Asian American college students* (pp. 73–80). New Directions for Student Services, no. 97. San Francisco, CA: Jossey-Bass.

American Association for Higher Education, American College Personnel Association, & National Association of Student Personnel Administrators (1998). *Powerful partnerships: A shared responsibility for learning.* Washington, DC: Authors.

American College Personnel Association. (1994). *The student learning imperative: Implications for student affairs.* Washington, DC: Author.

Cook, J. H., & Lewis, C. A. (Eds.) (2007). *Student and academic affairs collaboration: The divine comity.* Washington, DC: National Association of Student Personnel Administrators.

Degen, G., & Sheldahl, E. (2007). *The many hats of teaching in small colleges: The seamless web of student and academic affairs.* New Directions for Student Services, no 117. San Francisco, CA: Jossey-Bass.

Hurtado, S., Milem, J., Clayton-Pedersen, A., & Allen, W. (1999). Enacting diverse learning environments: Improving the climate for racial/ethnic diversity in higher education. *ASHE-ERIC Higher Education Report, 26*(8).

Keeling, R. P. (Ed.) (2004). *Learning reconsidered: A campus-wide focus on the student experience.* Washington, DC: National Association of Student Personnel Administrators and the American College Personnel Association.

Kellogg, K. (1999). *Collaboration: Student affairs and academic affairs working together to promote student learning.* Retrieved from ERIC database. (ED432940)

Kinzie, J., & Kuh, G. D. (2004). Going DEEP: Learning from campuses that share responsibility for student success. *About Campus, 9*(5), 2–8.

Kuh, G. D., Gonyea, R. M., & Palmer, M. (2001). The disengaged commuter student: Fact or fiction? *Commuter Perspectives, 27*(1), 2–5. Retrieved December 10, 2008, from http://nsse.iub.edu/pdf/commuter.pdf

Magolda, P. M. (2005). Proceed with caution: Uncommon wisdom about academic and student affairs partnerships. *About Campus, 9*(6), 16–21.

Martin, J., & Samuels, J. E. (2001). Lessons learned: Eight best practices for new partnerships. In A. Kezar, D. J. Hirsch, & C. Burack (Eds.), *Understanding the role of academic and student affairs collaboration in creating a successful learning environment* (pp. 89–100). New Directions for Higher Education, no. 116. San Francisco, CA: Jossey-Bass.

Milem, J. F., Chang, M. J., & antonio, a. l. (2005). *Making diversity work on campus: A research based perspective.* Washington, DC: Association of American Colleges and Universities.

Milem, J. F., & Umbach, P. D. (2008). Understanding the difference diversity makes: Faculty beliefs, attitudes, and behaviors. In S. R. Harper (Ed.), *Creating inclusive campus environments for cross-cultural learning and student engagement* (pp. 155–172). Washington, DC: National Association of Student Personnel Administrators.

O'Grady, C. (2000). Integrating service learning and multicultural education: An overview. In C. R. O'Grady (Ed.), *Integrating service learning and multicultural education in colleges and universities* (pp. 1–19). Mahwah, NJ: Lawrence Erlbaum Associates.

Pascarella, E. T., & Terenzini, P. (2005). *How college affects students: A third decade of research* (Vol. 2). San Francisco, CA: Jossey-Bass.

Pope, R. L., Reynolds, A. L., & Mueller, J. A. (2004). *Multicultural competence in student affairs.* San Francisco, CA: Jossey-Bass.

Shuford, B. C., & Palmer, C. J. (2004). Multicultural affairs. In J. D. MacKinnon & Associates, *Rentz's student affairs practice in higher education* (3rd ed., pp. 218–238). Springfield, IL: Charles C Thomas.

Walter, S. (2005). Moving beyond collections: Academic library outreach to multicultural student centers. *Reference Services Review, 33*(4). Retrieved December 10, 2008, from http://hdl.handle.net/1808/410

16

Working With the Majority

Jamie Washington

Claire and Jennifer, two White undergraduate students, would like to help with the multicultural student services office's events but are concerned that their presence would not be welcomed because they only see students of color at these events. On another campus, John, a second-year master's student in a student affairs preparation program, wonders if he could ever be competitive in a job search to be director of a multicultural student services office as a White man. He has a passion for these issues and strong skills in building trust and rapport across lines of difference but has never heard of a White person, let alone a White man, leading such an office on a college campus. Elsewhere, Paolo, an MSS director, feels his multicultural competence is stretched when trying to engage majority students about issues of oppression and diversity. He is unsure how to overcome this to more effectively recruit support for his office's initiatives.

MULTICULTURAL STUDENT SERVICES (MSS) units were first begun in predominantly White institutions (PWI) to serve the needs of Black and Latino students (see Shuford, Chapter 2), and this environment is where most MSS units still exist today (see Stewart & Bridges, Chapter 3). However, today's student populations not only reflect racial privilege, but class, sexual orientation, and religious privilege as well. Because of this, educating majority students has long been a fundamental component of MSS's philosophy and practice. As can be seen in the opening scenario, many issues must be addressed when tackling this topic. This chapter discusses ways in which diversity education and ally development can be practiced effectively under the umbrella of multicultural student services.

MSS offices have served as a resource for underrepresented students on predominantly White campuses for many years, providing academic, cultural, and social support and programs. Although this has been helpful on a small scale, in a climate where race-based programs, services, and offices are under attack, it is necessary to demonstrate that these offices serve to enhance the educational experience for all students. It should be noted that deciding to focus only on racial diversity on predominantly White campuses could lead to most White students (and many students of color, as well) feeling like the office is not for them. This dynamic continues to leave many of our students underprepared to engage effectively across difference and privilege. When engaging diversity with majority populations, it is important for them to see themselves as having an experience that matters. This is often better accomplished if they can connect to some part of their identities where they might also be underrepresented (e.g., sexual orientation, social class, religious identity).

For MSS to meet the needs of not only historically underrepresented students, but majority students as well, there are four major things to consider:

1. There must be clear direction and support from institutional leadership.
2. MSS will need to prepare its historically served students, faculty, and staff for the energy, time, and commitment needed for engaging with majority students.
3. MSS practitioners will need to focus on their own identities as members of multiple majority groups and how those identities intersect and impact their work.
4. MSS practitioners and those who have budgetary responsibility for the area will need to consider the implications of time, energy, and image of those who are now charged with creating programs and services that also address the learning needs for majority group members.

LEADERSHIP SUPPORT

Although MSS professionals might feel that their job is about the education of the entire student body, this philosophy might not be shared by their superiors. A vice president, provost, or president must clearly see that the mission of the office is broader than serving underrepresented students. This is important because it affects how resources are allocated and what programs and initiatives are supported. For example, a leadership and diversity conference might be seen as a project for the student life office, and, therefore, the MSS director's request to sponsor such an event might not be supported. However, if the MSS office is to serve all students, entering through the area of leadership might be a useful avenue.

In addition to senior administrative leadership being clear that programs and staffing patterns might need to be different, they must also be willing to have an honest conversation about the mission of the office. The title "multicultural" is often used to encompass all diversity issues, but the programs and services that are rewarded and given the most attention on many campuses are those that focus on race and ethnicity. Campus leadership must be clear in its mission for the MSS office. If the focus of the office is to serve racial and ethnic minorities and educate the rest of the campus on these issues, that needs to be clearly stated and the rationale shared by top leaders. However, if the office is charged with serving and meeting the needs of all underrepresented populations, that needs to be made clear as well. Senior leaders on a campus cannot abdicate responsibility for helping to shape the direction of the office. The mission and focus of the office must be in line with the direction of the institution.

MSS OFFICE CULTURAL ENVIRONMENTS

MSS offices have historically been staffed with students and professionals from underrepresented racial and ethnic populations. For these students and staff, the office becomes a safe haven, a place where they can be themselves. As a result, the office reflects the culture of those who are in it most. The music, art, norms about time, foods, celebrations, and humor represent the cultural traditions and beliefs of the group(s) that "live" in the space. This type of space is very important for racial minority students on predominantly

White campuses. This is often the only place on campus that does not feel like "their" space (i.e., belonging to and representing White people; Feagin, Vera, & Imani, 1996). Therefore, creating a space that is inviting to White students while maintaining the feeling of safety for racial minority students will take intentional energy. Additionally, if the office is meant to serve all underrepresented groups, creating the space for multiple underrepresented and privileged groups to feel comfortable can be very challenging.

Most people working in MSS offices chose the area because of their passion and commitment to serving underrepresented college students. Although they certainly welcome all students to participate in programs, the audiences they target in marketing these efforts are not usually majority students. If MSS practitioners are to reach majority students more effectively, attention will need to be given to staff and students as they move from an office culture that felt comfortable and familiar to most, to a culture in which everyone could initially be "walking on egg shells" in their attempts to not do or say the "wrong" thing.

This move requires cultivating an environment of trust and commitment. Individuals might often "work and/or school" their diversity engagements, meaning that they attend classes or work with people who are different than they are, but then often go home to communities that are largely monocultural. Thus, many people are not comfortable engaging across difference on a regular basis beyond superficial acquaintanceships. Yet, during the college experience, especially on residential campuses, students have the opportunity to work, school, and *home* their diversity engagements, requiring the multicultural awareness, knowledge, and skills to develop trusting, empathic, and caring relationships (Pope, Reynolds, & Mueller, 2004). Even on most commuter campuses, like community colleges, where the "path of least resistance" (Johnson, 2006) to superficially engage diversity runs deep, promoting the education and skill development to be willing to risk meaningful relationships across diversity is essential. Given this, team building, community norms, and developing a common language around issues of difference (Reason, Scales, & Roosa Milar, 2005) are necessary to create healthy multicultural learning environments for all students.

MSS STAFF IDENTITY AND COMPOSITION

As stated earlier, most staff members in MSS offices belong to underrepresented racial and ethnic groups. This has been a historic pattern that has served to help these student populations connect to the campus and feel that there are staff and faculty who might understand and be able to relate to their experiences. As offices become more focused on serving a broader constituency (both educating majority students and including more underrepresented groups in their missions), staff members must be more conscious of their own identities. Specifically, an MSS office that is staffed by racial/ethnic minorities must consider how their racial identities impact the way in which they engage not only their own groups, but now the majority group as well. Staff must consider in what parts of their identity they are privileged and what that means for engaging others at the intersections of identity, privilege, and oppression. This might best be illustrated in a story:

> A student from the predominantly White LGBT student organization comes to the MSS office requesting that information about the LGBT student organization be placed in the packets for the upcoming visitation weekend held for prospective students of color. When the director, a Black, heterosexual man, gets the request, he responds, "None of the students we've invited have requested this information and therefore I don't think it's necessary to go in the packets." When asked whether prospective students have requested any of the information in the packet, the director becomes defensive and states, "We are recruiting minority students, not gays."

This short story illustrates one of the tensions that can exist if staff members are not conscious of their multiple identities and areas of privilege and how those might impact their work. Engaging identity is an important part of the college experience. Most students engage this process both in and out of the classroom during the undergraduate years. However, unless they are put in a position or role that requires them to learn not only about the parts of their identities where they are underrepresented but the places where they are in the majority or dominant group, they can move about their entire college experience unaware that they, too, have privilege and power and, as a result, often are operating unconsciously out of that reality. The same blind spots might exist for professional staff working in MSS.

Acknowledging this also requires that we challenge the unspoken norm that the staff in MSS must be members of racial and ethnic minority groups to be most effective. Institutions must address the underlying assumptions in this practice and take responsibility for how it continues to "ghettoize" MSS offices. If the primary or only place on PWIs where people of color are located is in multicultural student services, then the message that the community often gets is that only "race" stuff happens there and that diversity and inclusion is only about people of color. All students and staff must learn to trust and engage across many types of differences. Students of color need White role models with whom they feel comfortable engaging issues of race. Likewise, White students need to see that it is acceptable to want to learn and engage across difference. When they see a program coordinator or an assistant director and maybe someday a director of an MSS office who looks like them, it begins to invite them into the dialogue in a different way. White students can begin to see why it would be important for them to be leaders in creating inclusive and welcoming communities and the role that representing the dominant culture can play in the conversation about celebrating differences and dismantling systems of power and privilege. This is also true for other dominant group members.

PREPARING STUDENTS FOR
A GLOBAL SOCIETY

In nearly every mission or campus vision statement or strategic plan, there is language that reflects a desire or commitment to prepare students for a global society. Although these statements exist on most campuses, the means to accomplish this goal is often left unclear. Many campus leaders operate under the notion that all we need to do is increase the numbers of underrepresented students. Although increased numbers might contribute positively to the overall campus climate by creating more opportunities for engagement, changing structural demographics does not ensure that students will have an experience that prepares them to engage not only what it means to be who they are, but also what it means to be who they are in relationship with the rest of the world (Hurtado, Milem, Clayton-Pedersen, & Allen, 1998).

MSS offices are in the best position to partner with faculty, community, and service-learning offices, as well as internships and study abroad programs, to create intentional opportunities for students not only to be in a different space and exposed to difference, but also to actively engage others within and across differences. These partnerships create a climate in which the MSS office can be an integral part of the learning for all students and not just those who the office has been thought to traditionally serve.

THE MSS CONTEXT

All MSS professionals must consider the context in which they operate as they attempt to broaden the office's mission and focus (see Petitt & McIntosh, Chapter 13). This context includes but is not limited to issues of origin, mission, and campus climate for MSS. Many of these questions were addressed by Stewart and Bridges (Chapter 3) in their demographic profile of MSS offices. With those data in mind, one should consider the following questions about the MSS office on a specific campus:

1. How was the office started? Was it started as a result of student unrest? Was there an outcry from the faculty? Was the office started based on an accreditation agency recommendation?
2. What does the office's mission statement include? Who is the office supposed to be serving, and who is it actually serving? How are these efforts being assessed? What does the campus leadership (e.g., senior student affairs officer, president) expect of the office?
3. How do "majority and minority" students see and experience the office? How do other faculty, staff, community members, and alumni see the office and its mission?

It is important to consider these questions as the office's focus is shifted to be more inclusive of serving and educating majority students. The implications for these responses are many and for this reason a deliberate and well-thought-out strategy must be considered.

Once there is a clear understanding of the context of MSS at a given campus, the staff can begin moving forward with a plan to meet the expanded mission; however, I want to offer three guiding questions to help this movement be successful. These are:

1. What are the costs and benefits of creating intentional programs to meet the learning needs of majority students?
2. What developmental models exist for race, gender, sexual orientation, and other social group identities that address majority identity development in these areas?
3. What are the dynamics and patterns of behavior that exist as majority and "minority" groups come together?

MSS offices also must be prepared to respond to the question of why their programs are being redesigned to include more majority students. Leaders must be able to talk about the benefits of creating opportunities for more intentional engagement between majority and underrepresented students. At the same time, there might also be a cost to this effort. The students of color might no longer see the MSS office or staff as being there for them, because they might seem to be giving more attention to majority engagement and learning than to meeting the support and empowerment needs of underrepresented students. The second question suggests that MSS professionals will have to shore up their learning about majority identity development. Much of the literature and training for professionals working in MSS offices has focused on the developmental needs and patterns of underrepresented students. As the mission and focus broadens, MSS staff will need to understand that developing racial, gender, and sexual orientation identity as a racial majority student is just as important a process as it is for the underrepresented student in any of the aforementioned groups.

The third question suggests that MSS professionals must pay more attention to the dynamics and patterns of behavior that occur when racial majority and underrepresented students at different developmental levels come together. Most partakers of the services and programs offered by MSS offices have been underrepresented students. Thus, there is an element of familiarity and comfort in most situations where this group is largely racially homogeneous. Because of the history of oppression and the lack of experience that most students bring for engaging across differences, there are likely to be dynamics of conflict and unconscious negative patterns of behavior as these groups spend more time together. MSS professionals will need to be grounded in how to engage these dynamics in ways that feel honoring and respectful to all involved.

CONCLUSION

The engagement of majority students by MSS offices helps to minimize the negative and often misinformed perception that MSS only caters to a small population of the campus community. Other added benefits of enhancing outreach and engagement to majority students include:

1. Potentially creating an audience of unexpected supporters.
2. Creating an opportunity for conversations to happen at a deeper level across difference.
3. Inviting faculty and staff members of majority groups to be more involved than just during orientation and special program months.
4. Illustrating to others that MSS practitioners have all of the transferable skills that their counterparts in student life and residential life have and thus are equally capable of moving to more generalist positions. This is important, given that it is often assumed that those who work in MSS can only work with underrepresented populations.

Our campuses are a microcosm of our society. They are becoming more and more diverse. Students bring diversity in every way imaginable and in some ways we have not begun to address as a profession. If MSS offices are to survive in this ever-changing world, they must stay true to their purpose of creating campus communities where all students can learn and grow to their fullest potential. The only difference now is that MSS practitioners need to work with all students, not just the ones who seek out their offices.

REFERENCES

Feagin, J. R., Vera, H., & Imani, N. (1996). *The agony of education: Black students at White colleges and universities*. New York, NY: Routledge.

Hurtado, S., Milem, J. F., Clayton-Pedersen, A. R., & Allen, W. R. (1998). Enhancing campus climates for racial/ethnic diversity: Educational policy and practice. *The Review of Higher Education, 21*, 279–302.

Johnson, A. G. (2006). *Privilege, power, and difference* (2nd ed.). Boston, MA: McGraw Hill.

Pope, R. L., Reynolds, A. L., & Mueller, J. A. (2004). *Multicultural competence in student affairs*. San Francisco, CA: Jossey-Bass.

Reason, R. D., Scales, T. C., & Roosa Millar, E. A. (2005). Encouraging the development of racial justice allies. In R. D. Reason, E. M. Broido, T. L. Davis, & N. J. Evans (Eds.), *Developing social justice allies* (pp. 55–66). New Directions for Student Services, no. 110. San Francisco, CA: Jossey-Bass.

17

Preparing Diversity Change Leaders

C. Carney Strange
Dafina Lazarus Stewart

Samantha, a White, female, first-year master's student in student affairs, really enjoyed her project in her student development theory course focusing on identity development. She expected she would like the required course on multicultural competence equally; however, her experience in that course left her angry and confused. By contrast, Ruben, a gay Latino man, and Abraham, a Jewish man, who are students in the same program, resented the theory course and found much more relevance in the multicultural competence course. These comments were expressed during a class break in another course, and the instructor overheard it. "Why would these three students have such different experiences in the same courses?" she mused to herself.

THE MANY CHALLENGES outlined in these chapters bespeak a post-secondary world that is both firm and fragile, but greatly enriched by the multicultural mix that characterizes its institutions and the students they serve. Meeting these challenges entails an understanding of not only the history and evolution of multicultural student services (MSS) and their functioning within and across a range of institutional types, but also the dynamics of collaborative political partnering that will continue to shape their success well into the future. In effect, bridge-building demands that those serving multicultural aims must come prepared as "cultural learners"

254

(Tierney, 1993), ready to "step out of [our] . . . spheres of influence and into the spheres of Others," to listen to "Others' stories . . . so that we might radically transform our own understandings," and to internalize "the Others' needs, wants, and desires . . . so well, that we incorporate these views in our own outlook" (p. 145). Thus, cross-cultural awareness implies "that the [cultural] learner sustains relationships across differences and works to create an environment in which these differences are able to be voiced and heard" (Tierney, 1993, p. 145).

Engaging in the kind of partnerships implicated here entails that student affairs professionals submit to the deep learning required for crossing differences that divide them and, from this transformative point, develop the skills necessary for successful collaboration. This is key to answering the faculty member's question in the opening scenario involving Samantha, Ruben, and Abraham's radically different experiences. For many in the field an important opportunity for doing so occurs first in the context of their graduate preparation. The question explored in this chapter is how best to approach this charge: preparing student affairs graduate students and new professionals to enter a diverse world as cultural learners who can serve as effective "diversity change leaders" (as used by Palmer, 1989).

DIVERSITY CHANGE PARADIGMS

Preparing diversity change leaders requires an understanding of basic world-views or paradigms that frame the multicultural experience and that guide our thinking about how best to prepare individuals to lead it. Judith Palmer (1989), in her seminal analysis of the challenges that face organizational change agents with regard to diversity concerns, described three such paradigms that "influence how we interpret facts and experiences, determine our actions, and give us a unique definition of diversity" (p. 15): Paradigm I ("The Golden Rule"), Paradigm II ("Right the Wrongs"), and Paradigm III ("Value the Differences"). According to Palmer, *The Golden Rule* paradigm assumes that everyone is an individual more similar to others than different. Differences that do exist are reflections of individual characteristics that should be appreciated as a matter of personal responsibility and morality. Those who subscribe to this first perspective resist programs focused on issues faced by specific groups and see the solution as "getting everyone to treat each other with respect."

The second paradigm, *Right the Wrongs*, begins with an assumption that specific groups in the larger society have been systematically disadvantaged, requiring remedies of justice and equality. Leaders who endorse this perspective focus on improving how organizations recruit, retain, develop, and reward one or two target groups. Consequently, majority members must learn how the target group feels, walk a mile in their shoes, so to speak, and face up to their negative prejudices. This approach inevitably involves polarities and oppositions that evoke confrontation and tension between groups as separate structures, and programs evolve in response to strong demands. However, this is seen as desirable in the struggle to bridge the gap and "rectify the injustice." When programs show positive progress for one target group, the issues are considered mostly resolved and another target group is then identified (Palmer, 1989).

The third perspective, *Value the Differences*, places importance on all kinds of identifiers (e.g., gender, race/ethnicity, sexual orientation, religion, age, ability, socioeconomic status), recognizing that diversity means consciously and sensitively using the talents of all the types in an organization. Norms must encompass many styles and approaches in pursuit of excellence. Fundamental to this paradigm is an appreciation for the heritage and culture of many different groups, as well as responsiveness to the uniqueness of each individual. Seeking a synergy of differences for better results (Palmer, 1989), this worldview emphasizes self-knowledge—that is, discovering one's own prejudices and strengths, and interpersonal skills, as well as specific learning about the culture or characteristics of many different groups and types.

As Palmer (1989) argued, each paradigm mandates different priorities. Advocates of Paradigm I gravitate to trouble spots within teams or between individuals, providing remedial or anticipatory action to smooth out friction. They prefer methods that do not dwell on a "group's" issues, such as those related to race, gender, or class membership, but instead help individuals work together smoothly. Paradigm II adherents focus singularly on the selected target group, viewing anything else as watering down the sources of the group's issues, and prefer methods that acknowledge and deal with them. Finally, Paradigm III proponents believe that a broad-range approach is imperative right from the start, preferring methods that demonstrate, in deed as well as word, that valuing diversity covers a broad spectrum of differences.

It is easy to see that encounters among these three differing perspectives can lead to some difficult tensions and potential missteps as each speaks past the other. For example, people who identify with Paradigm I value their "Golden Rule" outlook and believe that they are already sensitive and unprejudiced; they are shocked and hurt when those who advocate the "Right the Wrong" paradigm confront them on their lack of awareness of group differences. Paradigm II adherents are horrified by the "global" scope of Paradigm III, fearing that its "value all differences" orientation attempts to achieve too much. Paradigm III proponents believe that Paradigm I is dangerously ethnocentric with its "Golden Rule" and that Paradigm II is serving the needs of a few at the expense of many. Paradigm I people think that they are the same as Paradigm III and cannot understand why Paradigm II people appear impatient with them. These points are rarely articulated, but often ferment under the surface. Regardless, preparing individuals to understand and engage across these differences is a complex undertaking requiring a multipronged approach.

We turn now to two different strategies we employ in the graduate education of student affairs practitioners at the master's level, designed to elicit students' understandings of these concerns and to encourage them to develop their own approaches as emerging diversity change leaders. One is a model we characterize as a Cultural Diversity approach and the other a Social Justice approach. These two models differ in their goals, designs, rhetoric, and responses from participants. We next identify their respective pedagogical features, illustrate how each is implemented in a graduate curriculum, and consider their merits for preparing diversity change leaders. Last, we integrate their contributions to the challenges of each of Palmer's (1989) paradigms. Both of these approaches strive to nurture cultural learners.

CULTURAL DIVERSITY MODEL

Perhaps reflecting partially both Paradigm I (The Golden Rule) and Paradigm III (Value the Differences) assumptions is a pedagogical approach we are calling the Cultural Diversity Model. Its intent is to encourage understanding and appreciation of a wide range of differences among people, some of which extend from individual characteristics and some from group distinctions. Rather than institutions, this model is directed toward transforming perspectives of individuals through developing empathy, employing a language of personal transformation that emphasizes the importance of awareness, humility, knowledge, skills, and responsiveness. Its success is determined when individuals embrace differences through cognitive and affective assent, transforming fear to instincts of curiosity and empathy. This approach is implemented within our curriculum at Bowling Green State University in the form of the "Voice Project" (Strange & Alston, 1998), an integrated pedagogical strategy of cultural encounter that forms a key assignment in three of our core courses.

Cool!

The Voice Project requires students to select a "voice" other than their own, for which they will assume responsibility as an advocate in letting it be heard as part of class discussions and assignments over a sixteen-week term. The voice identity must be anchored principally in one of seven characteristics not shared by the student: gender, sexual orientation, race/ethnicity, age, religious belief, disability, or socioeconomic status. For example, an African American woman might consider the perspective of an Asian man; a heterosexual man could acquire the voice of a lesbian woman; or a traditional age student could pursue the voice of a returning adult learner. The expectation is that each student develops an expertise in a selected voice by examining relevant literature, accessing resources and personal contacts, observing and interacting in the context of individuals who are thought to live that voice, and interviewing people presumed to speak that voice. Furthermore, all students are expected to maintain a "voice journal" wherein they enter, on a weekly basis, their intellectual, personal, and experiential discoveries about their voice and any implications for the materials addressed in class. Finally, they are expected to let their voices be heard in class discussions.

Although the process of learning is prescribed, the content is entirely up to each student. As students' voices evolve across the term, they are encouraged to integrate their learning in various assignments and periodic examinations. To illustrate its use in exploring theories of campus environments, for example, students complete a voice-environment interaction analysis, wherein they select a college or university campus and conduct an assessment of the institution's capacity for including, securing, engaging, and inviting a student of their selected voice into the school's learning community. This involves examining the physical, human aggregate, organizational, and constructed features of an institution (Strange & Banning, 2001), as well as the characteristics attributed to their selected voice. In a similar manner, exam items are included in a course on student development theories, where implications of voice distinctions are considered for understanding students' paths of learning, growth, and development. In another example, students are asked to incorporate their voice into the design of an educational intervention to produce a particular outcome.

Presently, the Voice Project is integrated into three core courses in our graduate program: Theories of College Student Development, Theories of Campus Environments, and Educational Outcomes of American Colleges and Universities. In each course, students are asked to develop a voice different from the one they acquired during the previous term. The intended cumulative effect of this approach is that students develop an increasingly complex repertoire of understandings of identity differences they have applied to various questions and situations in student affairs, thereby broadening the range of strategies they can generate in response to the needs of an increasingly diverse student body. However, although this model is effective in changing individual perspectives, more is required to appreciate the insidious hegemonies that often surround these diversity experiences. Thus, we also provide for a learning approach that is rooted in questions of social justice.

SOCIAL JUSTICE MODEL

Consistent with the tenets of Paradigm II (Right the Wrong), and reflecting some of the insights of Paradigm III (Value the Differences), is another approach we use for preparing diversity change leaders in our master's program. The Social Justice Model focuses on acknowledging systemic practices that result in social inequities and how those inequities might also be reflected in the dynamics of the college experience. In our graduate curriculum, this approach is used in another required course called Multicultural Competence in Student Affairs, as well as in an elective course that trains social justice educators. The pedagogical goal of the Multicultural Competence course is twofold: first, to enhance student awareness and knowledge of how social systems operate to reproduce conditions of privilege and oppression. A second broad goal is to begin to equip students to challenge and transform these systems. In this model, the language of institutional change and systems thinking is emphasized, focusing on differences of power, privilege, and oppression among and within social groups.

In this course, students are introduced to Pope and Reynolds's (1997) characteristics of multicultural competence, comprising multicultural awareness, multicultural knowledge, and multicultural skills. These affective, cognitive, and behavioral attributes constitute a core competency for practitioners in student affairs according to Pope, Reynolds, and Mueller (2004). The *awareness* attributes emphasize cognizance of one's own and others' cultural influences and valuing the importance of cultural diversity. The *knowledge* characteristics reflect both a breadth and depth of understanding about cultural differences, how they can influence worldviews and interpersonal dynamics, and the systemic nature of privilege and oppression. The set of skills described by Pope and others seeks to put awareness and knowledge into action so that one can effectively build trust and rapport and communicate with those who are culturally different from oneself. The ability to design appropriate interventions in situations involving cultural differences is also included among multicultural skills. In this way, multicultural competence exhorts individuals to acknowledge and value all differences, as well as commit to redressing injustices perpetuated by discriminatory social systems and institutions. Ideally, the learning outcomes achieved through the Cultural Diversity Model described previously are effectively expanded in this course.

In the first half of the Multicultural Competence course students consider readings that define social groups (e.g., Young, 1990) and the systemic nature of privilege and oppression (e.g., Johnson, 2006), and debate the validity and efficacy of applying multicultural competence characteristics to individuals who do not subscribe to politically liberal views (see Stewart, 2008, for further discussion of this question). In the second half of the syllabus the class examines how to apply multicultural awareness, knowledge, and skills within the other core competencies identified by Pope and others (2004): theory and translation, administration and management, helping and advising, assessment and research, ethics and professional standards, and teaching and training. Discussion continues by examining other writing about how difficult dialogues around issues of diversity and difference challenge the limits of one's multicultural competence (e.g., Watt, 2007). Finally, the class engages in a discussion of privilege and diversity in higher education beyond student affairs (e.g., Maher & Tetreault, 2007).

Students in this course are evaluated in a number of ways. At the outset, they are asked to critically review, through the lens of multicultural competence, two texts that approach issues of difference from politically opposite viewpoints. Often the challenge for students is to see what might be multi-culturally "*in*competent" about an agreeable and comfortable point of view, while seeing what might be "competent" about a disagreeable and *un*comfortable point of view. The goal is to remind students that others' degree of multicultural competence cannot be determined solely by looking at the content of their views; also required is a recognition of the cognitive complexity with which they form those views (King & Baxter Magolda, 2005) while exploring their values about differences. Students are then asked to participate in and assess the multicultural competence of a diversity education program through its materials, participant evaluations, and discussion with the presenters. In addition, students pursue an ongoing project across the semester that has them identify a multicultural issue embedded within a particular student affairs functional area and develop an intervention strategy for addressing that issue that employs the characteristics of multicultural competence.

By the end of the semester, it is hoped that students have achieved the following outcomes: (a) greater awareness of the ways in which cultural differences shape how they see the world and how others see them; (b) recognition that, although individuals are not responsible for privilege and oppression, they are accountable for what they do about it; and (c) an increased sense of being better prepared to respond to multicultural issues in a competent manner, regardless of the functional area in which they work. Related to this last point, students also typically express a greater desire to build coalitions with professionals working in MSS, having realized the importance of such networks in spreading the work of creating welcoming and inclusive environments across campus.

ACHIEVING DIVERSITY CHANGE

Our analysis suggests that developing a diversity change capacity among graduate students and the leadership skills necessary for its implementation entails an immersion in a pluralistic or Paradigm III view. However, our experiences and observations also suggest that individuals tend to arrive at such a view from differing starting points, perhaps reflecting their own unique constructions of personal history and status within the larger culture. In our discussions that led to this analysis, for example, we were both attracted and resistant to one or the other model, relying on very different perspectives, words, and emphases to make our claims. On the one hand Carney, a Caucasian heterosexual man, found himself drawn first to a cultural diversity model that celebrated differences and focused on the inclusion of a rich multicultural heritage. Dafina (an African American lesbian woman), on the other hand, stood firmly on a critique of society's oppressive structures and affirming the goals of social justice. At times we seemed to be at cross-purposes, unable to reconcile, but for an insight that hit us both: Who we are matters in this debate. As a member of historically privileged groups, Carney was reluctant to enter the conversation through the language of oppression, preferring perhaps a more comfortable and secure discussion of interesting cultures. From the opening scenario, Samantha might also recognize greater affinity with this perspective for similar reasons. However, as a member of historically marginalized social groups, Dafina drew immediate strength from the promises of systemic change and the benefits of social equity and seemed suspicious of yet another foray into only appreciating differences while legitimizing structures of discrimination. Likewise, Ruben and Abraham might also understand their preference for the multicultural issues course in the same way.

If our experience reflects that of others, it is clear to us that how one self-identifies strongly influences how one approaches this topic. In our case, how we aligned with our respective cultures seemed to chart our initial pathways into the question of diversity. Once we understood that dynamic, we each were able to move forward in thinking about how to achieve our common goal—preparing student affairs professionals for success in a pluralistic society. Thus, we have concluded that whereas Paradigm I seems sufficient for the goals of a *diverse* society (where differences are appreciated but not necessarily engaged) and Paradigm II for a *just* society (where exchanges of power and control are equalized), we support the goal of Paradigm III to effect a social structure capable of sustaining engagement across differences for purposes of accomplishing what no individual or group can achieve alone. Regardless of starting point, our purpose is to transform both perspectives to a third and more complex view that combines the recognition of individual and group dynamics as they contribute to overall excellence (see Figure 17.1).

Figure 17.1. Relationship of diversity change paradigms.

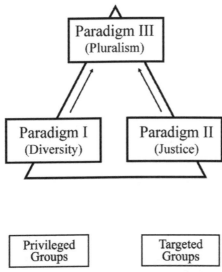

OTHER PHILOSOPHICAL PERSPECTIVES
TO CONSIDER

Kathleen Manning (2009) has presented seven philosophical perspectives that she sees as informing student affairs work on difference: political correctness, historical analysis, color-blind, diversity, cultural pluralism, anti-oppression, and social justice. Manning illustrates both positive and negative manifestations for each of these perspectives, except for the social justice perspective. A brief summary of these perspectives follows. Manning described political correctness as a potentially necessary first step for using language that is non-oppressive, but such changes in language do not necessarily indicate any change in underlying beliefs. The historical analysis perspective, although important to gain greater knowledge, might reinforce dominant culture paradigms when histories are produced by the victors. Moreover, overreliance on historical analysis might lead to a fatalistic approach believing that "nothing will ever change" (Manning, 2009, p. 13). The color-blind approach sees all people as equal because all people are human, believing that inequities can be cured simply by educating individuals or changing policies. Diversity (also known as structural diversity) focuses on creating a critical mass of underrepresented social groups on campus, but "does not change the power structure to more equitable forms" (Manning, 2009, p. 14). The cultural pluralism perspective engages difference through either assimilation or acculturation approaches. An anti-oppression orientation recognizes the root of oppression in all isms but can become paternalistic, doing *for* oppressed people instead of working *with* them. This approach is also focused on causes of oppression. By contrast, the final perspective Manning described, social justice, is focused on outcomes of hope, equity, and fairness. The emphasis on this approach is on activism. Manning warned that many educators in student affairs believe that the social justice perspective informs their work but it really could be another one of the seven perspectives in disguise.

Relating Manning's (2009) list to Palmer's (1989) three paradigms, one can see some overlap across the models. The political correctness, colorblind, and cultural pluralism perspectives share Paradigm I's focus on doing the right thing and take an individual versus systemic approach to rectifying inequity. Paradigm II parallels the historical analysis, diversity, and anti-oppression approaches discussed by Manning. These perspectives share a focus on rectifying oppression and recognizing the causes of oppression. However, Manning's summary points out an important distinction between the anti-oppression and social justice philosophies that is masked in Palmer's discussion. Paradigm III's cultural pluralism approach seems not to have a corollary in Manning's list of perspectives, Manning's social justice philosophy does not seem to be represented fully among Palmer's three paradigms. Nevertheless, as Manning points out, the emphasis of Paradigm III on understanding oppression, pursuing transformational change within institutions, and developing self-efficacy does reflect the goals of the social justice philosophy described by Manning.

Manning's (2009) discussion also has implications for preparing diversity change leaders. The Voice Project discussed in this chapter might be popular with students and effective in building empathy and capacity to relate to others across lines of difference; however, "cultural invasion" (Manning, 2009, p. 15) is a possible negative outcome that educators should be aware of. Cultural invasion is when an individual uses the cultural knowledge they have gained from others to manipulate power and control or engage in cultural voyeurism, where culturally different others are exoticized. As a result of this, when we ask students to conduct a Voice Project, we encourage them to seek opportunities to gain cultural knowledge through actually engaging others who reflect their chosen voice. Additionally, students are warned to remember that their newfound knowledge is not complete and might not be accurate for specific individuals within that voice group.

The Multicultural Competence class tends to employ the historical analysis, anti-oppression, and social justice approaches discussed by Manning (2009). Therefore, it is vulnerable to the fatalism that might follow the historical analysis approach, and students might resist the emphasis on developing the self-efficacy and practical skills to engage activism required by the social justice approach. These forms of resistance can undermine achievement of the course's learning objectives. To overcome these issues, Dafina has used illustrations of transformative efforts that have rectified instances of institutional oppression to demonstrate that the past does not have to determine the future. Moreover, Dafina emphasizes interpersonal communication skills to build students' confidence in addressing communication issues involving difference. This is a helpful first step for students to impact student and staff experiences with the institution on a daily basis in the interpersonal exchanges that often reproduce systems of dominance.

CONCLUSION

Diversity change leaders developed in the manner described here can build bridges to connect previously disengaged groups to each other and to the campus. Such leaders can also usher in new visions and practices of community that embrace heterogeneity instead of homogeneity (Tierney, 1993). Moreover, with more student affairs professionals trained to be diversity change leaders, the work of creating welcoming, inclusive spaces for all cultural differences will be done throughout the campus, not just in the MSS office. When *every professional* is a diversity change leader, there is truly no wrong door and no zone that is not safe.

REFERENCES

Johnson, A. G. (2006). *Privilege, power, and difference* (2nd ed.). New York, NY: McGraw Hill.

King, P. M., & Baxter Magolda, M. B. (2005). A developmental model of intercultural maturity. *Journal of College Student Development, 46,* 571–592.

Maher, F. A., & Tetreault, M. K. T. (2007). *Privilege and diversity in the academy.* New York, NY: Routledge.

Manning, K. (2009). Philosophical underpinnings of student affairs work on difference. *About Campus, 14*(2), 11–17. doi: 10.1002/abc.284

Palmer, J. (1989). Three paradigms for diversity change leaders. *OD Practitioner: Journal of the Organization Development Network, 21*(1), 15–18.

Pope, R. L., & Reynolds, A. L. (1997). Student affairs core competences: Integrating multicultural awareness, knowledge, and skills. *Journal of College Student Development, 38,* 266–277.

Pope, R., Reynolds, A., & Mueller, J. (2004). *Multicultural competence in student affairs.* San Francisco, CA: Jossey-Bass.

Stewart, D. L. (2008). Confronting the politics of multicultural competence. *About Campus, 13*(1), 10–17. doi: 10.1002/abc.242

Strange, C. C., & Alston, L. (1998). Voicing differences: Encouraging multicultural learning. *Journal of College Student Development, 39,* 87–99.

Strange, C. C., & Banning, J. H. (2001). *Educating by design: Creating campus learning environments that work.* San Francisco, CA: Jossey-Bass.

Tierney, W. G. (1993). *Building communities of difference: Higher education in the 21st century.* Westport, CT: Bergin & Garvey.

Watt, S. K. (Ed.). (2007). Difficult dialogues, privilege, and social justice [Special issue]. *The College Student Affairs Journal, 26*(2), pp. 114–126.

Young, I. M. (1990). Five faces of oppression. In *Justice and the politics of difference* (pp. 39–65). Princeton, NJ: Princeton University Press.

18

Multicultural Competence and Social Justice Advocacy

Robert D. Reason
Kenjus T. Watson

A group of students called a meeting to complain to Sue, the director of multicultural affairs, that the office was not focused enough on social justice issues and should be more involved in getting unisex bathrooms designated on campus, adding domestic partner benefits for faculty and staff, and pushing for a prayer room for Muslim students to be created on campus. Sue was bewildered by the students' demands and felt that it was more important to facilitate more effective cross-cultural dialogue and equip students with the resources necessary to be successful citizens of a pluralistic campus and global society. In her mind, as greater cross-cultural competence spread, the changes the students were seeking would also come.

THE ROLES, FUNCTIONS, ORGANIZATION, and even names of multicultural student services (MSS) offices often reflect the philosophy that guides those offices. In practice, two major perspectives can guide the approach that student affairs professionals take in these offices: a multicultural competency approach and a social justice advocacy approach. In Chapter 17, Strange and Stewart also discuss multicultural competence and social justice as important frameworks in educating diversity change leaders in graduate preparation programs. Like Strange and Stewart, we do not present multicultural competence and social justice as mutually exclusive. In fact, we argue that community is best served when these two approaches are merged; the two approaches have distinct strengths and weaknesses and encourage different types of actions. Moving the discussion from graduate preparation to student affairs practice for full-time professionals raises some unique issues not covered in Chapter 17. The opening vignette involving Sue highlights some of these differences. This chapter provides an overview of these two approaches relative to the work of multicultural community building and provides examples of good practices blending the two traditions.

As we strive to provide educational services for *all* students, it is imperative to ground our work in theoretical foundations of multiculturalism and social justice (Adams, Bell, & Griffin, 1997). Principles of Hardiman and Jackson's (1997) social identity theory are often present throughout discussions concerning social justice. According to Hardiman and Jackson, members of socially constructed groups (e.g., race, gender, sexuality, class) measure their psychological success through continuous comparisons with other groups. Group members obtain positive self-evaluation through collective acquisition of societal goods that increase their standard of living. Thus, groups engage in competition for property, education, wealth, meaningful work, and familial success (Miller, 1999). However, because inequitable power and privilege stratify the distribution of goods along hierarchical lines in our society, some groups (e.g., men, Whites, heterosexuals) are more likely to perceive success than are others (e.g., women, Chicanos, LGBTQ community; Adams et al., 1997; Gurin & Nagda, 2006; Miller, 1999).

The social identity perspective designates social groups as either dominant or subordinated (Hardiman & Jackson, 1997). Thus, social group identities position humans as either dominant *agents* or subordinated *targets* of oppression (Adams et al., 1997). The nomenclature employed within social identity theory highlights group members' roles in reproducing systems of injustice. More specifically, targets are *subordinated* to and *dominated* by agents of oppression.

The principles of social identity theory (Hardiman & Jackson, 1997) are the basis for our discussion of the multicultural competency and social justice perspectives. Inherent in each framework is the assumption that resources are inequitably distributed among socially constructed groups.

This inequitable distribution impedes intergroup interaction and engagement. With this understanding in mind, we explore potential benefits and disadvantages of using the multicultural competency and social justice perspectives in working with students.

A MULTICULTURAL COMPETENCE PERSPECTIVE

Adams (1997) traced the roots of multiculturalism and multicultural education in the United States back to the 1940s and 1950s. She concluded that multicultural educators' efforts in this era focused on increasing exposure to difference in attempts to improve respect and communication among social identity groups. It was during this time that Allport (1954) introduced his oft-cited contact hypothesis, which reinforced the need to couple education with exposure to diverse others in order to reduce prejudice. This understanding laid the foundation for contemporary understandings of multicultural competence.

More recently, Talbot (2003) defined multiculturalism as "a state of being in which an individual feels comfortable and communicates effectively with people from any culture, in any situation, because she or he has developed the necessary knowledge and skills to do so" (p. 426). In Talbot's definition, an individual demonstrates multicultural competence by learning about different cultures and adapting to different settings with little discomfort. Grounding in the original understandings of multiculturalism (Adams, 1997) is evident in Talbot's emphasis on comfort and skill development.

Much of the recent writing upon which a multicultural approach is built comes from the counseling literature and couples personal development with skill development. Sue and Sue (2008), for example, emphasize personal development in their definition of multicultural competence. Sue and Sue employ Pedersen's (1988) model of awareness, knowledge, and skill to frame the characteristics of a multiculturally competent counselor. According to this approach, individuals are multiculturally competent when they recognize themselves as cultural beings (awareness), are familiar with others who are culturally different (knowledge), and have the ability to communicate across those differences in a sensitive and culturally appropriate manner (skills).

Proponents of the multicultural competency perspective have several goals in common, but the primary goal can be assumed to be the minimization of discomfort with intergroup communication (Sue & Torino, 2005). The focus on creating comfortable spaces for intergroup dialog is laudable, although even Sue and Sue (2008) admit that this comfort is sometimes privileged over the recognition of differences. The primacy of comfort and interaction is necessary from a multicultural competence perspective because of its emphasis on inclusiveness, skill development, and individual growth (Sue & Torino, 2005). However, if comfort comes at the cost of appreciating difference, then multiculturalism might ignore the realities of target group members—a serious, potential weakness of this approach. Ignoring the realities of target group members' lived oppression can lessen the emphasis on creating structural changes to further social justice.

More recently, Pope, Reynolds, and Mueller (2004) adapted the discussion of multicultural competence in counseling to be more directly applicable to the work of student affairs professionals. In so doing, these authors expanded the definition of multicultural competence, incorporating action and advocacy. The perspective forwarded by Pope and her colleagues avoids many of the weaknesses, described previously, inherent in other multicultural competence perspectives, and moves us closer to a blending of multicultural competence and social justice.

Pope and her colleagues (2004) position multicultural competence as essential for all student affairs professionals, not simply those charged with leading multicultural student services. They suggested that multicultural competence is transcendent, positing that multicultural awareness, knowledge, and skill should permeate all areas of a professional's work (e.g., administration, teaching and training, assessment and research). Again, this expansion of the definition moves multicultural competence from its clinical counseling roots toward a practical application in student affairs.

Pope and others (2004) defined multicultural competence much as others have: Multicultural competence is the "awareness, knowledge, and skills necessary to work effectively across cultural groups and to work with complex diversity issues" (p. xiv), but these authors argued for a dynamic definition that changes to meet the needs of an evolving context. One change incorporated for student affairs practitioners is the understanding that awareness, knowledge, and skills are "necessary, but not sufficient" (Pope et al., p. 14) for effective student affairs work. Expanding on Sue (2001), Pope and colleagues included intervention and advocacy as necessary skills for multicultural competence and began to refocus the discussion toward institutional change.

A SOCIAL JUSTICE PERSPECTIVE

Since its inception in Hellenistic society, the contemporary construction of "social justice" has occupied a precarious position in both definition and subsequent practice (Miller, 1999). Educators have sought to identify those *necessary* and *essential* characteristics that define a *just society* (Mayhew & Fernandez, 2007). According to Mayhew and Fernandez (2007), "increasingly, institutions are being charged with cultivating students' commitment to issues related to social justice" (p. 55). This dynamic intensified the academic discourse concerning the nuances of social change. Despite the lack of general agreement among scholars, we offer a tentative operational definition to engage in a productive dialogue concerning the multiple advantages and pitfalls in adopting a professional practice rooted in advocacy. Agreeing with Bell (1997), we see social justice as "including a vision of a society in which the distribution of resources is equitable and all members are physically and psychologically safe and secure" (p. 3). Underlying the following discussion is our belief that student affairs professionals should be advocates allied against injustice (Evans & Reason, 2001; Reason, Broido, Davis, & Evans, 2005).

Several key components of social justice are endorsed by most advocates, activists, and allies. The underlying assumption in the majority of arguments for social justice is that the world is unjust in the distribution of resources (Bell, 1997). This recognition serves as the foundational catalyst for social justice actions, which are defined as "behaviors taken on behalf of [the] goal" of social equity (Reason & Davis, 2005, p. 7). Advocates' impulse to act against injustice begins with an awareness of the oppression and privileges they possess in relation to their social identities (Bell, 1997; Mayhew & Fernandez, 2007).

A primary strength of employing a social justice advocacy perspective in multicultural practice is the requisite emphasis on social action and change. Student-based social justice activism has challenged colleges and universities to better exhibit their "multicultural" missions by becoming increasingly diverse and inclusive (Cunningham, 2007; Freedman, 2007; Mayhew & Fernandez, 2007). For example, after initially ignoring the outcries of members of the lesbian, gay, bisexual, transgender, and questioning (LGBTQ) community and their allies, many high-profile universities have implemented gender-neutral housing options and single, lockable restrooms on campus (Canal, 2007). Although admirable, these seemingly inclusive institutional gestures are the result of constant, strategic, and often unpopular actions of LGBTQ justice advocates. This victory illustrates one of the major strengths of using an activist perspective in our work. By aggressively promoting social justice on college campuses, advocates help produce climates that are necessary for student learning and growth.

Like multicultural competence, the social justice perspective, if accepted uncritically, is not without its weaknesses. Young (2006) argued that most discussions of social justice "focus too narrowly on issues of distribution" (p. 98), ignoring the power that oppression holds in most societies. The author claimed that the focus on equal distribution fails individuals who do not fit exclusive, normative trends instituted by dominant groups (e.g., English as a first language, Judeo-Christian, and competitive orientation). According to Young, the "ideals of impartiality and neutrality . . . tend to assume default social norms that position some people as deviant" (p. 98). Advocates who intentionally examine "oppression" claim that one of the major privileges associated with dominant group status is the "luxury" to see oneself as a *neutral* individual who exists outside social group designation (Bell, 1997, p. 9). Indeed, broad and effective social justice action "requires simultaneous attention to personal and systemic levels of power, privilege, and inequity" (Mayhew & Fernandez, 2007, p. 75).

Further, although advocates strive to develop campuses that feature progressive, familial, and civil communities, some worry that social justice efforts can produce very different campus climates. Considerable concern exists that the social justice activism of students, faculty, and administrators might contribute to disjointed environments where conservative values are unfairly denigrated and neutral-minded students are forced to make inauthentic ideological commitments (Cunningham, 2007; Freedman, 2007; Watson, 2008). Although some students protest university associations with sweatshop-produced clothing, others want to be free to show their school pride *in peace*. As student affairs professionals, we often occupy uncertain positions in regard to such movements. Many non-politicized students look to us as neutral voices of reason, while upper-level administrators and fellow colleagues might be involved in frustrating negotiations with the student activists. If we choose to stand with the students who are protesting our institutions' relationships with sweatshop labor, our peers might perceive us as disruptive agitators, and other students might consider us biased accommodators. How can we affirm our commitment for social justice while continuing to support *all* students and work within the administration?

Related to this difficult inquiry are ever-increasing charges of indoctrination by external critics (Watson, 2008). Social justice-minded student affairs professionals and instructors are often accused of indoctrination if they used pedagogical methods to "pressure" students into "unwillingly" adopting distinct political perspectives (Freedman, 2007). Numerous diversity and social justice training programs have come under increased scrutiny since a high profile incident at the University of Delaware, in which a social justice–oriented residence hall program was suspended amid charges of indoctrination (Watson, 2008). This increased scrutiny threatens the very existence of activist educators. As a result, educational leaders and administrators increasingly ask themselves, "How is it possible to teach for social justice without engaging in indoctrination?" (Freedman, 2007, p. 445).

Despite this dilemma, critical educators and activists have no qualms concerning the nature of their vocation. Some scholars (Applebaum, 2008; Bell, 1997) answer affirmatively to the charge of entering the classroom with the agenda of *changing* students' minds. Others deny the charges of indoctrination (Reason et al., 2005); rather, they claim that critical pedagogy is primarily concerned with bringing about change through education with willing and active participants. However, incidental indoctrination might be a necessary dynamic to thwart the greater evil of oppression. Essentially, interrupting the status quo on college campuses might require social justice advocates to use controversial methods in order to create campus environments that are equitable and safe for all community members—a goal of the social justice perspective.

A COMBINED PERSPECTIVE

Although these two approaches to multicultural work in student affairs were presented in distinct sections, we recognize that they are not mutually exclusive. In fact, we agree with Pope and others (2004): A developmental approach that combines both multicultural competency and social justice is the most educationally powerful approach. Each approach alone, taken to an extreme, likely will be ineffective. A multicultural competence approach risks privileging comfort over change. The use of more assertive, controversial methods for the sake of social justice risks alienating the very people and institutions in need of change. What is needed is an approach that balances advocating for justice with skill building for cross-cultural engagement.

In this section, we provide examples from our campus of two multicultural offices that successfully combine these two approaches: the Paul Robeson Cultural Center (PRCC) and the Lesbian, Gay, Bisexual, Transgender, and Ally Student Resource Center (LGBTA SRC) of Pennsylvania State University. We also address the principles of intergroup dialogues, a set of principles and activities taking place on many campuses across the country. We believe each exemplifies a possible balance between a focus on multicultural competency and social justice action that proves educationally powerful.

Although the PRCC and LGBTA SRC employ different balances between multicultural competency and social justice, each assumes a developmental approach to its work, meeting students (both target and agent group members) where they are and attempting to move them toward goals of increased multicultural competence and social justice. Each offers a range of programmatic activities that provide challenge and support for students. Each presents programs that attempt to teach target and agent students about the histories and contributions (knowledge), the issues of oppression still facing the specific populations (awareness), and the characteristics and techniques to interact across difference (skill). Importantly, each office builds upon the foundation in multicultural skills to increase students' abilities to advocate for social justice.

The Paul Robeson Cultural Center—Striking a Balance

Jenkins (2008) provided a five-point programming framework employed by the PRCC staff that includes specific programmatic efforts in cultural education, cultural engagement, cultural student development, cultural community building, and cultural environmental enhancement. Descriptions of activities in each area focus on student learning and skill development. Clearly, the framework and its consequent activities can be assumed to have a multicultural competence foundation. Jenkins contended that this comprehensive framework allows the PRCC to become "a dynamic center that understands and appreciates aspects of various cultures and enacts learning, engagement, and interaction grounded in this understanding and appreciation" (p. 28).

A closer reading of the five-point framework (Jenkins, 2008) highlights several opportunities to employ a more activist, social justice approach. This reading reinforces our observations of PRCC activities over the last several years. Under the area of cultural student development, for example, Jenkins described a literacy program housed in the PRCC that performs outreach activities in the local prison. The PRCC's commitment to social justice is evident through its invitation to campus community members to interact and build relationships with individuals who have been devastatingly affected by the injustices of the prison industrial complex.

Although not mentioned in the article, PRCC staff members have led the effort each year to present the Tunnel of Oppression, an experiential program that encourages students to gain a greater awareness of multiple forms of oppression in our society. Although this is certainly a knowledge- and awareness-raising event, participants are provided with information about how to act upon their new knowledge, including information about specific state and national policy initiatives and contact information for policy makers.

The PRCC at Penn State University has found a balance between multicultural competency initiatives and social justice initiatives. Although most of the goals and activities listed under the five-point plan presented by Jenkins (2008) would fall within our definition of multicultural competency, other activities certainly take a social justice stance. Some activities, like the Tunnel of Oppression, blend goals of increasing multicultural competence development with calls for (and tools for) social justice action.

The LGBTA SRC—Striking a Different Balance

We again draw upon an office on our campus for an example of programmatic activities that strike a different balance between multicultural competence and social justice. Like the PRCC, the LGBTA SRC employs a comprehensive model when approaching its work. Students and staff members engage in activities meant to increase the multicultural competence of queer and straight students around issues of sexuality and gender. Students who engage with this office, however, tend to assume a social justice advocacy perspective in much of what they do, engaging in reasoned and intentional behaviors meant to disrupt the status quo around issues of sexuality and gender. In many of the ways Hamrick (1998) described, the staff members of the LGBTA SRC recognize and affirm the value of this social justice perspective and assist students to channel their energies in meaningful and productive ways.

Many of the formal activities sanctioned by the LGBTA SRC have the goals of awareness building, knowledge generation, and skill development—the goals of multicultural competence. Further, efforts to increase the inclusiveness of the community are often in the forefront of programmatic activities. When one enters the LGBTA SRC, the decorations, resources, and staffing convey a sense of inclusion and awareness building. Staff members intentionally display art depicting racially and ethnically diverse LGBT individuals. Educational materials address the common and unique experiences of sexual minorities in various racial, ethnic, and religious groups. Trained student panelists lead discussions, called "Straight Talks," in most first-year seminars and many residence hall floors. There is also an educational outreach effort to the Greek-letter community.

Along with an intentional focus on creating inclusive environments and educating all students about issues and concerns of the lesbian, gay, bisexual, and transgender community, the LGBTA SRC staff members have found a way to "welcome activist energies" (Rankin, Roosa Millar, & Mathias, 2007, p. 92) in their students. During situations similar to the fictional case study presented by Rankin and her colleagues (2007), LGBTA SRC staff members assisted students in channeling activist energies in ways that further the cause of social justice. Although each campus officer must find his or her own balance between supporting student activism and supporting campus administration (often the target of student activism), assisting students to plan legal, productive, and safe demonstrations against unjust policy or practice falls under the purview of MSS administrators.

Disrupting the status quo, whether reactively in response to an unjust policy or practice or proactively to encourage others to examine assumptions of normalcy, is a social justice function (Reason & Davis, 2005). One event, the annual Valentine's Day Kiss-In, serves this function. The Kiss-In, during which same-sex couples engage in a public kiss at the center of campus, is meant to disrupt people's assumptions about who engages in "normal" intimate behaviors. In so doing these students, with the support of LGBTA SRC staff members, are challenging heterosexist assumptions about intimacy on a "holiday" meant to celebrate traditional couples. In a similar manner, an annual LGBTA SRC–sponsored drag show disrupts assumptions about gender conformity.

The staff and students who work in the LGBTA SRC intentionally combine educational and inclusive activities with disruptive, thought-provoking activities—combining multicultural competency with social justice advocacy. In essence, they effectively *challenge* inequitable and problematic campus and societal dynamics, while offering *support* to staff, faculty, and students as we struggle to become a more welcoming, inclusive, and socially just community.

Intentionally Engaging With Balance—Intergroup Dialogue

Intergroup dialogues (IGDs) are characterized by honest, sustained, and carefully facilitated encounters between self-identified members of two or more historically conflicted, yet equally represented, social groups (Alimo, Kelly, & Clark, 2002; Nagda & Gurin, 2007). IGD participants are encouraged and guided through structured "dialogic engagements" (speaking, listening, and asking questions) across and within their social identity groups by trained facilitators (Nagda & Gurin, 2007, p. 35). Increasing intergroup understanding is one of the commonly shared goals of most IGD programs. This desire for multicultural awareness is often mediated through specific pedagogical interventions (inter- and intra-group dialogue, self-reflective writing, critical reading, and related activities) that address such concepts as intergroup difference, privilege, power, oppression, and action in a developmental manner (Nagda, 2006; Nagda & Gurin, 2007). Given this definition, it is reasonable to perceive IGD as a contemporary effort to produce the necessary components for progressive cross-cultural understanding via the contact hypothesis (Allport, 1954).

However, IGDs differ from other discussion-based diversity initiatives in several ways, most importantly the ultimate goal of such engagement. For example, several student affairs interventions promote discussions across difference for the sake of building participants' multicultural competence (Watson, 2008). IGD scholars and practitioners, on the other hand, "have developed [dialogue groups] as vehicles through which social justice . . . is taught and practiced" (Alimo et al., 2002, p. 49) in addition to furthering intergroup understanding.

Ratnesh Nagda and Patricia Gurin (2007), renowned innovators of the IGD programs, recently worked within a diverse multi-university research group of scholars, practitioners, faculty, administrators, and staff from nine IGD-practicing institutions across the country. In addition to conducting a national study on effects of race and gender IGDs, the multi-university group collaboratively conceptualized IGDs as occurring across a unique four-stage pedagogical process. These "stages" are designated as group beginnings, exploring differences and commonalities of experience, exploring and dialoguing about issues of conflict, and action planning and alliance building (Alimo et al., 2002; Nagda & Gurin, 2007). Within each stage participants "build relationships across cultural and power differences, . . . raise consciousness of inequalities, . . . explore the similarities and differences in experiences across identity groups, and . . . strengthen individual and collective capacities to promote social justice" (Nagda & Gurin, 2007, p. 35).

Because IGD builds multicultural competence while inspiring collaborative efforts toward progressive social change, it might represent another successful amalgamation of the multicultural competence and social justice advocacy approaches discussed in this chapter. In fact, IGD might actually improve upon our treatment of *balance* owing to its unique characteristics. IGD groups feature both development processes and subsequent social justice action (Alimo et al., 2002; Nagda, 2006; Nagda & Gurin, 2007). Such intentional blending of awareness with action is absent from other approaches to multicultural and social justice education (Nagda & Gurin, 2007).

CONCLUSION

We have provided a brief historical understanding of the principles, goals, strengths, and weaknesses of two approaches to building diverse communities through the work of MSS offices: the multicultural competence approach and the social justice approach. Although presented in distinct sections for illustrative purposes, the two approaches must not be understood to be mutually exclusive. In fact, we argue, through the use of three examples, that integrating the approaches presents powerful educational opportunities.

Finding a balance between the multicultural competence and social justice approaches allows MSS professionals to combine knowledge, awareness, and skill building with activism and advocacy directed at institutional change (Pope et al., 2004). Such balance can be struck in single programmatic efforts (e.g., intergroup dialogues) or through a curricular approach that intentionally combines multicultural competence development activities (e.g., Straight Talks Panels) with more disruptive, social justice–oriented activities (e.g., Valentine's Day Same-Sex Kiss-In). This blended approach takes as its ultimate goal to provide students the competencies necessary to function effectively within a diverse society, including effectively engaging in activism that creates change.

REFERENCES

Adams, M. (1997). Pedagogical frameworks for social justice education. In M. Adams, L. A. Bell, & P. Griffin (Eds.), *Teaching for diversity and social justice: A sourcebook* (pp. 30–43). New York, NY: Routledge.

Adams, M., Bell, L. A., & Griffin, P. (Eds.). (1997). *Teaching for diversity and social justice: A sourcebook.* New York, NY: Routledge.

Alimo, C., Kelly, R., & Clark, C. (2002). Diversity initiatives in higher education: Intergroup dialogue program student outcomes and implications for campus radical climate: A case study. *Multicultural Education, 10*(1), 49–53.

Allport, G. W. (1954). *The nature of prejudice.* Cambridge, MA: Addison-Wesley.

Applebaum, B. (2008). Voice—for whose benefit? Identity—at whose expense? Changing minds—at what cost? A rejoinder to Jackson. *Journal of Moral Education, 37,* 239–243.

Bell, L. A. (1997). Theoretical foundations of social justice education. In M. Adams, L. A. Bell, & P. Griffin (Eds.), *Teaching for diversity and social justice: A sourcebook* (pp. 1–15). New York, NY: Routledge.

Canal, E. A. (2007, September 1). Emerson makes restrooms gender-neutral: Joins other schools after student pleas. *The Boston Globe.* Retrieved from http://www.boston .com/news/local/articles/2007/09/01/emerson_makes_restrooms_gender_neutral/

Cunningham, F. (2007). The university and social justice. *Journal of Academic Ethics, 5,* 153–162. doi: 10.1007/s10805–007–9031-y

Evans, N. J., & Reason, R. D. (2001). Guiding principles: A review and analysis of student affairs philosophical statements. *Journal of College Student Development, 42*, 359–377.

Freedman, E. B. (2007). Is teaching for social justice undemocratic? *Harvard Educational Review, 77,* 442–473.

Gurin, P., & Nagda, B. A. (2006). Getting to the what, how and why of diversity on campus. *Educational Researcher, 35*(1), 20–24.

Hamrick, F. A. (1998). Democratic citizenship and student activism. *Journal of College Student Development, 39,* 449–460.

Hardiman, R., & Jackson, B. W. (1997). Conceptual foundations for social justice courses. In M. Adams, L. A. Bell, & P. Griffin (Eds.), *Teaching for diversity and social justice: A sourcebook* (pp. 16–29). New York, NY: Routledge.

Jenkins, T. S. (2008). The five-point plan: A practical framework for campus cultural centers. *About Campus, 13*(2), 25–28.

Mayhew, M. J., & Fernandez, S. D. (2007). Pedagogical practices that contribute to social justice outcomes. *The Review of Higher Education, 31,* 55–80.

Miller, D. (1999). *Principles of social justice.* Cambridge, MA: Harvard University Press.

Nagda, B. R. A. (2006). Breaking barriers, crossing borders, building bridges: Communication processes in intergroup dialogues. *Journal of Social Issues, 62*(3), 553–576.

Nagda, B. R. A., & Gurin, P. (2007). Intergroup dialogue: A critical-dialogic approach to learning about difference, inequality, and social justice. In M. Kaplan & A. T. Miller (Eds.), *Scholarship of multicultural teaching and learning* (pp. 35–45). New Directions for Teaching and Learning, no. 111. San Francisco, CA: Wiley Periodicals.

Pedersen, P. D. (1988). *Handbook for developing multicultural awareness.* Alexandria, VA: American Association of Counseling and Development.

Pope, R. L., Reynolds, A. L., & Mueller, J. A. (2004). *Multicultural competence in student affairs.* San Francisco, CA: Jossey-Bass.

Rankin, S. R., Roosa Millar, E. A., & Mathias, C. (2007). Safe campuses for students: Systemic transformation through re(a)wakening senior leaders. In J. F. L. Jackson & M. C. Terrell (Eds.), *Creating and maintaining safe college campuses: A sourcebook for evaluating and enhancing safety programs* (pp. 75–98). Sterling, VA: Stylus.

Reason, R. D., Broido, E. M., Davis, T. L., & Evans, N. J. (Eds.). (2005). *Developing social justice allies.* New Directions for Student Services, no. 110. San Francisco, CA: Jossey-Bass.

Reason, R. D., & Davis, T. L. (2005). Antecedents, precursors, and concurrent concepts in the development of social justice attitudes and actions. In R. D.

Reason, E. M. Broido, T. L. Davis, N. J. Evans (Eds.), *Developing social justice allies* (pp. 5–15). New Directions for Student Services, no. 110. San Francisco, CA: Jossey-Bass.

Sue, D. W. (2001). *Counseling the culturally different: Theory and practice.* New York, NY: Wiley.

Sue, D. W., & Sue, D. (2008). *Counseling the culturally diverse: Theory and practice* (5th ed.). Hoboken, NJ: John Wiley & Sons.

Sue, D. W., & Torino, G. C. (2005). Racial-cultural competence: Awareness, knowledge, and skills. In R. T. Carter (Ed.), *Handbook of racial-cultural psychology and counseling* (pp. 3–18). Hoboken, NJ: John Wiley & Sons.

Talbot, D. M. (2003). Multiculturalism. In S. R. Komives, D. B. Woodard Jr., & Associates (Eds.), *Student services: A handbook for the profession* (4th ed., pp. 423–446). San Francisco, CA: Jossey-Bass.

Watson, J. (2008). When diversity training goes awry. *Diverse Issues in Higher Education, 24*(25), 11–13.

Young, I. M. (2006). Education in the context of structural injustice: A symposium response. *Educational Philosophy and Theory, 38,* 93–103.

19

Conclusion

Re-Visioning the Future of Multicultural Student Services

Kathleen Manning
Frank Michael Muñoz

During the last session block of a national student affairs conference, a workshop discussing the future of multicultural student services was held. The presenters asked the audience the following questions to begin the session: "Is working ourselves out of a job still an appropriate goal for multicultural educators? Is it better to diffuse our work across campus, taking a decentralized approach and making diversity 'everyone's job'? In this time of heightened scrutiny of programs designated for certain minority populations on campus, how do we remain relevant?" A lively debate among the session attendees ensued, who were suddenly energized despite their conference fatigue.

IN 1991, KATHLEEN MANNING AND PATRICE COLEMAN-BOAT-WRIGHT expressed a vision for higher education in an article entitled, "Student Affairs Initiatives Toward a Multicultural University." According to this vision, higher education institutions could and would transform themselves from monoculturalism to multiculturalism through changes in attitudes, behaviors, and assumptions. The 1991 article outlined structural changes necessary for an institution to transform itself to better meet the needs of all students. The authors challenged student affairs administrators and others in higher education to transform the ways of operating in university life. With this change, higher education institutions would become more socially just as well as practice approaches to multiculturalism that better served students.

When colleges and universities transformed themselves from monocultural to multicultural institutions, Manning and Coleman-Boatwright (1991) posited that specialized student services would no longer serve *all* the needs of students from underrepresented groups. Instead, *all* offices would shift from their emphasis of mainly serving dominant culture students to serving *all* students. *All* administrators, staff, and faculty, not just those from underrepresented groups and their allies, would understand social justice and translate that knowledge into practice. Racism, homophobia, classism, religious persecution, and other forms of oppression impacting students would be challenged and, it is hoped, eliminated.

Since 1991, structural diversity (i.e., numbers of diverse students) in higher education has radically changed. Our campuses are now more diverse on every measure: sexual orientation, class, religion, socioeconomic status, race, and ability, among others. Power and authority are shifting, language use is expanding, leadership styles are diversifying, and cultural competence is increasing. Despite these meaningful changes, we are not yet at the point of the transformation envisioned by Manning and Coleman-Boatwright (1991).

Readers who have devotedly engaged the other chapters in this text might now be deliberating the same questions as the presenters posed in the opening vignette. But truly such questions have implications not only for multicultural student services (MSS), but for the campus in general. In this chapter, we explore theoretical understandings with noteworthy potential to reframe student affairs practice, including MSS. We make suggestions to transform higher education administration to more inclusive and just forms. Although staff members in MSS have long embraced many of the practices advocated in this chapter, we argue that higher education institutions are long overdue for transformed practices in *all* campus offices and departments. Without a transformed institutional and leadership approach, MSS will, by necessity, continue to shoulder the responsibility of serving students from underrepresented populations.

The transformations and reframing suggested are made in the context of critical race theory (CRT), a theoretical perspective not yet embraced widely in student affairs practice. The changes yet to be experienced on college campuses warrant a theoretical perspective with the depth and richness necessary to work with today's students. CRT can provide that perspective.

CRITICAL RACE THEORY
AND HIGHER EDUCATION

As discussed by Patton, Ranero, and Everett (Chapter 4), CRT emerged in the 1970s and 1980s as legal scholars challenged prevailing racial injustice and highlighted the persistent presence of racism in American jurisprudence (Bell, 1992; DeCuir & Dixson, 2004; Delgado, 1995; Ladson-Billings, 1998; Matsuda, Lawrence, Delgado, & Crenshaw, 1993). Early CRT scholars embraced a vantage point that highlighted systems and artifacts of racism and oppression while simultaneously working toward their elimination. Developing as a powerful analysis and tool for social critique, CRT now has a substantial following of lawmakers, educators, academics, and organizers who embrace its tenets and transformative potential.

Within education, Ladson-Billings and Tate (1995) asserted that race had yet to be seriously interrogated and theorized by educational researchers. Their work, "Toward a Critical Race Theory of Education," began a scholarly discourse about the utility of CRT as an analytical framework for examining educational issues, particularly those relating to racism and oppression. Their CRT-guided analysis of prevalent educational inequalities attracted the attention of educators looking for new ways to analyze and understand students and educational processes (Dixson & Rousseau, 2006). In particular, Ladson-Billings and Tate proposed an analysis of race and educational (in)equity that relied heavily on legal, social science, and educational discourses. Their analysis introduced educational researchers and practitioners to a theoretical framework that challenged the basic assumptions and understandings of educational inequity.

Since education's first encounters with CRT, scholars and practitioners have found it to be a robust analytical tool for examining educational environments and its key players (see Patton et al., Chapter 4). In particular, scholars of CRT and education make known the experiences of students, faculty, and staff of color (Teranishi, 2002; Villalpando & Bernal, 2002; Yosso, 2005), examine notions of (in)equality in education (Rousseau & Tate, 2003), and expose the dangers of color blindness (Ladson-Billings, 1995). We encourage readers to review Dixson and Rousseau (2006) for an elaboration of these themes, as well as the discussion by Patton, Ranero, and Everett in this volume. The theory avoids oversimplification by embracing the consciousness-raising of feminism, the interdisciplinarity of ethnic and women's studies, and the political activism of queer studies. CRT has become an important tool used by scholars to augment and enrich research on the experiences of underrepresented groups at higher education institutions (see Delgado Bernal, 2002; Parker & Lynn, 2002; Solórzano & Yosso, 2002).

Over the last decade, scholars have further tailored the tenets of CRT to fit the terrain of education. Although articulations of these tenets vary by author and project, there are at least five premises guiding the work of critical race theorists in education (see Delgado Bernal, 2002; Smith, Yosso, & Solórzano, 2007; Solórzano & Yosso, 2002; Villalpando, 2003):

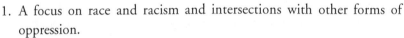

1. A focus on race and racism and intersections with other forms of oppression.
2. A challenge to dominant ideologies.
3. An understanding of the importance of experiential knowledge.
4. An interdisciplinary and historically informed contextual approach.
5. A dedication to working toward social justice and social justice practice.

Given the collaborative manner of its central tenets and the complexity with which it examines systems of oppression (e.g., homophobia, racism, sexism, ageism, ableism), CRT holds great promise as a lens through which to reconceptualize approaches to MSS.

In this chapter we use CRT to discuss the ways that majority culture characteristics (e.g., White, heterosexual, middle or upper class, able-bodied, Christian) and ways of operating (e.g., singular authority figure, top-down decision making, elite leadership structures) are systemically embodied in individual perspectives and privileged in institutional structures. We begin the discussion by focusing on the CRT tenets, illustrated with vignettes unique to student affairs practice, and then apply those principles as a theoretical perspective from which to view future practice in MSS and student affairs.

A Focus on Race and Racism and Intersections With Other Forms of Oppression

The Office of ALANA (African, Latino, Asian, Native American) Student Services has a long history of serving students of color. Despite the office's clear focus, students come there seeking relief from homophobia (if they are persons of color and gay, lesbian, bisexual, or transgender), sexism (if women), ableism (if they have learning, physical, or psychological disabilities), and regionalism (when they come from a different part of the country than where the institution is located). ALANA Student Services staff know they must work with students from the totality of their experiences and identities. In response to a need expressed by LGBT (lesbian, gay, bisexual, and transgender) students of color, the office started QPOC (Queer People of Color). This group meets weekly as a way for LGBT students of color to gather, discuss issues, form community, and defend against isolation.

Critical race theorists use the oppressive forms of race and racism as a vantage point from which student experiences can be understood. The centrality of these elements underscores the key assumption that race and racism are embedded in the structures, functions, and policies of institutions of higher education. Some CRT critics decry the assumption that racism is a permanent part of U.S. society. There are two important responses to this criticism. First, though progress toward racial equity has been made, racism persists. Even in the wake of the first African American president, race continues to function as a way to stratify society.

The concept of *intersectionality* broadens CRT's critical gaze to include race and racism's entanglement with other forms of subordination such as sexism, classism, and homophobia (Crenshaw, 1989; Matsuda et al., 1993). CRT's simultaneous recognition of the centrality and intersectionality of race and racism provides theoretical space for the examination of all forms of oppression, including areas of overlap and interaction. Any inequitable system based on identity (e.g., women's inequitable pay, LGBT people's denied marriage rights) relies on the oppressive mechanisms that also define race and racism. *Any* form of oppression will be eliminated only by attacking the root causes of *all* oppressions. Some scholars reference the *intercentricity* of race to emphasize both the centrality of race and racism to CRT analysis *and* the intersections with other forms of oppression (Solórzano & Yosso, 2002; Yosso, 2005). There is a clear commitment among CRT theorists to examine the many layers of identity and experiences that shape the lives of individuals. Regardless of the identity or identities expressed, there is a continued influence of multiple and intersecting forms of oppression. CRT, as an analysis, theory, and set of assumptions upon which to base practice, offers hope. Its racial realism is tempered by a commitment to challenge and destroy oppression.

In student affairs, we cannot understand one oppression without understanding how multiple oppressions interact, amplify, and change the dynamic at hand. Neither can we work on one oppression (e.g., homophobia) without understanding the impact of other related oppressions (e.g., classism). CRT recognizes that individuals and communities possess multiple intersecting identities and considers these varied terrains in its analysis. This sophisticated analysis assists student affairs educators as they seek to understand how systems of oppression are expressed in institutional contexts. This centering of the racialized experience and simultaneous recognition of people as possessors of multiple identities situates CRT as a potent and responsive tool for addressing inequity on college campuses.

A Challenge to Dominant Ideologies

> *During a severe budget crisis on campus, cutting 100 staff members was proposed as one way to balance the budget. Often the first positions to be cut during budget crises, the affected staff members included the lowest paid campus employees. Despite student protests calling for a response, the president refused to commit to a cut in his pay beyond the raise freeze for employees earning more than $75,000. Staff jobs were considered to be superfluous, expendable, and of little value, whereas executive-level positions were assumed to be essential, indispensable, and worthy of high pay, even during times of challenging budget situations.*

CRT challenges institutional claims of color blindness, meritocracy, objectivity, and equal opportunity (Villalpando, 2003). In this rejection, the theory highlights how these dominant ways of thinking about race and oppression preserve current power inequalities and perpetuate the status quo. Delgado Bernal (2002) articulates this tenet as giving "meaning to the creation of culturally and linguistically relevant ways of knowing and understanding and to the importance of rethinking the traditional notion of what counts as knowledge" (p. 109). In other words, CRT rejects theories or worldviews that ignore or misconstrue the realities and experiences of underrepresented groups. As a race-aware epistemology with a powerful analysis of oppression, CRT seeks alternative pedagogical frameworks and proposes new ways of learning and understanding knowledge.

An Understanding of the Importance of Experiential Knowledge

> *Taking attendance is a well-established faculty practice in higher education. Students barely look up when this ritual is performed at the start of each semester or class. For transgender students, a minimally uncomfortable and maximally unsafe "outing" occurs when their given name does not match their gender expression. Faced with several choices, a student can decide not to respond and be penalized as absent; privately "out" themselves to the professor after class; or "out" themselves publicly to the professor and class during roll. This experience is repeated over and over in classes as transgender students navigate institutions where gender is woven into every system and process. For those who are not gender variant, the labyrinth of gendered processes is invisible.*

CRT holds that the historically silenced voices of underrepresented peoples are vital parts of a rich and informed discourse about oppression. Indeed, educational researchers using CRT recognize students and communities of color as loci of knowledge regarding racism and other experiences of oppression. Critical race theorists and researchers use a unique methodology, counterstorytelling, to expose accounts that dispute the dominant culture narrative (e.g., rugged individualism, Protestant work ethic, working hard will result in just rewards).

Solórzano and Yosso (2002) define counterstorytelling as a "method of telling the stories of those people whose experiences are not often told" (p.

32). Similar to the transgender students' experience told in the vignette, Delgado (1989) explained that these counterstories challenge dominant understandings about race, power, and oppression. They present alternative conceptions of reality. Counterstorytelling provides knowledge, data, and context invisible to most dominant culture researchers and educators. Through this powerful research methodology (Solórzano & Yosso, 2002), underrepresented groups can name their reality, promote their psychological well-being, and strengthen community (Delgado, 1989).

An Interdisciplinary and Historically Informed Contextual Approach

Statistics and research on demographic change point to increasing numbers of college attendees who have disabilities, are "out" LGBT students, are more racially diverse, and occupy a wide range of socioeconomic classes. Despite these predictions, institutional and administrative practices remain focused on the typical high schools for admissions recruitment, the traditional ways of teaching classes, and the standard practices for working with college students.

CRT advocates an interdisciplinary approach that incorporates psychology, sociology, racial and ethnic studies, gender studies, history, education, and other areas to understand and transform educational experiences. Transgressing traditional discipline-bound approaches, a CRT approach uses knowledge and methods outside education to more fully understand oppressive forces at play in schools, colleges, and other educational settings, including student affairs.

CRT challenges trends toward ahistoricism that characterize educational research concerning race and ethnicity (Villalpando, 2003). Similar to the racial analysis conducted within CRT, oppression related to all underrepresented groups suffers from an inadequate analysis of history and context. Using CRT, identities and oppressions become historical *and* contemporary artifacts to be understood and eliminated using interdisciplinary methods. Historical accounts, psychological considerations, context built through sociological and anthropological research, and experiential knowledge built through counterstorytelling combine to present a richer, more complete picture of human living.

A Dedication to Working Toward Social Justice and Social Justice Practice

For years, the student affairs division embraced a commitment to diversity. Expressed as tolerance for others and a dedication to building diverse residential life environments, the division felt that it was on the cutting edge of practice. One spring, a coalition of diverse students occupied the vice president of student affairs' office to protest their treatment on campus. Through stories told during the occupation, students relayed cases of discrimination by campus police, harassment by staff, and systematic exclusion from paid student leadership positions. The vice president and her staff were shocked to discover that their "commitment to diversity" was inadequate to serve the current needs of diverse students on campus. She immediately convened a cabinet meeting where they discussed ways to bring their knowledge and practice up to date through division-wide training, examination of policies, and change of practices.

CRT is an activist theoretical framework with the goal of political and social change (Delgado Bernal, 2002). Villalpando (2003) conceives of this as a "commitment to social justice and praxis" (p. 623), similar to the ongoing dialectical relationship between educational theory and practice as theorized by Freire (1970).

Postmodern theorists, including critical race theorists, have helped educators realize that there is no neutral environment. Every environment—including classrooms, residence halls, college offices, and student unions—is marked in raced, gendered, and classed ways. CRT acknowledges the presence of these factors and actively challenges them within and through the processes of education. Solórzano and Yosso (2002) situate this concept in higher education as an ongoing social justice project that works to eliminate racism, sexism, and poverty alongside the empowerment of disenfranchised groups.

When CRT and education are fused through action and practice, the liberation of people of color and other oppressed peoples is possible. In addition, educators, using CRT, can have a positive impact on the educational experiences of underrepresented groups.

As scholarship incorporating education and critical race theory enters its second decade, there remains great space for this work to develop. In their 10-year retrospective of CRT in education, Dixson and Rousseau (2006) reemphasized the importance of this commitment to transformative change. To them, CRT is not only a framework for discovering and understanding oppression but can provoke strategic opposition to these forces.

CRT as a theoretical framework has real-life utility in the analysis and transformation of problems in student affairs, higher education, and beyond. It is a tool for understanding educational disparities and the lived experiences of underrepresented groups in higher education institutions. Student affairs practitioners can use CRT to frame their observations, recommendations, and policies. This practice then becomes part of a larger, concerted effort to dismantle enduring inequities across education and society as a whole.

A TRANSFORMED CAMPUS
TO SERVE ALL STUDENTS

As argued previously, CRT is a theoretical framework with the potential to understand various forms of oppression by educators within MSS and across the campus generally. Beyond this reflective aspect of the theory, its activist orientation provides a powerful guide and catalyst for the transformation of structures, organizations, and administrative practices. Reflection and action combine to create praxis; human action with the potential to transform the world (Freire, 1970).

This section applies CRT to student affairs practice as a way to illustrate possible changes in institutional structure, form, and content. These changes can transform a college or university to become one more responsive to the needs of all students. The illustrations of practice applied to CRT outlined in what follows (a) recognize marginalized and multiple identities, (b) realize a fuller social justice expression, (c) shift power to more equitable forms, (d) change leadership styles to recognize multicultural as opposed to mainstream leadership, and (e) achieve substantive structural change. These practice-oriented illustrations model ways CRT could be applied to a student affairs context specifically and higher education generally. These practices can also be ways to reframe multicultural student services.

Recognition of Marginalized and Multiple Identities

In his groundbreaking book, *The Pedagogy of the Oppressed,* Freire (1970) eloquently discussed the basic human right to "name your world," an essential mechanism for self-efficacy. From ethnic slurs to the micro-aggressions discussed in CRT, language and labeling are powerful means to define the reality and identity of others. Oppression is effectively advanced when the dominant culture usurps the right to name others. To illustrate the power of naming your world, we use transgender students and preferred name use as an example of this dynamic.

Transgender students exercise their gender expression and identity in a variety of public and private ways. Despite this powerful self-definition, these gender variant expressions are rarely reflected, reinforced, or recognized in sanctioned, institutional ways. In other words, if a transgender student is using a preferred name that better reflects zir[1] gender identity than a legal name, the legal name continues to be used on class rosters, advisors' lists, and other official documents. The institutionalized structures that govern name use are rigidly built into bureaucratic and administrative procedures, and the preferred name is not accommodated in the computer systems that regulate many campus procedures. Because university systems were built on mainstream conceptions of identity, a student's world (e.g., multiraciality, gender queer, transgender) might not be represented in the institutional structures governing colleges and universities. The student is not allowed to name zir world. Rather, the world is named for zir.

People from marginalized or underrepresented groups are becoming more empowered to "name their world" (Freire, 1970). Increased knowledge within higher education about social justice and the effect of legislation (e.g., legalized gay marriage), among other developments, increases the presence and power of underrepresented groups. With the increased presence of students with multiple and layered identities, it is impossible to "check one box." Symbolically and metaphorically, a singular box rarely represents the full range of identities characterizing an individual. Students with multiple identities are spurring a powerful self-naming process institutionalized through initiatives outlined in the previous chapters: recognition of queer people of color, attention paid to the intersection of culture and religion,

---

[1] These alternate pronouns are preferred by some gender variant students. They are used here to dismantle the gender binary (see Green & Peterson, 2003–2004).

and coalition formation between lesbian, gay, bisexual, transgender, queer, and allied (LGBTQA) and MSS offices, to name a few.

The burgeoning practice of naming and claiming multiple identities and working with the implications of those intersects with the first CRT premise: a focus on race and racism and their intersections with other forms of oppression. From this perspective, students, faculty, staff, and administrators name their realities and have those multiple realities recognized in institutionalized campus forms. The ongoing challenge to any singular expression of identity means that students and campus offices are acknowledging that intersecting identities have a profound effect on students' needs, development, and worldviews.

Fuller Realization of Social Justice

The change in practice of "other-naming" to "self-naming" reflects one example of the more complete realization of campus social justice currently occurring on college campuses. Past practice in student affairs embraced a variety of approaches generally grouped under the term *diversity*. With more knowledge about and experience with underrepresented students, greater delineation of the variety of approaches beyond "diversity" has occurred. Manning (2009) suggested several more clearly demarcated and articulated approaches to the area often called "diversity": political correctness, historical analysis, difference blindness, diversity, cultural pluralism, anti-oppression, and social justice. A social justice approach is supplanting less-mature perspectives to work in this area. As discussed further by Reason and Watson (Chapter 18), social justice entails hope, equity, and fairness (Manning, 2009) and values the right of people to name their world (Freire, 1970).

The recognition of multilayered identities is further advanced by the abandonment of the word *diversity* as a concept and philosophical underpinning for student affairs practice. *Diversity* euphemistically waters down the fact that oppression is permanent, a CRT tenet. Diversity fails to recognize the histories and traditions of any individual group by aggregating dissimilar people within an overgeneralized term (e.g., *LGBT, people of color*). These terms ignore multiple identities, disguise the unique needs of different groups of people, and disrespect and underestimate human beings by pretending that their disparate needs are common and straightforward. Although more precise terms for *diversity, multiculturalism, people of color,* and *LGBT* are difficult to locate, we are confident that future efforts in student affairs will discover better ways to more precisely express a commitment to social justice rather than diversity.

Shift in Power to More Equitable Forms

As our campuses become more diverse across all measures of identity, several questions beg to be addressed: What does social justice look like when a critical mass of formerly underrepresented students is achieved? How will multicultural student services evolve? How will student affairs practice change? Over the past 20 years, the demographic nature of higher education has changed such that today's students are more diverse on every measure. This increased structural diversity has created challenges about how campus practices reflect racialized, gendered, religious, classed, and other identity-based ways of operating. The presence of a critical mass of diverse students challenges how power is structured on campus. *Why do we continue to have a predominance of White men in upper administration?* The increase has altered the expression of multiple student voices on campus. *Who runs for student government positions? What issues are valued?* The parameters for "legitimate" knowledge, sanctioned topics, and suitable behavior are rapidly evolving. *Should Black, queer, and women's studies be recognized as majors with the appropriate resources allocated to ensure their success?*

Another challenge to legitimacy addresses the centrality or marginalization of MSS on campus. As higher education demographics shift to reflect increased structural diversity on campus, the voices of LGBT students, students from economically diverse backgrounds, women, students of color, and other underrepresented groups will dislodge, in some circumstances, and in others, add to, the traditionally privileged voice (i.e., White, male, heterosexual, middle to upper class, Christian). With that change, the power structure will shift. The issues introduced and advocated by students will challenge the legacies of inclusion and exclusion that will undoubtedly require remedy within the organizational structure.

The second tenet of CRT addresses the dynamics of the power shift that is occurring and growing on colleges and universities. Rather than euphemistically referring to race and racism, sexual orientation, gender, and class as *diversity* or *cultural pluralism*, this theoretical perspective names the dynamic of racism and oppression and claims these as permanent features of U.S. life.

The claims of progress achieved under the banner of diversity are placed in the context of the ever-present need to substantially transform the power structure to shift from elite forms to ones with wider access to power and privilege for all.

For example, when power shifts, presidential retreats, strategic planning processes, and other administrative leadership activities will involve the full participation of formerly underrepresented campus groups. The counterstories, as advanced by CRT, of these formerly marginalized members will be included in campus decision making and planning. The center will expand through the inclusion of members formerly marginalized and isolated at the outer reaches of campus. These expanded communities will be respected as sites of knowledge about a wide range of issues, not just diversity-related topics. And, the predominant leadership style will switch from the traditional mainstream culture approach to newer forms of multicultural leadership (Bordas, 2007).

Change in Leadership Styles

Mainstream leadership is characterized by competition, individualism, veneration of youth, and a present focus (including immediate gratification; Bordas, 2007). Most higher education offices employ mainstream leadership both in expression (i.e., who occupies those leadership positions) and nature (i.e., how leadership is exercised). In other words, even when leadership positions are occupied by women, LGBT individuals, or people of color, these people are appointed because they enact a mainstream style of leadership and willingly adjust their styles to reflect a mainstream approach.

Emerging from communities of color and other marginalized settings, multicultural leadership does not resemble mainstream leadership in practice or perspective (Bordas, 2007). Relying on its own traditions and emanating from a collective orientation valued within marginalized communities, the group takes precedence over the individual. One does not assign or designate oneself as the leader in a multicultural leadership setting. Rather, the group designates the leader, who then accepts the role of first among equals—a position taken on as service, not personal advancement. Group empowerment is valued, and individual self-aggrandizement is shunned. Consensus decision making is practiced in a manner that emphasizes the "good of the whole" over the advancement of the individual or elite few. Multicultural leadership techniques are expected and valued in collectivist settings where mainstream leadership practices would be rejected and ineffective (Bordas, 2007).

Despite the prevalence of mainstream leadership in higher education, pockets of multicultural leadership exist on campuses. With the increase in people from underrepresented groups and amplified social justice on campuses, multicultural leadership can be implemented even further in student affairs offices and divisions, with increasingly successful results. This approach can enact the vision long advocated by MSS to better serve all students in equitable and just ways. Most notably, MSS has traditionally been a location where multicultural leadership (e.g., communal orientation and emphasis, understanding of the historical ramifications of oppression, community as a means of support and success; Bordas, 2007) has been expressed and acted upon. This area of student affairs practice has always differed from the norm in its use of activism and empowerment. These offices are enclaves and safe havens where people from underrepresented groups can escape from the pressures and oppression of mainstream leadership.

Substantive Structural Change

The successful adoption of the practices of multicultural leadership necessitates structural changes from the traditional hierarchy to flat, web, and/or circular organizational structures (Helgesen, 1995; Zohar, 1997). These newer approaches support consensus and participation; they promote structural and cultural change. Curriculum transformation models are used here as an illustration of the shift away from hierarchy.

Curricular change predominantly takes one of two forms: The first is the "add and stir" method, and the second, an integrated approach. In the first, change is made but lacks the deep, structural modification necessary to transform the curriculum or institution. Classes in ethnic, Black, or gender and sexuality studies are "allowed" to occur but in marginal ways (e.g., as a minor rather than an academic major). The mainstream curriculum, academic core, and general education requirements remain dominant-culture-oriented, little changed by these curricular innovations.

The second approach to transformation occurs when the curriculum is fundamentally changed to reflect all perspectives present within an institution, country, or setting. This approach is truly transformational because the principles and assumptions (e.g., what is valued as knowledge, how knowledge is created, who is represented) undergirding the curriculum are changed. Expansive worldviews, diverse cultural perspectives, all-embracing approaches to gender and sexual identity, and various ways to view the world (e.g., ethnically, religiously, spiritually) are built into the foundation of the curriculum.

As people with multiple identities gain voice, campuses achieve a fuller realization of social justice, power shifts to more equitable forms, leadership styles shift to more just models, and organizational structures change to be more inclusive. Multicultural student services will surely emerge as a major campus influence. Undergoing the same fundamental and substantive multicultural transformations as the curriculum, MSS will travel from the periphery of the campus to the center. As advocated in this book, multicultural student services, given the pervasive presence of oppression in U.S. institutions, will continue to be required on college campuses. The need for safe havens and enclaves provided by an office of MSS for underrepresented groups will continue. But a transformed, integrated approach to practice regarding social justice means that more campus offices will embrace and assist with the traditional mission of MSS. Efforts to serve underrepresented populations will be transformed from an additive to an integrative approach. *All* offices will serve *all* students. For this change to meet the goal of institutional transformation, all offices must sincerely embrace a commitment to cultural competence and socially just approaches to serving students.

Through change created as a result of demographic shifts, increased knowledge and cultural competence, advocacy, and commitment to social justice, students from underrepresented groups will no longer be viewed as "extraordinary visitors" on college campuses. Instead, these students will be viewed as full participants who can approach any office and be served in ways previously emphasized by MSS offices, offices with diverse staff, and/or majority staff allies who embrace a social justice approach.

SUMMARY

For the last 20 years, student affairs professionals have taken significant leadership in the area of advocacy for students from marginalized groups. Through a discussion of CRT and social justice perspectives, this chapter proposes a transformation in student affairs practice toward a re-visioned approach. The vision shifts practice toward social justice and organizational structures and shifts leadership toward inclusion, justice, and fairness. In this vision, students learn and develop within a democratic environment that prepares them for lives in a more just and equitable society.

The world in which we currently live is complex, interrelated, and troubled. The substantial issues of our time—global warming, ethnic conflicts, and economic turmoil—can only be solved through collaborative efforts. The solutions to these issues are found in interpersonal relationships forged across difference. The student affairs vision of education of the "whole student" has evolved into one of social justice, fairness, and equity. We are certainly up to the task.

REFERENCES

Bell, D. (1992). *Faces at the bottom of the well: The permanence of racism.* New York, NY: Basic Books.

Bordas, J. (2007). *Salsa, soul, and spirit: Leadership for a multicultural age.* San Francisco, CA: Berrett-Koehler Publishers.

Crenshaw, K. (1989). Demarginalizing the intersection of race and sex: A Black feminist critique of antidiscrimination doctrine, feminist theory and antiracist politics. *University of Chicago Legal Forum, 1989,* 139–167.

DeCuir, J. T., & Dixson, A. D. (2004). "So when it comes out, they aren't that surprised that it is there": Using critical race theory as a tool of analysis of race and racism in education. *Educational Researcher, 33*(5), 26–31.

Delgado, R. (1989). Storytelling for oppositionists and others: A plea for narrative. *Michigan Law Review, 87,* 2411–2441.

Delgado, R. (1995). *Critical race theory: The cutting edge.* Philadelphia, PA: Temple University Press.

Delgado Bernal, D. (2002). Critical race theory, LatCrit theory, and critical raced-gendered epistemologies: Recognizing students of color as holders and creators of knowledge. *Qualitative Inquiry, 8,* 105–126.

Dixson, A. D., & Rousseau, C. K. (Eds.). (2006). *Critical race theory in education: All God's children got a song.* New York, NY: Routledge.

Freire, P. (1970). *The pedagogy of the oppressed* (M. B. Ramos, Trans.). New York, NY: Seabury.

Green, E. R., & Peterson, E. N. (2003–2004). *LGBTQI terminology.* Retrieved from http://out.vcr.edu/programs/edmaterials.htm

Helgesen, S. (1995). *The web of inclusion*. New York, NY: Doubleday.

Ladson-Billings, G. J. (1995). Toward a theory of culturally relevant pedagogy. *American Education Research Journal, 35,* 465–491.

Ladson-Billings, G. J. (1998). Just what is critical race theory and what's it doing in a nice field like education? *International Journal of Qualitative Studies in Education, 11,* 7–24.

Ladson-Billings, G. J., & Tate, W. (1995). Toward a critical race theory of education. *Teachers College Record, 97,* 47–68.

Manning, K. (2009). Philosophical underpinnings of student affairs work on difference. *About Campus, 14*(2), 11–17. doi: 10.1002/abc.284

Manning, K., & Coleman-Boatwright, P. (1991). Student affairs initiatives toward a multicultural university. *Journal of College Student Development, 32,* 367–374.

Matsuda, M. J., Lawrence, C. R., Delgado, R., & Crenshaw, K. W. (1993). *Words that wound: Critical race theory, assaultive speech, and the First Amendment.* Boulder, CO: Westview Press.

Parker, L., & Lynn, M. (2002). What's race got to do with it? Critical race theory's conflicts with and connections to qualitative research methodology and epistemology. *Qualitative Inquiry, 8,* 7–22.

Rousseau, C., & Tate, W. F. (2003). No time like the present: Reflecting on equity in school mathematics. *Theory Into Practice, 42,* 210–216.

Smith, W. A., Yosso, T. J., & Solórzano, D. G. (2007). Racial primes and Black misandry on historically White campuses: Toward critical race accountability in educational administration. *Education Administration Quarterly, 43*(5), 559–585.

Solórzano, D. G., & Yosso, T. J. (2002). Critical race methodology: Counter-storytelling as an analytical framework for education research. *Qualitative Inquiry, 8,* 23–44.

Teranishi, R. T. (2002). Asian Pacific Americans and critical race theory: An examination of school racial climate. *Equity & Excellence in Education, 35,* 144–154.

Villalpando, O. (2003). Self-segregation or self-preservation? A critical race theory and Latina/o critical theory analysis of a study of Chicana/o college students. *International Journal of Qualitative Studies in Education, 16,* 619–646.

Villalpando, O., & Bernal, D. D. (2002). A critical race theory analysis of barriers that impede the success of faculty of color. In W. Smith, P. Altbach, & K. Lomotey (Eds.), *The racial crisis in American higher education* (2nd ed., pp. 243–270). New York: State University of New York Press.

Yosso, T. J. (2005). Whose culture has capital? A critical race theory discussion of community cultural wealth. *Race, Ethnicity, and Education, 8,* 69–91.

Zohar, D. (1997). *ReWiring the corporate brain.* San Francisco, CA: Berrett-Koehler.

About the Editor

DAFINA LAZARUS STEWART is associate professor of Higher Education and Student Affairs at Bowling Green State University and joined the faculty in 2005. Prior to her faculty career, Dr. Stewart served briefly at Kenyon College in Multicultural Affairs. Her research and writing focus on issues of diversity, multiculturalism, and the identity and experiences of African American college students.

About the Contributors

MARY GRACE A. ALMANDREZ is a seasoned educator, conference presenter, and training facilitator. As a founder of multicultural affairs departments at three private, liberal arts institutions, Dr. Almandrez has successfully developed and implemented campus-wide initiatives that integrate social justice with leadership development.

STANLEY BAZILE is the director/assistant to the vice president of Academic Affairs and Enrollment Services at Cumberland County College (NJ). Dr. Bazile maintains an active research agenda that examines student retention, transfer, and success of community college students.

BRIAN K. BRIDGES is the vice provost for Diversity, Access, and Equity at Ohio University. Dr. Bridges served as lead author on the monograph *Broadening the Leadership Spectrum: Advancing Diversity in the American College Presidency* and co-coordinated the *At Home in the World* initiative designed to cultivate collaboration between multicultural education and internationalization efforts on college campuses, during his previous tenure at the American Council on Education.

301

Carretta A. Cooke is currently the assistant to the vice president for Student Affairs at Northwestern University. She has served in a variety of student affairs positions at different types of higher education institutions. Her professional interests include social justice and equity, campus crisis management, retention, the role of inclusion on college campuses, and the role of multicultural affairs offices in the twenty-first century. She has worked in multicultural affairs for more than 20 years.

Kimberly Everett earned a BS in Elementary Education and an MEd in Student Affairs from Iowa State University. Ms. Everett has served as assistant director of Residence Life at the University of West Georgia and multicultural liaison officer for the College of Engineering at Iowa State University. She currently serves as an advisor for the Iowa State TRIO Student Support Services Program while pursuing a PhD in Educational Leadership and Policy Studies.

Kimberly M. Ferguson is now the dean of students at Spelman College and has held several prior positions in multicultural affairs, student activities, and judicial affairs. Ms. Ferguson has also been a consultant on faculty development with the Great Lakes Colleges Association and INROADS and has served on numerous boards and committees in Ohio. She is currently pursuing her PhD in higher education administration from Ohio University.

Walter M. Kimbrough is the twelfth president of Philander Smith College in Little Rock, Arkansas. Prior to Philander Smith, Dr. Kimbrough served at Albany State University, Old Dominion University, Georgia State University, and Emory University in various student affairs and academic affairs functional areas.

Corinne Maekawa Kodama is a former associate director for the Asian American Resource and Cultural Center at the University of Illinois at Chicago. Ms. Kodama has published research on student development issues and identity development for Asian American students. Her experience in higher education has taken her to public institutions across the country, working in a wide variety of functional areas. She is currently pursuing a doctorate in Higher Education Administration at Loyola University Chicago.

V. Leilani Kupo received her doctorate in Higher Education Administration from Bowling Green State University. Dr. Kupo's research agenda includes understanding First Nations/Indigenous community members' experiences with higher education in both U.S. and international contexts and examining how power and oppression impact access, retention, and the overall experience of marginalized students in the academy.

Felicia J. Lee is currently chief of staff for the Division of Student Affairs at the University of California–Berkeley. Dr. Lee is an executive coach with clients in higher education and in nonprofit organizations. She has consulted extensively with private and public colleges and universities as well as non-profit agencies on issues of student leadership and diversity, strategic planning, conflict resolution, and staff development.

Robert Longwell-Grice is the director of academic services for the School of Education at the University of Wisconsin–Milwaukee and a faculty member in their higher education administration program. He received his doctorate in educational and counseling psychology, with an emphasis in college student personnel, from the University of Louisville. His interest in tribal college administration began in 1978 when he lived and worked on the Rosebud Reservation in South Dakota and attended Sinte Gleska College.

Kathleen Manning has experienced student affairs from the perspectives of both an administrator and faculty member. She is currently professor in the Higher Education and Student Affairs Administration program at the University of Vermont. Dr. Manning's research and writing interests include social justice, qualitative research methodology, and student affairs organizational models. She currently serves as the executive editor of the *Journal of Student Affairs Research and Practice.*

Dorian L. McCoy is assistant professor in the Higher Education and Student Affairs program at the University of Vermont. His current research includes defining and documenting aspects of "extreme" predominantly White institutions and issues of access for historically underrepresented populations in higher education. Dr. McCoy has more than 10 years of administrative experience in residential life and human resource management at the University of Florida and Louisiana State University.

DAVID MCINTOSH is a doctoral candidate in Higher Education Administration at Texas A&M University. He assumed the role as coordinator of Campus Diversity Initiatives at Texas A&M University in September 2007. His research interests include whiteness studies and barriers to success for traditionally underrepresented people within higher education. He also has experience consulting in outcomes-based assessment for both academic and administrative units.

FRANK MICHAEL MUÑOZ currently serves as the event coordinator for the Dudley H. Davis Center at the University of Vermont. Mr. Muñoz's professional interests lie in student union management and its intersections with social justice work and environmental stewardship. His scholarship focuses on critical race theory, campus planning and architecture, sense of place, and the experiences of historically underrepresented students in higher education.

NICHOLAS A. NEGRETE currently serves as the assistant director of Cross Cultural Centers at California State University–Los Angeles. His past research and experiences have been focused on the transgender student experience at University of Vermont and support programs for students who identify as queer people of color.

LORI D. PATTON is associate professor of Higher Education in the Morgridge College of Education at the University of Denver. She has a wide range of administrative experiences in student affairs functional areas, including multicultural programming and recruitment, Greek life, and residence life. Dr. Patton Davis's research spans broadly across social justice issues in higher education, with a particular focus on race, gender, and sexual identities, and is often grounded in critical race theory.

BECKY PETITT is assistant vice president for Diversity at Texas A&M University. Dr. Petitt's research interests include institutional discrimination based on class, gender, and race within complex higher education institutions, social inequality, organizational development, and organizational change. Dr. Petitt is a nationally recognized consultant, specializing in diversity in higher education, leadership, and organizational development.

CHRISTOPHER PURCELL currently serves as the program coordinator in the Center for Lesbian, Gay, Bisexual, and Transgender Life at Duke University.

Academically and professionally, his foci have been exploring the power of personal narrative writing and developing innovative programming initiatives addressing the intersections of identity.

Jessica Ranero is a doctoral candidate in the Educational Leadership and Policy Studies program at Iowa State University. Her research interests include social justice, the role of multicultural affairs at predominantly White institutions, and critical race theory in education. Before returning to school full time, she worked in multicultural affairs for seven years.

Robert D. Reason is associate professor of Education in the College Student Affairs and Higher Education programs at Penn State University. He is also senior research associate at the Center for the Study of Higher Education. Dr. Reason studies student development in college environments, specifically related to the development of social justice attitudes.

Les D. Riding In is a member of the Osage Tribe and currently a student development specialist with the Honors College at UT–Arlington. Dr. Riding In's research concentrates on how higher education is a vehicle for ensuring American Indian tribal sovereignty. He is also the chair of the Native American and Tribal College interest group of the National Association of Academic Advisors.

Kevin D. Rome Sr. currently serves as the vice president for Student Affairs at North Carolina Central University. Dr. Rome is very active in the arena of higher education and has been highly recognized by several professional associations for his research, publications, presentations, and other scholarly work. He has been a keynote presenter and seminar leader for a large diversity of colleges, universities, churches, and fraternal organizations.

Bettina C. Shuford currently serves as assistant vice president for Student Affairs at Bowling Green State University. Dr. Shuford's research interests, publications, and presentations have focused on functions in multicultural affairs offices, assessment of multicultural affairs programs, student development and retention of students of color, affirmative action, and African American women in student affairs.

JENNY L. SMALL is a recent graduate of the University of Michigan, receiving a PhD from the Center for the Study of Higher and Postsecondary Education. Her research has focused on the spiritual lives and faith identities of religiously diverse college students and how college students use language to define these elements of their identities.

C. CARNEY STRANGE is professor of Higher Education and Student Affairs at Bowling Green State University, where he has served as a faculty member since 1978. His courses focus on student development, the design and impact of educational environments, dimensions of student spirituality, and methods of qualitative research.

KISA J. TAKESUE is associate dean of Student Life and oversees diversity initiatives within the division of Campus Life and Student Services at Brown University. She has worked collaboratively with faculty and academic deans to develop and implement a wide range of diversity-related programs, particularly those that serve students of color and international students.

TIMEKA L. THOMAS-RASHID currently serves as director of the Center of Student Involvement at Kent State University, overseeing the university's leadership, student organizations, civic engagement, and sorority and fraternity programs. Dr. Thomas-Rashid's research interests and presentations have focused on the areas of Black women's leadership, the history of Blacks in higher education, and minority student development.

JAMIE WASHINGTON serves as the president and founder of the Washington Consulting Group, a multicultural organizational development firm based in Baltimore, Maryland. Rev. Dr. Washington has served as an educator and administrator in higher education for more than 25 years. He is a founding faculty member of the Social Justice Training Institute for professional and personal development of practitioners in their skills and competencies in designing and facilitating culture change through a diversity lens.

KENJUS T. WATSON serves as assistant director of the Intergroup Dialogue Program at Occidental College. His research interests concern the educational and social psychological outcomes of intergroup dialogues, particularly identity development, diversity efforts at colleges and universities, intergroup conflict, and collaborative action across social groups.

Eboni M. Zamani-Gallaher is professor of Educational Leadership and coordinator of the Community College Leadership Program in the Department of Leadership and Counseling at Eastern Michigan University. Dr. Zamani-Gallaher's teaching, research, and consulting activities largely include psychosocial adjustment and transition of marginalized collegians, transfer, access policies, women in leadership, and institutional practices affecting work and family balance.

Index

Millennial Generation, 108
Miller, D., 268
minority-serving institutions. *see* historically
  Black institutions; tribal colleges
minority students. *see* diverse student populations; students of color
Misa, C. M., 86
Misa-Escalante, K., 68
Morales, E. S., 85
Morehouse College
  affiliation, 171
  challenges facing, 180–182
  demographics, 171
  development of, 170–171
  diversity at, 171–173
  dress code at, 175
  gender identity at, 174–175
  identity salience at, 176–177
  multiculturalism at, 177–180, 182
  religious issues at, 173–174
  sexual orientation issues at, 175
  social class at, 175–176
  students' geographic background at, 176
MSS leader
  academic advising by, 51–52, 222
  educational requirements for, 47–48
  and office staff, 49–50
  professional development for, 118–119
  reporting line issues, 47
  responsibilities of, 48–49
  salary of, 48
  title of, 46–47
Mueller, J. A., 59, 98, 118, 119
multicultural awareness. *see* cultural
  awareness
Multicultural Center at Humboldt State
  University, 111
multicultural competence
  abilities of professional with, 205–206
  defined, 148, 270
  features of, 195
  perspective, 269–271
  and professional development, 118–119
  as a requirement, 204–205
  and social justice model, 259–261,
    271–274

multicultural educators
  barriers faced by, 141–145
  and campus climate issues, 147
  hiring, 148–149
  and identity development, 111
  and inclusive programming, 149–150
  professional development for, 118
  retention efforts by, 147–148
multiculturalism
  at Black colleges, 169, 171–172
  and color blindness approach, 75
  in curriculum, 177–178, 190
  defined, 269
  for developing global citizens, 146
  at liberal arts colleges, 133, 136
  at Morehouse College, 177–180, 182
  resistance to, 142
  at tribal colleges, 190–191
multicultural leadership, 295–296
multicultural organizational development
  (MOD) theory, 204–206, 212
multicultural programming
  and ethnic student services, 133–135
  national grants for, 235
  support for, 34
multicultural speakers, 173, 174, 237–238
Multicultural Student Leadership Training
  Program, 161
multicultural students
  and gender identity, 43
  identification of, 42–43
  involvement from, 55
multicultural student services (MSS). *see also*
  collaboration efforts; integrated
  services; students of color
  assessment of, 206–212
  audit of, 207
  at Black institutions, 32, 169–170, 182
  budget issues, 50, 137
  campus attitude towards, 54–55
  case study, 223–225
  and color blindness approach, 31, 74–76
  at community colleges, 159–164
  conclusion about, 58–60
  context of, 251–252
  and cultural environments, 247–248
  development of, 30–33, 38–39

ACPA titles available from Stylus

The First Generation Student Experience
Implications for Campus Practice, and Strategies for Improving Persistence and Success
Jeff Davis

"Jeff Davis does an excellent job of defining, deciphering, and discussing the experiences, issues, and successes of first generation college students on both the individual and institutional levels. However, the real richness of this resource comes from the voices of students themselves. Hearing their stories through personal narratives illustrates both the diversity of background yet the commonality of challenge that first generation college students experience in their transitions into and through higher education. The content of this book has the power to inspire higher educators to examine their commitment to the success of first generation college students, provides concrete recommendations for practice in service to this growing population of undergraduates, and, thus, brings us several steps closer to an answer."—***Jennifer R. Keup***, *Director, National Resource Center for The First-Year Experience and Students in Transition*

Empowering Women in Higher Education and Student Affairs
Theory, Research, Narratives, and Practice from Feminist Perspectives
Edited by Penny A. Pasque and Shelley Errington Nicholson
Foreword by Linda J. Sax

How do we interrupt the current paradigms of sexism in the academy? How do we construct a new and inclusive gender paradigm that resists the dominant values of the patriarchy? And why are these agendas important not just for women, but for higher education as a whole?

These are the questions that these extensive and rich analyses of the historical and contemporary roles of women in higher education—as administrators, faculty, students, and student affairs professionals—seek constructively to answer. In doing so they address the intersection of gender and women's other social identities, such as of race, ethnicity, sexual orientation, class, and ability.

Also from Stylus

Culture Centers in Higher Education
Perspectives on Identity, Theory, and Practice
Edited by Lori Patton
Foreword by Gloria Ladson-Billings

"Lori Patton's book is stunning! It has closed the decades-long absence of a definitive compilation to inform Culture Center communities as they function in American Higher Education. As many colleges and universities struggle with issues of recruitment and retention of underrepresented students, this work provides a splendid blueprint for the development of Culture Centers for years to come."—***Willena Kimpson Price***, *Director African American Cultural Center, University of Connecticut, Storrs*

"As our nation becomes increasingly diverse, these centers serve as models of social justice and thus this book is a must read for all who want to ensure that their institution provides environments that exude academic success and achieve graduation for all students with their soul and identity whole."—***Mildred García***, *President, California State University, Dominguez Hills*

"I highly recommend this book for anyone interested in better understanding the challenges of race and ethnicity on U.S. campuses and the importance culture centers play in the lives of students."—***Robert Rhoads***, *UCLA Graduate School of Education and Information Studies*

22883 Quicksilver Drive
Sterling, VA 20166-2102

Subscribe to our e-mail alerts: www.Styluspub.com